Nick Malgieri's
bread

Nick Malgieri, former Executive Pastry Chef at Windows on the World and 1996 inductee into Who's Who of Food and Beverage in America, is currently director of the baking programme at the Institute of Culinary Education in New York City. The author of 10 cookbooks, Nick's recipes have been published in *The New York Times*, *The Washington Post*, *Food & Wine*, *Gourmet*, and *Ladies' Home Journal*. He is a contributing editor for *Desserts Professional* and a frequent contributor to *Saveur*. Nick has appeared on national morning shows and local television throughout the United States, as well as on Food Network and Martha Stewart. Visit him online at www.nickmalgieri.com.

Nick Malgieri's
bread

over 60 breads, rolls and cakes plus
delicious recipes using them

photography by
Romulo Yanes

Kyle Books

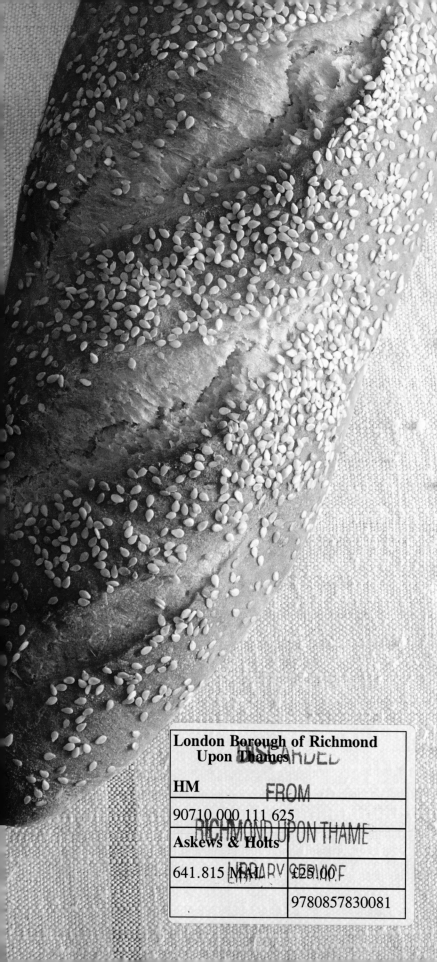

Dedication

For **Miriam Brickman**, **Kyra Effren**, **Sandy Leonard**, and **Nancy Nicholas**, devoted friends whose kindness and support are endless.

First published in Great Britain in 2012 by Kyle Books
an imprint of Kyle Cathie Limited
23 Howland Street
London
W1T 4AY
general.enquiries@kylebooks.com
www.kylebooks.com

10 9 8 7 6 5 4 3 2 1

Text © 2012 Nick Malgieri
Photographs © 2012 Romulo Yanes
Book design © 2012 Kyle Books

ISBN 978-0-85783-008-1

Project editor Anja Schmidt
Angliciser Lee Faber
Designer Dirk Kaufman
Photographer Romulo Yanes
Food styling Paul Grimes
Prop styling Megan Hedgpeth
Production by Gemma John & Nic Jones

A Cataloguing in Publication record for this title is available from the British Library.

Colour reproduction by Scanhouse
Printed and bound in China by C & C Offset co., Ltd.

Fifty years ago, great bread was everywhere. Small family-owned bakeries that prepared a variety of flavourful loaves, rolls and sometimes simple sweets like breakfast buns were so common that shoppers often made stops at several different bakeries for their favourites among the offerings of each. In the all-Italian inner city neighbourhood where I was born, there were three or four bread bakeries (and an equal number of pastry shops) within a few streets of each other. Then, industrial bakers decided to try their hand at what they labelled 'French bread' or 'Italian bread'. They shipped these loaves to supermarkets, and as the pace of life quickened and no longer left time for leisurely food shopping in the neighbourhood, people accustomed to eating good bread started to settle for industrially baked imitations. The decrease in revenue that befell small single-unit bakeries, and the need for younger generations of the families that owned them to seek higher education rather than settle into the family business, were all that was needed for the closings to start, mostly when owners became too old to do all the heavy work of making bread themselves. A few remained, though many bakeries that survived switched to easier production methods, such as using machines to form loaves that had once been lovingly shaped by hand. They began to rely on convenience products, ranging from dough improvers that made handling easier to 'just add water' mixes that completely replaced the doughs that had once been made from fresh ingredients.

Fortunately, the pendulum is swinging back. Dedicated young bakers from all over the world are bringing back the traditions of real bread, rejecting the conveniences of machines, flavour-destroying improvers, and fast mixing methods and returning to old ways of baking bread that tastes as appealing as it looks. Of course, the factories are jumping right on the bandwagon: in almost any supermarket, you'll find industrially made loaves identified as 'artisan bread' in big letters on the wrapping. In fact, I no longer use the term 'artisan bread' now that it's frequently applied to bread that's industrially made.

My professional birth was into the world of pastry and dessert – I've had to grow into bread. I've hammered bread experts with questions, worked beside them when I could and conducted endless experiments, including an entire summer spent cultivating sourdough starters from nothing more than flour and water. And I've tasted all over the world, from Paris, Istanbul, Melbourne and Palermo, to Cape Town, Bangkok and right back home to New York City, researching formulas and techniques as I encountered outstanding breads.

BAKING BREAD AT HOME

Bread is a book about baking bread at home. You don't need a wood-burning oven, a steam-injection system for the oven you have, a spiral mixer or a proof box to duplicate the recipes here. I developed all the bread and other recipes at the counter in my Manhattan apartment kitchen and baked all the breads in my single-oven electric stove. I've used a KitchenAid stand mixer and a pizza stone for some, but most of the breads may be mixed by hand and baked on or in a tin. Your only investments are a few inexpensive ingredients, some time and concentration and a desire to prepare bread with love for both the process and those for whom you bake it.

The range of breads here covers many different textures, flavours, styles, national traditions and methods of preparation. I've written explanations for how and why the steps in the breadmaking process work the way they do, relying on experts who provided scientific information that I then expressed in simple and easily understandable terms. Baking a loaf of bread shouldn't have anything in common with studying for a biochemistry exam. Using these recipes, you will make delicious home-made bread with a minimum investment of today's most precious and scarce commodity: time. Breads that utilise starters or other pre-fermented components, or are made from slow-rise doughs, require a little advance planning, but don't significantly increase the amount of active time you'll need to spend baking bread.

COOKING WITH BREAD

Bread has also afforded me the pleasure of sharing some of my favourite recipes for both savoury and sweet dishes that include bread as an ingredient. Friends and colleagues from all over the world, themselves bread bakers, pastry chefs, chefs, restaurateurs, cookery book authors, culinary and baking instructors and home bakers and cooks have shared favourites from among their recipes. These are grouped at the end of each chapter.

Mastering a few simple steps is all it takes to bake great bread at home and to prepare salads, soups, sandwiches, main courses and sweets that expand its use. And once you do, you'll be amazed at how easy and natural it is.

New York City
September 2011

7

chapter one

Ingredients & Equipment

Understanding the nature of the ingredients needed to bake good bread makes the process less of a mystery and assures good results. The descriptions of the ingredients that follow are meant to be a guide for purchasing the correct ones for the recipes that require them and not a complete scientific explanation of their nature.

Wheat flour, water, yeast and salt are the main components of bread dough and are at the top of the list, followed by flours made from other grains, sweeteners and fats, all of which figure in speciality bread formulas. Most are easily available in supermarkets and health food shops, while less common ingredients are easy to buy online. Throughout the book I've concentrated on ingredients that you can easily find on a supermarket shelf, but regional preferences and the emphasis on convenience products in today's food shops might make it necessary, as it is for me in New York City, to visit several shops for just the basics. Online sources for difficult-to-find ingredients are listed in the recipes that use those particular ingredients.

FLOUR

Today's wheat flour is milled from a grain whose botanical name is *Triticum aestivum*. The immediate ancestors of today's wheat came about when wild grasses of different types were brought under cultivation in the Middle East about 10,000 years ago. What we now know as wheat resulted from accidental cross-breeding and from farmers selecting plants with larger grains that remain attached to the stem during harvesting (eliminating waste) as seed stock for further planting. What we would still recognise as bread today came into existence in Egypt shortly after 6,000 BCE.

Milling wheat into flour: when wheat reaches the mill it is usually washed to adjust its water content. After that, the wheat berries are crushed and forced air removes the bran or outer skin and the germ, the part at the base of the berry that would sprout into a new plant. What remains is the internal part of the grain, or endosperm. Repeated crushing and sifting of the endosperm results in fine powder that becomes flour. Depending on the type of flour being produced, several different batches might be mixed to achieve the correct balance of starch, the major part of flour, and protein, the factor that determines the flour's strength.

In general, strong flour has a higher protein content than weak flour; strong flour is produced from hard wheat and weaker flour from soft wheat. Hard and soft wheat are so named according to the actual texture of the wheat berry itself.

Of the thirty-odd proteins in wheat, two specifically influence the texture of dough made from flour: glutenin and gliadin. When flour is moistened and mixed to a dough, those proteins change shape and form gluten, a web of elastic strands in the dough. The percentage of protein in the flour is only one factor that determines the nature of the gluten formed in a dough. Other factors, such as the amount of liquid added to the flour, mixing speed and duration, the presence of other ingredients and resting time, all contribute to the quality of gluten. Gliadin, by the way, is the element in flour that causes terrible problems for people afflicted with coeliac disease or gluten intolerance.

Flour that is chemically bleached with benzyl peroxide is capable of quickly forming a strong gluten in dough and is favoured by industrial bakers, but smaller scale commercial bakers and home bakers prefer chemical-free unbleached flour whose colour is naturally lightened through aging.

Most white flour available today to both bakers and consumers has been enriched with vitamins and minerals added to the flour to boost its nutritional content with no influence on gluten development. Occasionally, you might see ascorbic acid (vitamin C) listed separately on the ingredient panel of a sack of flour. It acts as a dough conditioner and was much favoured by Professor Calvel (see page 17), but its use today has pretty much fallen away. Its presence can also complicate matters when you're making a sourdough starter from scratch, so I don't recommend flour that contains it.

FLOURS COMMONLY USED FOR BREADMAKING

STRONG WHITE BREAD FLOUR is used in most of the recipes in this book. It has a protein content of approximately 12%, though that may vary by as much as half a percentage point during different seasons.

PLAIN FLOUR has a protein content of 10.5%. It's fine to use for many non-bread recipes, and while it may also be used to make bread, it works well only in the hands of a baker experienced in determining the quality of the gluten formed in a dough by eye and by touch. I freely admit that I'm not one of them and I'm guessing that you aren't either, so for actual bread formulas bread flour is always preferable.

WHOLEMEAL FLOUR has a high protein content of 13.5% to 14%, but its gluten-forming capabilities are diluted by the presence of the bran or skin of the wheat berry, which also imparts a slightly bitter flavour. Recently more available, white wholemeal flour is made from white as opposed to red wheat berries and its bran is less tough and bitter. Bread you make from it won't look like wholemeal bread, but it may be used interchangeably in the formulas.

STRONG WHOLEMEAL BREAD FLOUR is usually stone-ground wholemeal flour that retains 100% of the wheat berries used for it.

This is in direct contrast to most wholemeal flours that are assembled from the miller's formula for specific percentages of white flour, bran and germ mixed together after separate milling.

DURUM WHEAT FLOUR, protein content 14%, is made from a different species related to common wheat called *Triticum durum* (durum means 'hard' in Latin) and is the hardest of all hard wheat. There is a great deal of confusion in both package labelling and recipes with regard to durum wheat products. *Triticum durum* is also used to make semolina, a granular meal very similar in appearance to maize meal. To make matters worse, much semolina is labelled as 'semolina flour' though it isn't flour at all, but a more finely milled meal that's still granular in texture. Semolina is used to make a soft mush like polenta or grits, a certain type of gnocchi and some pastry fillings in Italy. Durum wheat flour looks and feels like flour and is what is used to make semolina bread, as well as dry pasta like spaghetti.

VERY STRONG WHITE BREAD FLOUR, protein content 13%–14%, is a very strong flour preferred by bagel makers and is also used to boost the gluten strength in doughs made with other grains such as rye that have little or no gluten development potential. Depending on where you live, it may be easy or difficult to find in a retail shop, but online sources such as www.barryfarm.com and www.kingarthurflour.com carry it, albeit at a premium price. Also check out www.shipton-mill.com. The results won't be exactly the same, but strong white bread flour can be an adequate substitute.

SPELT FLOUR is made from a grain, *Triticum spelta*, that some scientists believe is an ancestor of modern wheat, while others classify it as a subspecies. Its high protein content of 13%, like wholemeal flour's, doesn't translate to gluten-forming potential, but it has good nutritional value. To my taste, spelt bread has a much more appealing

Top to bottom: *Dark rye flour, cracked rye flour, medium rye flour, rye meal, light rye flour.*

flavour than wholemeal bread. Spelt is often confused with another similar grain called emmer, or *Triticum dicoccum,* which is known as farro in Italy, but to add to the confusion, large grains of spelt may also be called 'farro grande'. Spelt may be safely consumed by some people with wheat sensitivities, but not by those afflicted with coeliac disease.

RYE FLOUR is made from rye grain that is not the same as ornamental rye grass. Rye, or *Secale cereale,* belongs to the same botanical tribe as wheat but behaves very differently in a dough. It has the same amount of gliadin as wheat flour does, but a much lower amount of glutenin and is consequently unable to form a strong gluten. Rye flour's high proportion of soluble fibre is what makes rye doughs soft and sticky. Doughs made from a majority of rye flour result in dense, cakey breads; medium amounts of rye mixed with a strong white flour can produce better textured breads and often use a combination of sourdough and yeast as leavening.

Light or white rye flour is the equivalent of white flour that has had the bran and germ removed.

Medium or medium white rye is darker in colour and has some of the bran and germ added back after milling, mostly to improve the colour of the finished bread.

Dark rye flour is the rye equivalent of wholemeal flour and has the bran and germ included.

Rye meal is a coarsely milled version of dark rye flour and is sometimes called pumpernickel flour.

MAIZE MEAL has a very minor place in breadmaking, though small amounts can be added for flavour and colour. Maize contains no gluten-forming proteins but, in combination with an equal amount of white flour, makes a good baking powder–leavened bread.

OAT FLOUR is made from oat groats, the endosperm and germ of *Avena sativa* that has had its bran removed. Oats contain the highest proportion of both soluble fibre and nutritional proteins of any grain, but the absence of glutenin and gliadin prevent it from being made into bread on its own. The flavour and nutritional value of oat flour make it appropriate in small amounts in a multigrain bread.

BARLEY has a place in breadmaking, though barley flour is seldom used to make actual bread. When barley grain is soaked and allowed to sprout, it is dried and made into malt. Adding powdered malt or malt syrup to a bread dough introduces enzymes, which help break down the sugars in flour to make them available to yeast as food. Malt may also be made from wheat and rye, though barley malt is the most common form.

WATER is essential to breadmaking, though other liquids such as milk, buttermilk and even yogurt may be used in combination with it. Water with a high chlorine or mineral content can sometimes contribute a strong flavour to bread. Because of most tap water's high chlorine content, I always use spring water or distilled water when initially cultivating a sourdough starter.

SALT is another essential in breadmaking, though there are some rare salt-free breads like the Pane Sciocco on page 113. While all salt ultimately derives from sea water, common salt is mined from underground deposits of evaporated sea water formed during geological shifts that occurred millions of years ago. Sea salt, on the other hand, is made directly from sea water allowed to evaporate until the salt is left behind and has a finer flavour. Always look at the content description of a container of sea salt and only buy the type that has no anti-caking additives, which might distort its flavour.

Kosher salt is a coarse salt intended to be used in the preparation of kosher meat. It's popular as both a sprinkling and cooking salt because it's easy to grab a large pinch. Never substitute kosher salt for fine salt — the larger grains of kosher salt mean you won't get the same amount of saltiness when you measure

by volume. Also, kosher salt added along with flour in a dough won't dissolve as easily as fine salt. If you can't find kosher salt, try substituting lightly crushed Maldon sea salt.

Pretzel salt has coarse opaque white grains meant for sprinkling on pretzels or bread.

YEAST

The term yeast or baker's yeast refers to a plant organism whose botanical name is *Sacchromyces cerevisiae*, which means 'sugar [eating] fungus of beer'. Yeast was originally a by-product of beer making, and some brewing companies still manufacture yeast, but today *S. cerevisiae* is grown in a culture medium containing specific amounts of nitrogen, dextrose and amino acids to foster its growth.

When yeast meets the other ingredients in a bread dough, the organisms feed on the starches in the flour and during their life cycle give off carbon dioxide gas and ethanol.

All the recipes in this book were developed and tested using Red Star active dry yeast and SAF instant yeast. If you intend to do more than occasional bread baking, it's worthwhile to buy a vacuum-sealed package of either, which costs much less in the long run than a tenth of the quantity of yeast purchased in sachets. When I open a large package of dry or instant yeast, I fill a small container that holds a couple of ounces and keep it ready to use at room temperature. The rest goes into a large plastic container with a tight cover. I write the expiration date of the yeast on the cover of the container and store it in the refrigerator: chilling will keep it fresh longer.

Cream yeast is a semi-liquid form of yeast siphoned off from the growing medium. Industrial bakers use cream yeast because it can be transported in tanks and delivered via pipeline to refrigeration systems in factories.

Compressed yeast is made from cream yeast that has had most of its moisture removed by pressure. Sometimes referred

to as fresh yeast, it used to be much more commonly available in supermarkets than it is today. Sold in large blocks and smaller wrapped pieces, it's still used by some commercial bakers. If you're interested in trying compressed yeast, you can probably buy some from a friendly bagel shop or retail bakery, but more and more commercial bakers have switched to instant yeast (see below). For the small quantities of dough in this book, 10g of compressed yeast is equal to a 7g sachet of dried or instant yeast.

Active dried yeast only came into existence when it was developed for use in military kitchens during World War II. Liquid yeast is shot into a forced air drying chamber to make active dried yeast. Today's active dried yeast is available in much smaller, easier to soften granules than previously. I categorically avoid active dried yeast in large granules.

Instant yeast, developed in the 1970s, is very finely granulated and is made using a different dehydration system than that used for active dried yeast and contains more live yeast cells per granule. It's possible to add instant yeast directly to a bread dough, but since all the recipes here call for either active dried yeast or instant yeast, I've called for whisking it into liquid too.

Other names for instant yeast are bread machine, fast acting, quick rise and rapid rise yeast.

SUGAR

Aside from recipes for enriched breads like *panettone* and buns, where it contributes obvious sweetness, small quantities of sugar in different forms can be added to bread doughs as extra food for yeast. Nourishing the yeast with added sugar is especially important in doughs that have a long fermentation time, since the yeast feeds constantly and might eventually exhaust the supply of natural sugars in the flour. If that occurs, there is little sugar remaining in the dough to promote a well caramelised crust colour and a pale, unappetising crust may result. Large amounts

Turbinado sugar and demerara sugar are slightly less refined sugars that retain some of the natural molasses rather than having it added back to them. Their granular form (the crystals are large) makes them easier to use and their flavour is superior to that of standard light brown sugar, but as they aren't as readily available, I use light brown sugar in most of my recipes here.

FATS

While fats contribute flavour, richness and tenderness to doughs, too much fat, like too much sugar, can interfere with gluten development. This is why high butter content doughs like brioche have the butter added at the end of mixing, after the dough has developed a good gluten structure.

Unsalted butter is used throughout this book. If you have a large freezer and do a lot of baking it would be worthwhile to purchase a 40 x 250g case of butter from a wholesale source. The price can be less than half what a supermarket charges. Beware of sales on butter in retail shops when the butter is being dumped because it has started to become stale. Old butter oxidises and becomes darker on the surface and then has a stale or 'refrigerator' taste. If you scratch a piece of butter and see that the colour is lighter right below the surface, it's oxidised and no longer fresh.

Olive oil is sometimes used for its flavour, especially in and on focaccia. Extra-virgin olive oil is fine for this purpose, but for baking an inexpensive one is fine. For greasing bowls that hold fermenting dough I sometimes use a pure olive oil that has a mild flavour and a low price.

Lard or rendered pork fat is used in some ethnic doughs. Good lard is called leaf lard and is

of sugar can interfere with a dough's ability to form strong gluten. For this reason, most recipes for enriched breads and buns have a smaller amount of sugar in the actual dough with more added on the dough, as in the Cinnamon Knots on page 210, or in the form of a glaze or icing after baking.

Sucrose, the refined sugar we commonly use for baking, isn't immediately available as food for yeast until a natural enzyme present in the yeast, invertase, converts it to glucose and fructose, both simple sugars.

Malt (see barley, opposite) has a different action in bread dough. Amylase, a natural enzyme in malt, helps to convert the natural sugars in flour more efficiently into food for yeast. The actual sugars in malt have less to do with nourishing the yeast than the extra amylase (there is some

also naturally present in flour) it provides, though added malt can have a good influence on the development of crust colour.

Diastatic malt has active enzymes, while non-diastatic malt has had the enzymes deactivated during the refining process. Diastatic malt is available as powder or syrup. In the recipes here I've used organic malt syrup that's easy to find in a health food shop. Following Professor Calvel's example, I always add a little malt when beginning to cultivate a new sourdough starter.

Moist brown sugar, whether light or dark, is made from refined sugar that has had some of the molasses extracted during refining added back for flavour, colour and moisture. I prefer light brown sugar – the darker type can sometimes have a strong and obvious molasses flavour.

rendered from the hard white fat surrounding the kidneys. Beef suet is exactly the same, but ground and not rendered before use. Contrary to contemporary belief, a small amount of lard in a bread dough cannot cause immediate cardiac failure and it has a subtle, savoury flavour that can't be duplicated by anything else. Freshly rendered leaf lard, available at speciality shops or online, is entirely natural and healthier in every way than vile-tasting vegetable shortening that's chemically rendered, whether or not it contains trans fats.

Safflower oil is my top choice for a vegetable oil and the one I use is expeller-pressed and not extracted chemically, like most of the oils on the supermarket shelf. It's much more expensive than those other oils, but so little is used at a time that the expense is negligible.

Information about speciality ingredients such as dried or fresh fruit, cured or fresh meat, and fish, cheese, herbs and spices is covered in the introduction to the recipe that uses the ingredient.

EQUIPMENT

Primitive bakers who made the first breads thousands of years ago used their eyes and hands for measuring, mixing, dividing and forming loaves of bread. A wooden trough functioned as a mixer, as a vessel for bulk fermentation, as a bench for forming and as a proofing cabinet. A board to slide the loaves into and back out of the oven completed the baker's supply of equipment.

'Minimalist' bread baking like this is still practised in some parts of the world, but both commercial and home bakers today rely on specialised equipment to make the process easier and less time-consuming.

What follows here is a list of essential pieces of equipment and aside from a mixer, most of them are inexpensive. They're listed in the same sequence as they are used in preparing a loaf of bread, starting with measuring the ingredients and moving on to mixing, fermenting, forming, proofing, baking

and cooling. Online sources for purchasing difficult-to-find pieces are included at the end of the recipes that utilise them.

INGREDIENT STORAGE

I use clear plastic 4-litre square containers with lids that allow stacking for my most used flours and sugars, plus smaller ones that hold about a litre for salt, cocoa powder, and speciality flours that are used in small quantities. The former are made by Rubber Maid. The smaller ones come from the Container Store and because they're not necessarily made for direct contact with food, I line them with a plastic food storage bag and close the bag before covering the container.

SCALES

My kitchen scale is an electronic digital postal scale that can measure up to 25kg. It measures kilos, grams, pounds, ounces and decimal fractions of pounds. You can easily find electronic digital scales at good kitchen shops and online. No matter what kind of digital scale you buy today, it is going to be capable of weighing both pounds and ounces and kilos and grams. One with a larger weigh plate is more practical than one with a tiny one. All the ingredients in all the bread recipes are stated in metric weights with smaller quantities expressed as teaspoons or tablespoons. If you're not familiar with using a scale, read the instruction booklet or sheet that accompanies it, test its accuracy with 250g of butter, and you're off and running.

VOLUME MEASURE

Standard measuring cups and measuring spoons are necessary for volume measurement. A couple of sets of measuring spoons are also practical when you need to measure both dry and liquid ingredients in the same recipe.

Liquid measure cups are glass or clear plastic, and newer plastic ones have the amounts inside the cup so you don't have to crouch down next to your kitchen counter to see the amount of liquid in the cup. Lately I've noticed some large variations in liquid measure cups so I have weighed all the liquids in these bread recipes.

MIXERS

I have a 4.7 litre tilt-head KitchenAid mixer that I used to develop and test every recipe in this book. If you do a lot of baking it's practical to invest in extra bowls and attachments. The bowl and dough hook are the most used for the recipes here and even if you only have one of each, you can move from one batch to another without washing either, as long as you start with the lightest coloured and less flavoured dough and move to the darker one or those that have solid elements added. The flat beater or paddle is used in a few recipes for looser doughs.

I haven't used the food processor for mixing doughs in this book, but as long as you use the plastic dough blade and watch for the signs of the developing dough stated in the recipes, rather than adhering to the suggested amounts of times for using the mixer, it should work well. Keep in mind that a food processor only has one high speed, so it's easy to over-mix when using it.

You'll need some sturdy stainless steel bowls for hand mixing and fermenting doughs.

HAND TOOLS

WHISK: a small pointed-end whisk with thin flexible wires is best for mixing yeast in liquid.

SILICONE SPATULAS: these are heatproof and function well for both mixing and when cooking. Several sizes make it easy to do preliminary mixing of smaller and larger quantities of dough.

PLASTIC SCRAPERS: these are helpful for scraping soft dough out of bowls and moving it on the work surface.

BENCH SCRAPER: the rectangular dull metal blade may be attached to a wood or plastic handle or be made from a single piece of metal. Whichever you choose, it's used for cutting dough into pieces, keeping dough from sticking to the surface and scraping the surface clear of excess flour.

ROLLING PIN: the kind I favour is straight and without handles. I bought a fancy white nylon rolling pin years ago in Paris when they were all the rage and it sits in a pile with other unused rolling pins, because I always reach for the old reliable one that I bought for four dollars about 25 years ago. Small rolling pins with handles are useless, because they're only meant to roll out dough for a 23cm pie. Large, heavy rolling pins with handles are for rolling large pieces of croissant or Danish dough by hand.

BRUSHES: new silicone brushes with thin bristles are fine, though the ones with a round bead at the end of each bristle are meant for basting rather than brushing. I have a few natural bristle brushes I like; if you buy one, make sure to buy one with black bristles that are more easily visible if the brush sheds a little.

Left: *Mixing dough by machine.*

PIZZA WHEEL: this can be used to cut focaccia and other flatbreads, as well as to cut strips of dough. Never use it for cutting buns that are formed from a piece of rolled up dough, because it flattens them beyond recognition.

FORMING AND PROOFING

BANNETON: this is a French basket in a variety of shapes that may also be lined with heavy canvas, for proofing formed loaves. I've called for it very few times in this book, and when I tested the recipes that call for one, I substituted a 23cm diameter bread basket lined with a coarse-weave napkin that easily holds the flour rubbed into it to keep the dough from sticking.

COUCHES: these are canvas cloths that are floured and placed on a tin and then pleated between each addition of formed baguettes so that the breads proof up against each other and don't spread out. A couple of coarse textured flat-weave kitchen towels are an inexpensive alternative.

BAKING TINS: for most tin-baked loaves I call for a 23 x 12.5 x 7.5cm tin that holds approximately 1.7 litres/900g. The *pain de mie* is baked in a 23 x 10 x 10cm covered Pullman tin, or a 39 x 10 x 10cm tin. Some of the sweetened breads call for tube tins, which may be either one or two-piece 3.8-litre tins. One recipe calls for a 3.8-litre Bundt tin, while another uses a smaller 1.2-litre fluted tin for a *Gugelhupf*. *Panettone* and similar breads are baked in 7.5cm deep tins that are 23cm in diameter or 23cm springform tins. A couple of recipes call for 20- and 23cm tins that are 5cm deep and for metal 23 x 33 x 5cm tins.

BAKER'S PEEL: made from wood or metal, a peel can make sliding a loaf onto a heated tin or pizza stone easy. If you've never used one before, fill a plastic bag with flour and tie it securely closed. Practise sliding the bag from the peel onto a pizza stone in a cold oven to get the knack of the movement, which is easy to master.

BAKING SHEET: These may be either swiss roll tins with sides or flat baking sheets. Whichever you choose, they should be made from heavy gauge aluminium, not the flimsy kind. A stack of commercial aluminium half-sheet tins is practical if you do a lot of baking and they're perfect for cookies, too.

SPRAY BOTTLE: once filled with water, a spray bottle is helpful for spraying a loaf before and during baking.

ROASTING TIN OR CAST IRON FRYING PAN: these may be used for steaming the oven at the beginning of baking. Each is placed directly on the bottom of the oven to heat when you turn the oven on. For the roasting tin, I fill a half litre measure with hot water and quickly open the door and throw the water into the pan, averting my face from the blast of steam that escapes before the oven is fully closed again. For the frying pan, it's better to use a cup of ice cubes.

COOLING AND SERVING

COOLING RACKS: both round and rectangular are useful for cooling baked bread.

BREAD KNIFE: this is essential for cutting bread. The serrated blade can stay sharp longer if you remember to lift the loaf off the cutting board when the knife is about to pass through the bottom of the loaf. This avoids crushing the edge of the blade against the board, which would eventually dull it. Serrated knives can't be sharpened like flat-edged knife blades.

A round wooden board or the same basket you use as a substitute banneton, or even a banneton lined with a clean napkin, are all attractive ways to serve bread at the table.

chapter two

The Essentials of Breadmaking

Styles in breadmaking have changed in the past 50 years and much of this is due to the efforts of the late Professor Raymond Calvel of the *École Française de Meunerie* (French School of Milling) in Paris. Calvel first became known to an American public when Julia Child visited him at his school bakery on one of her 1971 *French Chef* TV episodes, which resulted in what Julia would later call her '750 days of bread' when she brought her newly acquired knowledge back to the United States and translated it for use with American ingredients and home kitchens.

Calvel is best remembered for his books *La Boulangerie Moderne* (Modern Breadmaking), which first appeared in 1965, and his *Le Goût du Pain* (The Taste of Bread), published in 1990 and translated into English a few years later, both of which have influenced almost every professional bread baker worldwide since their appearance. Today's bread owes its natural chewy quality to Calvel, who discouraged the violently fast mixing so common in the past and encouraged the use of softer doughs that acquire strength and elasticity through gentle mixing and cool temperatures. This chapter is devoted to the steps in the process of producing fine home-made bread, from measuring the ingredients to the end of the mixing process. Details about shaping breads are in the chapters appropriate to the different shapes and techniques for baking in a baking tin or on a baking stone and for steaming in the oven are in their respective chapters. To make it easy to locate these shaping and baking processes, a list identifying them and the pages where they appear is provided at the end of this chapter after a list of definitions of terms used in the bread baking process.

Mixing a batch of bread dough can be almost as simple as stirring a spoonful of sugar into a cup of coffee, but a scientific explanation of what happens when you combine flour, water, yeast and salt has filled many a thick book. Fortunately, as long as the dough is mixed according to simple and easy-to-follow instructions, your dough and resulting bread will be excellent. Here's a short and clear explanation of what's happening as you're getting a batch of dough ready for shaping and baking, with all the steps expanded further below.

HOW BREAD COMES ABOUT

When you mix flour and liquid together, two of the proteins in the flour, glutenin and gliadin, change shape – the scientific term is denature – and form strands of gluten. Everything related to the form and texture of the resulting bread depends on the quality of the gluten formed in the dough. Gentle mixing, slow fermentation and cool temperatures produce the best gluten – one that will efficiently hold in the gases formed during fermentation (below) and help the dough hold a shape accurately when formed into a loaf.

Adding yeast and salt to the already complex mixture of flour and liquid imparts flavour, growth and appealing crust colour to the dough. As soon as yeast organisms arrive in the friendly environment of a bread dough, they wake up and begin their life cycle, feeding off the starches in the dough and producing carbon dioxide gas (as we do when we exhale the oxygen we've breathed in) and alcohol; then, fermentation begins. The gas is what makes the dough rise or increase in size, but it does this well only if the dough has a good gluten structure to keep the gases trapped in the dough. The alcohol combines with the salt added to the dough to create the unique flavour we associate with fine bread. Adding other ingredients, such as sugar or fat, complicates the process somewhat, but fortunately the yeast can adjust to the presence of these elements through the action of enzymes, which help it to digest the starches and sugars in the dough.

Mixing four simple ingredients together causes texture and flavour to develop in the dough; their interaction is as intertwined as the individual strands of fibre that, once joined, make a strong rope. The guidelines for successfully completing the process are explained in detail below in easy-to-understand (and easy-to-execute) steps. Each step plays a part in the process of creating bread that's as beautiful to behold as it is delicious to taste.

The bread recipes in the chapters that follow have complete instructions for mixing the dough by machine. That process is explained here, as is the process for mixing the dough by hand.

Before starting to bake one of the breads here for the first time, review all the explanations below for more detailed instructions on each step.

1. MEASURING INGREDIENTS: in all the bread recipes, I've given metric weights for ingredients, along with typical home baking volume measurements. I haven't given pounds and ounces because it's easier to measure odd amounts with numbers of grams than with portions of ounces. Here's how each ingredient of a typical bread formula is easily measured.

Flour: measure by weight in grams.

Water: measure by weight in grams, as for flour.

Yeast: measure by volume with standard measuring spoons except when using one 7g sachet. Most scales available for home use aren't sensitive enough to measure accurately amounts that differ from each other by a gram or two.

Salt: measure by volume with standard measuring spoons.

2. YEAST AND STARTERS: always make sure that any yeast or pre-ferment is at room temperature, especially if it was stored in the refrigerator.

<< For the sake of consistency, dried yeast, whether active dried or instant, is added to room temperature water, about 24°C, before being mixed with flour and other ingredients, although you might see formulas in other sources where instant yeast is added directly to the flour. This would require that liquid of a different temperature be added to the dough when using instant yeast, and for this reason I've stuck to whisking the yeast into water no matter which type you're using.

All the pre-ferments in this book are soft enough to be combined easily with other dough ingredients.

3. PRIMARY MIXING **>>**: this refers to the initial mixing of the liquid and dry ingredients in a bread dough. Most formulas here instruct you to use a rubber spatula to stir the ingredients together, whether you intend to continue mixing by hand or by machine. If you intend to knead by hand, cover the bowl and let the dough rest for 10 minutes, then begin kneading.

KNEADING BY HAND **>far>**: to continue mixing a soft dough by hand, scrape the dough from the bowl to a lightly floured work surface. Lightly flour the top of the dough and, grasping it with one hand, lift the dough and fling it against the work surface, folding over the end in your hand to the far end of the dough. Use a bench scraper in the other hand to scrape the dough off the work surface, lifting it again from the end closest to you and repeating the fling-fold-scrape movements. Repeat until the dough is smooth and elastic. To save time and effort, you can knead for a few minutes, drop the dough back into the bowl, cover it and let it rest for 10 or 15 minutes. Continue and the dough will quickly become smoother and more elastic.

To knead a firm dough by hand, place the dough on a lightly floured surface and gently press it into a fat disc. Fold it in half towards you and use the heels of both hands placed over the overlapped area to push it away from you. Turn the piece of dough 90 degrees and repeat the fold, press, and turn, continuing until the dough is smooth and elastic. You can also knead a little and let the dough rest before continuing as for the soft dough, above. Some doughs that only need to be stirred together without further mixing are also identified as per the instructions in the recipe.

After the dough is fully mixed by hand or by machine, it should be elastic enough to pull away from the side of the bowl, leaving it clean. The ideal temperature of the dough at this point is 24°C–26°C.

To mix by machine, follow the instructions in the individual bread recipes in the chapters that follow.

4. RESTING DURING MIXING: whether mixed by hand or by machine, most of the bread recipes in this book alternate short rest periods with short periods of mixing. This gives the flour time to absorb the liquid fully at several stages during mixing. It makes for a smoother dough with less use of energy, whether electrical or manual and also promotes steady and even gluten development, which imparts a gentle elasticity to the dough, rather than a rubbery quality that would make the dough difficult to shape. If you've never tried this technique before, you'll be amazed at how a dough becomes smoother and more elastic after a short rest.

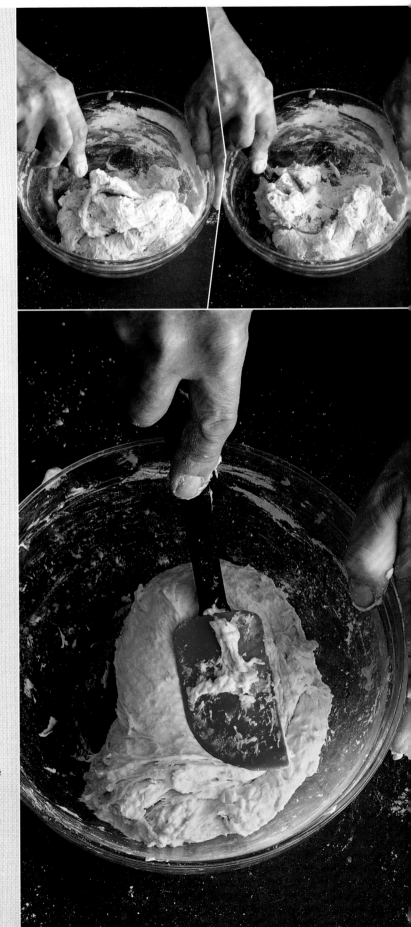

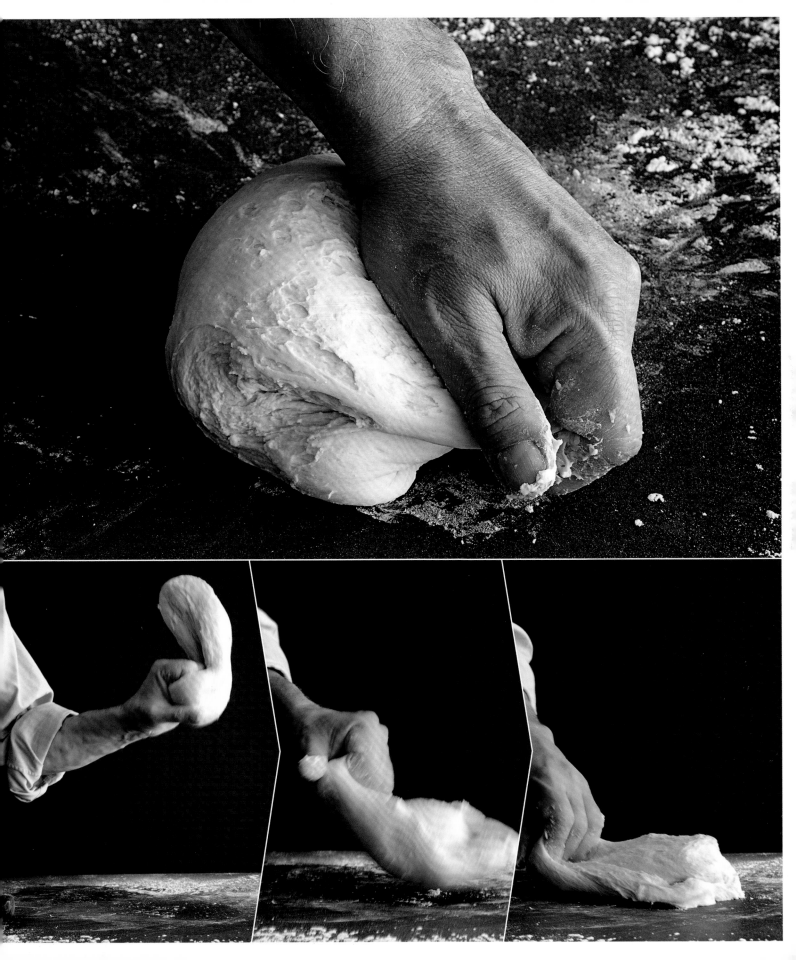

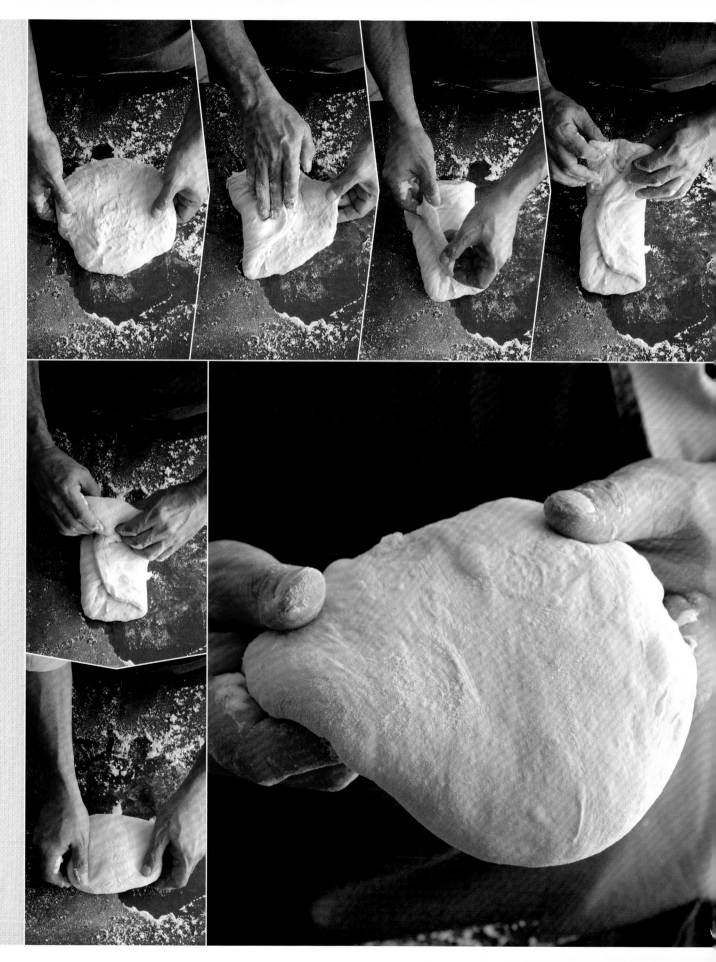

Right: The top piece of dough before it's turned; the bottom is a nicely turned piece of dough.

5. **≪ TURNING THE DOUGH:** although there are several different ways to accomplish this step, they are all geared towards the same result: making the dough smoother and more elastic. To turn a batch of dough, invert it smooth top side downward from the bowl or container where it's fermenting to a floured work surface. Gently pull the dough horizontally to about a 50% increase in width. If the dough is very soft, use a bench scraper to fold the right and left sides of the dough in to overlap at the middle. Just use your hands for a dough that's firmer. Roll the dough swiss roll-style towards you (or away from you, as in the photo) from the top and drop it back into the bowl seam side down. In some doughs this step is repeated immediately or after the dough has started to ferment again, but see individual recipes for specific instructions.

6. **FERMENTING THE DOUGH:** fermentation starts a few minutes after the ingredients are mixed together, but only becomes visible after mixing has been completed. Fermentation is measured in this book by the dough's increase in volume over its previous size. The ideal room temperature for fermentation is 24°C. Time estimates for dough bulk increase are just that – fermenting to the size indicated will take longer if it's cooler in the room and be faster if it's warmer. Taking longer is generally better; when fermentation is rushed in an overly warm environment, the resulting dough doesn't have enough time to develop good flavour and texture.

7. **FULLY FERMENTED DOUGH:** each specific type of dough in the chapters that follow calls for specific increases in volume in order to be considered fully fermented and ready to be shaped. When you press a fully fermented dough with a fingertip, it holds the mark you've made.

The recipes that follow contain instructions for shaping, proofing and baking once the dough has fermented as indicated.

bread baking terms defined

GLUTEN

When bread dough is mixed, strands of gluten develop as a result of the denaturation (change of shape) of two proteins in flour, glutenin and gliadin. All wheat flours, as well as some non-wheat flours, are capable of forming gluten when mixed with liquid. Bread doughs require a fairly strong gluten both to hold in the gases generated by fermentation and to have the degree of internal structure necessary to promote a good rise when baked. Under-mixing or using a flour that's too weak will keep the dough from forming a strong enough gluten, and over-mixing will partially destroy the structure already formed in the dough. Most of the recipes in this book use a mixing system that includes a brief rest after the initial mixing, when the gluten strands relax and regroup so that the dough easily becomes smooth and elastic during its final mixing. Turning the dough once or several times during the dough's fermentation further tones and strengthens the gluten, imparting a gentle, manageable elasticity to the dough.

FERMENTATION

Panary fermentation is the process whereby a bread dough ferments due to the life cycle of the yeast in it. The yeast feeds on carbohydrates in the dough and during its life cycle produces carbon dioxide gas (that makes the dough rise), alcohol and enzymes. Bulk fermentation refers to the initial fermentation of bread dough after the ingredients have been mixed.

PRE-FERMENTS

A pre-ferment or sponge is a small quantity of dough that's mixed from part of the flour, all or part of the yeast or other leavening in the dough and part of the liquid. Pre-ferments produce enzymes that favourably influence the structure of the final dough and the texture and flavour of the baked bread. A firm pre-ferment is sometimes known by its Italian name, *biga*. A poolish (see page 107) is less firm, and contains a higher proportion of liquid in relation to the weight of the flour.

NATURAL PRE-FERMENTS

Sourdough starter, a mixture of flour, water, and sometimes malt and salt, ferments naturally from the native yeasts in the flour. The 'sour' in sourdough comes from the action of a bacterium known as a *Lactobacillus*, present everywhere, that lives in symbiosis with the natural yeasts and produces lactic acid during its life cycle.

Levain is the French name for sourdough starter and *lievito madre* (literally 'mother yeast') is the Italian name. In French bread formulas, the sponge or pre-ferment made using sourdough is referred to as the *levain*.

YEAST-BASED PRE-FERMENTS

Aside from using a sponge and poolish, defined above, there are several other systems for adding a pre-ferment to a bread dough. Saving a small amount of dough from a batch and keeping it cold to add to the next day's dough is referred to as using 'old dough'. The French name for old dough is *pâte fermentée* (fermented dough). Another pre-ferment known by the French name of *levain-levure* (yeast starter) is a starter made from flour, water and yeast that apes sourdough. As in sourdough use, some of the *levain-levure* is used in the dough and a portion is fed and allowed to ferment until the process is repeated the next day. Begun principally as a way to save money on yeast, the *levain-levure* system isn't used outside the world of commercial baking in France.

RESTING/FORMING/PROOFING

After bulk fermentation, dough often needs to rest between the steps of forming it into a loaf or rolls. Dividing the dough into separate units and then leaving them partially formed and allowing them to rest so that the gluten has time to relax is known as bench proofing. After the dough is formed, the final rising before baking is known as proofing to distinguish it from bulk fermentation. A loaf that proofs too long before baking is said to be over-proofed and will not rise well in the oven and might even collapse.

SLASHING/SCORING

Making cuts in the surface of a completely proofed loaf is known as slashing or scoring, and allows for the increased expansion during baking; without slashing, the surface of the loaf might crack or expand irregularly, compromising its appearance.

BAKING

The final rise that a bread dough makes in the oven is known as oven spring. Oven spring relies on a well-developed gluten structure and the right degree of proofing for success. Spraying the surface of a loaf with water before and during the initial few minutes of baking prevents the crust from hardening too quickly and allows for maximum expansion. Introducing steam into the oven while bread is baking by pouring water or ice onto a heated pan also helps and plays a role in developing a crisp crust. While good, none of these systems fully mimics the live steam introduced into a real baker's oven.

FORMING/SHAPING BREADS

BAKING METHODS

chapter three

One-Step Breads

If you want to try baking bread for the first time or you're short on time for bread baking, these recipes will give you a great loaf with a minimum of time and effort. I've provided instructions for machine mixing, but you'll find the methods for mixing by hand in Chapter 2. The one-step or straight dough method refers to the fact that all the ingredients are mixed to a dough in a fast continuous process, rather than using a pre-ferment or starter that needs to be made in advance. For ease and convenience in baking, all these breads are baked on a flat baking sheet and don't need to be slid onto a heated baking sheet or baking stone already in the oven. Spraying the loaves with water before and during the first few minutes of baking is an important step. Though it won't necessarily make a very crisp crust (the fairly dense crumb of these loaves retains too much water after baking to allow that), it does help the loaves to rise evenly and to their full potential by preventing the crust from hardening before the dough is fully risen. There's an old bread baker's trick to getting a crisp crust without using a steam-injection oven: After the bread is baked and cooled, pop it back into a preheated 180°C/gas mark 4 oven for 3–4 minutes and then cool on a rack again – this is best done close to the time you want to serve the bread.

You can be as creative as you like by adding nuts, dried fruit or seasonings, such as spices or fresh or dried herbs, to these loaves. See the recipes for Fig and Almond Bread (page 32) and Fennel and Black Pepper Bread (page 33) for guidelines on quantities to use.

Makes one 23–25cm round loaf

275g room-temperature tap water, about 24°C

7g sachet fine granulated active dried yeast or
    instant yeast

400g strong white bread flour

1 ½ teaspoons fine sea salt

Olive or vegetable oil for the bowl

One heavy baking sheet or pizza pan dusted
    with maize meal or lined with parchment paper,
    plus a spray bottle filled with warm water

If you've never baked bread before or you want a bread that's easy and relatively quick to prepare, look no further. This dough may be mixed by machine or by hand, plus it's easy to shape into a loaf. Once you've baked this one, you'll want to try some of the others in this chapter. All the other recipes in this chapter are mixed the same way and with one exception, all are formed the same way too.

1. Pour the water into the bowl of an electric mixer and whisk in the yeast. Wait 30 seconds and whisk again.

2. Use a large rubber spatula to stir the flour into the yeast and water mixture a little at a time. Make sure all the flour is mixed into the liquid and there isn't any clinging to the side of the bowl.

3. Place the bowl on the mixer and attach the dough hook. Mix on the lowest speed until the dough comes together around the dough hook, 1–2 minutes. Stop the mixer and pull the dough away from the hook; let the dough rest for 15 minutes.

4. Increase the mixer speed to low/medium, sprinkle in the salt and mix until the dough is smooth and elastic, 2–3 minutes longer.

5. Scrape the dough into an oiled bowl and turn it over so that the top is oiled. Cover the bowl with clingfilm and let the dough ferment until it starts to puff, about 30 minutes.

6. Scrape the dough onto a floured work surface, flour your hands, and gently flatten the dough to a disc. Fold the two sides in to overlap at the middle, then roll the top towards you all the way to the end, swiss roll-style. Invert, flatten and repeat. Place the dough back in the bowl seam side down and cover. Let the dough ferment until fully doubled in bulk, about 30 minutes.

7. To form the dough into a boule-shaped loaf, use a flexible plastic scraper to slide it from the bowl to a floured work surface; try not to deflate the dough. Fold the edges of the dough all around its perimeter into the centre. Round the loaf by pushing against the bottom of the dough all around with the sides of your hands held palms upward. The dough will quickly form an even sphere.

8. Place the dough on the prepared baking sheet and cover it with a tea towel or piece of sprayed or oiled clingfilm. Let the dough rest until it starts to puff again, about 30 minutes. Set a rack in the middle level of the oven and preheat to 230°C/gas mark 8.

9. Once the dough is proofed about 50% larger, flour the palms of your hands and gently press to flatten it to about 4cm thick. Use an X-Acto knife or single edge razor blade to cut 4 slashes in the form of a square at the edges of the loaf and a 3mm-deep slash across the diameter of the loaf, then generously spray it with water. Place it in the oven.

10. Wait 5 minutes, then open the oven and spray the loaf again and reduce the oven temperature to 220°C/gas mark 7. Bake the loaf until it is well risen and deep golden and the internal temperature reads 93°C on an instant read thermometer, 20–30 minutes.

11. Cool the loaf on a rack. Keep the bread loosely covered at room temperature on the day it's baked. Wrap and freeze for longer storage. Reheat at 180°C/gas mark 4 for 5 minutes and cool before serving.

Makes one 23–25cm round loaf

340g room-temperature tap water, about 24°C

7g sachet fine granulated active dried yeast or instant yeast

460g strong wholemeal bread flour

2 teaspoons fine sea salt

Oil for the bowl

One heavy baking sheet or pizza pan dusted with maize meal or lined with parchment paper, plus a spray bottle filled with warm water

QUICK CHANGES

Add 120g coarsely chopped walnuts or hazelnuts to the dough at the end of step 4, continuing to mix for another minute or so to distribute the nuts. Add the same amount of raisins or dried currants to the dough along with or instead of the nuts.

B read made entirely from wholemeal flour has more nutritional fibre than white bread. The sweet flavour of wheat comes through loud and clear, though, and that flavour can be emphasised by using an organic stone-ground wholemeal flour that has much more intrinsic flavour than one made by an industrial miller. Thinly sliced, this bread is perfect with cheese, especially if you add some nuts and/or dried fruit to the dough.

1. Pour the water into the bowl of an electric mixer and whisk in the yeast. Wait 30 seconds and whisk again.

2. Use a rubber spatula to stir the flour into the yeast mixture a little at a time. Make sure all the flour is mixed and there isn't any clinging to the side of the bowl.

3. Place the bowl on the mixer and attach the dough hook. Mix on the lowest speed until the dough comes together around the dough hook, 1–2 minutes. Stop the mixer and pull the dough away from the hook; let the dough rest for 15 minutes.

4. Increase the mixer speed to low/medium and sprinkle in the salt; mix until the dough is smooth and elastic, 2–3 minutes longer.

5. Scrape the dough into an oiled bowl and turn it over so that the top is oiled. Cover the bowl with clingfilm and let the dough ferment until it starts to puff, about 30 minutes.

6. See step 6, page 28.

7. See step 7, page 28.

8. Place the dough on the prepared baking sheet and cover it with a flat-weave tea towel or piece of sprayed or oiled clingfilm and let the dough rest until it starts to puff again, about 30 minutes.

9. Set a rack in the middle level of the oven and preheat to 230°C/gas mark 8.

10. Once the dough is proofed to about 50% larger than its original size, flour the palms of your hands and gently press to flatten it to about 2.5cm thick. Use an X-Acto knife or single-edge razor blade to cut a diagonal lattice pattern on the top of the loaf, then generously spray it with water. Place the baking sheet in the oven.

11. Wait 5 minutes, spray the loaf again, then reduce the oven temperature to 220°C/gas mark 7. Bake the loaf until it is well risen and deep golden and the internal temperature reads 93°C on an instant read thermometer, 20–30 minutes.

12. Cool the loaf on a rack. Keep the bread loosely covered at room temperature on the day it's baked. Wrap and freeze for longer storage. Reheat at 180°C/gas mark 4 for 5 minutes and cool before serving.

An almost daily food in the Veneto region of Italy, as well as in Ticino, Switzerland's Italian-speaking canton, polenta is made from maize meal and water slowly cooked together until creamy. Dense versions of polenta are often served with braised or roasted meats, while lighter, creamy polenta is often paired with shellfish or cheese. If you decide not to add cheese to the dough, try a slice of this bread lightly toasted and still warm, spread with Gorgonzola dolce and a tiny drizzle of honey, a perfect marriage of textures and flavours.

1. Pour the water into the bowl of an electric mixer and whisk in the yeast. Wait 30 seconds and whisk again.

2. In a separate bowl, combine the flour, maize meal and cheese, if using, and use a rubber spatula to stir this into the yeast mixture a little at a time. Make sure all the flour mixture is mixed in and there isn't any clinging to the side of the bowl.

3. Place the bowl on the mixer and attach the dough hook. Mix on the lowest speed until the dough comes together around the dough hook, 1–2 minutes. Stop the mixer and pull the dough away from the hook; let the dough rest for 15 minutes.

4. Increase the mixer speed to low/medium and sprinkle in the salt. Mix until the dough is smooth and elastic, about 2–3 minutes. The dough will be very soft and sticky.

5. Scrape the dough into an oiled bowl and turn it over so that the top is oiled. Cover with clingfilm and let the dough ferment until it starts to puff, about 30 minutes.

6. See step 6, page 28.

7. See step 7, page 28.

8. Place the dough on the prepared baking sheet and cover it with a flat-weave tea towel or piece of sprayed or oiled clingfilm and let the dough rest until it starts to puff again, about 30 minutes.

9. Set a rack in the middle level of the oven and preheat to 230°C/gas mark 8.

10. Once the dough is proofed to about 50% larger than its original size, flour the palms of your hands and gently press to flatten it to about 2.5cm thick. Use an X-Acto knife or single-edge razor blade to cut a shallow slash across the diameter of the loaf, then cut another at a 90-degree angle to the first, making a cross shape. Be careful not to cut too deeply into this dough because it's so soft; deep cuts will cause the loaf to open too widely while it is baking. Generously spray the loaf with water. Place the baking sheet in the oven.

11. Wait 5 minutes, spray the loaf again, then reduce the oven temperature to 220°C/gas mark 7. Bake the loaf until it is well risen and deep golden and the internal temperature reads 93°C on an instant read thermometer, 20–30 minutes.

12. Cool the loaf on a rack. Keep the bread loosely covered at room temperature on the day it's baked. Wrap and freeze for longer storage. Reheat at 180°C/gas mark 4 for 5 minutes and cool before serving.

Makes one 25cm round loaf

340g room-temperature tap water, about 24°C

7g sachet fine granulated active dried yeast or instant yeast

400g strong white bread flour

120g stone-ground yellow maize meal

45g finely grated Parmigiano Reggiano cheese, optional

1 ½ teaspoons fine sea salt

Olive or vegetable oil for the bowl

One heavy baking sheet or pizza pan dusted with maize meal or lined with parchment paper, plus a spray bottle filled with warm water

polenta bread

Makes two small 20cm round loaves

230g dried Calimyrna figs

375g room-temperature tap water, about 24ºC

7g sachet fine granulated active dried yeast or instant yeast

400g strong white bread flour

130g strong wholemeal bread flour

1 tablespoon sugar

2 teaspoons salt

150g whole unblanched almonds, coarsely chopped and lightly toasted

Olive or vegetable oil for the bowl

15g unsalted butter, melted, for brushing the loaves after baking

One 30 x 45.5cm swiss roll pan dusted with maize meal or lined with parchment paper, plus a spray bottle filled with warm water

---

QUICK CHANGES

Substitute diced dried apricots or pitted dates, dried cherries or cranberries, or a mixture of raisins and sultanas for the figs.

My friend Ann Nurse has been a loyal customer of Royal Crown Bakery in Brooklyn, New York, for years, and whenever I see her she gives me a couple of their fig and walnut loaves. When I was planning which breads to include in this book, I embarked on an attempt to recreate the flavour, with almonds instead of walnuts. Ann and I both agreed that there might be a little sugar in the dough, and that it looked and tasted as though there might also be a little wholemeal flour. It took a few tries, but I'm happy with the result.

1. Snip the stems from the figs; if they're at all hard or dried out, put them in a bowl and cover them with boiling water. Let them steep for 15 minutes, then drain and pat dry with kitchen paper before cutting into 1cm dice.

2. Pour the water into the bowl of an electric mixer and whisk in the yeast. Wait 30 seconds and whisk again.

3. Combine the strong white bread flour, wholemeal flour and sugar and use a large rubber spatula to stir them into the yeast liquid a little at a time. Make sure all the flour is mixed into the liquid and there isn't any clinging to the side of the bowl.

4. Place the bowl on the mixer and attach the dough hook. Mix on the lowest speed until the dough comes together around the dough hook, 1–2 minutes. Stop the mixer and pull the dough away from the hook; let the dough rest for 15 minutes.

5. Increase the mixer speed to low/medium and sprinkle in the salt. Mix until the dough is smoother and more elastic, 2–3 minutes longer. Add the figs and almonds and mix 1 further minute to distribute them.

6. Scrape the dough into an oiled bowl and turn it over so that the top is oiled. Cover with clingfilm and let the dough ferment until it starts to puff, about 30 minutes.

7. See step 6, page 28.

8. See step 7, page 28. Divide the dough into 2 equal pieces. Round each by pushing against the bottom of the dough all around with the sides of your hands held palms upward. The dough will quickly form an even sphere.

9. Place the loaves several centimetres apart on the prepared baking sheet, cover with a flat-weave tea towel and let rest until they start to puff, about 30 minutes. Set a rack in the middle level of the oven and preheat to 230°C/gas mark 8.

10. Once the loaves are proofed about 50% larger, flour the palms of your hands and gently press to flatten them to about 2.5cm thick. Use a single-edge razor blade to cut a deep slash across the diameter of each loaf, and another at a 90-degree angle to the first. Generously spray the loaves with water. Place the baking sheet in the oven.

11. Wait 5 minutes, spray the loaves again, then reduce the oven temperature to 200°C/gas mark 6. Bake until well risen and deep golden, with an internal temperature of 93°C on an instant-read thermometer, 20–30 minutes.

12. Place the baked loaves on a rack, brush them all over with the melted butter and let cool completely. Keep the bread loosely covered at room temperature on the day it's baked. Wrap and freeze for longer storage. Reheat at 190°C for 5 minutes and cool before serving.

The seasonings in this slightly spicy bread recall the Neapolitan savoury ring cookies called *taralli*. Though there are many different types of *taralli*, both savoury and sweet, fennel seeds and pepper are the most commonly used savoury seasonings. I decided to add eggs to the dough for this bread, as they are used in the most delicate *taralli*, prepared only as an Easter treat. I decided to bake this bread as a ring, though you can shape it into a round loaf like the other breads in this chapter. This is a fine bread to serve with strongly flavoured starters or snacks, such as dried sausage, smoked meat or smoked or aged cheese. It has no place alongside delicately seasoned dishes, which it would overwhelm.

1. Pour the water into the bowl of an electric mixer and whisk in the yeast. Wait 30 seconds and whisk again, then whisk in the oil and eggs.

2. Combine the flour, fennel seeds and pepper and use a large rubber spatula to stir this mixture into the liquid a little at a time. Make sure all the flour is mixed into the liquid and there isn't any clinging to the side of the bowl.

3. Place the bowl on the mixer and attach the dough hook. Mix on the lowest speed until the dough comes together around the dough hook, 1–2 minutes. Stop the mixer and pull the dough away from the hook; let the dough rest for 15 minutes.

4. Increase the mixer speed to low/medium and sprinkle in the salt. Mix until the dough is smooth and elastic, 2–3 minutes longer.

5. Scrape the dough into an oiled bowl and turn it over so that the top is oiled. Cover with clingfilm and let the dough ferment until it starts to puff, about 30 minutes.

6. See step 6, page 28.

7. To shape the dough, invert it so that the smooth side is underneath and pull it into a rough square. Roll the piece of dough from the top towards you, swiss roll-style, to make a cylinder. Roll the cylinder under the palms of both hands to lengthen and extend it to about 65–75cm in length. Sprinkle a few drops of water on the two ends, overlap them to form a circle and roll under the palm of your hand to make them the same thickness as the rest of the ring.

8. Transfer the loaf to the prepared baking sheet. Cover with a flat-weave tea towel or piece of sprayed or oiled clingfilm and let rest until it starts to puff again, about 30 minutes. Set a rack in the middle level of the oven and preheat to 230°C/gas mark 8.

9. Once the loaf is about 50% larger than its original size, use an X-Acto knife or single-edge razor blade to cut 4 or 5 straight overlapping slashes along the top of the ring. Generously spray the loaf with water. Place the baking sheet in the oven.

10. Wait 5 minutes, spray the loaf again, then reduce the oven temperature to 220°C/gas mark 7. Bake the loaf until it is well risen, deep golden, and the internal temperature reads 93°C on an instant read thermometer, 20–30 minutes.

11. Cool the loaf on a rack. Keep the bread loosely covered at room temperature on the day it's baked. Wrap and freeze for longer storage. Reheat at 180°C/gas mark 4 for 5 minutes and cool before serving.

Makes one large ring loaf, about 30cm in diameter, or two smaller ones

225g room-temperature tap water, about 24°C

7g sachet fine granulated active dried yeast or instant yeast

4 tablespoons olive oil

3 medium eggs, at room temperature

525g strong white bread flour

1 tablespoon fennel seeds

1 tablespoon coarsely ground black pepper

2 teaspoons fine sea salt

Olive or vegetable oil for the bowl

One heavy baking sheet or pizza pan dusted with maize meal or lined with parchment paper, plus a spray bottle filled with warm water

QUICK CHANGES

For a spicier loaf, replace the black pepper with crushed red pepper. You can also replace the fennel seeds with 2–3 tablespoons chopped fresh rosemary leaves.

fennel & black pepper bread

mexican-style meatballs

Makes 12 meatballs in sauce, 4–6 servings

SALSA VERDE

570g tomatillos (available online), husked and rinsed

2 small jalapeño chillies, rinsed and stemmed

2 small cloves garlic, smashed and peeled

½ teaspoon ground cumin

15g coriander leaves and upper stems, rinsed and drained

240ml chicken or vegetable stock or the water from cooking the vegetables

1 tablespoon vegetable oil, such as safflower or rapeseed

1½ teaspoons salt

ALBÓNDIGAS

3 medium eggs

120ml milk, heated to a simmer

85g fresh breadcrumbs (see box, page 36)

450g beef mince

3 thin slices (about 50g) boiled ham, finely chopped

½ small white onion (about 50g), peeled and grated on the largest holes of a box grater

1 tablespoon chopped fresh mint

½ teaspoon salt

¼ teaspoon freshly ground black pepper

Chopped coriander, finely chopped white onion and crumbled Mexican *queso fresco* for serving

---

QUICK CHANGES

ALBÓNDIGAS ENCHIPOTLADAS: Substitute 2 tinned chipotle chillies in adobo sauce for the jalapeños, and omit the coriander.

When I asked my friend Roberto Santibañez, chef/owner of Fonda in Brooklyn, New York, and on Avenue B in Manhattan, about *albóndigas* (al-BONE-dee-gahs) he told me his grandmother brought her meatball ingredients to a butcher in Mexico City and asked him to run them through the meat grinder along with the beef she purchased there. I doubt your local butcher would take your request seriously if you showed up with the ham, onion and hard-boiled eggs for this recipe, but it's easy enough to make these meatballs at home without a meat grinder. Unlike Italian-style meatballs, these are not cooked in oil first, but just dropped into the pot of simmering sauce. Serve with steamed white rice.

1. For the *salsa verde*, put the tomatillos and chiles into a 23cm-wide by 10cm-deep saucepan or Dutch oven. (The size of the pan is important so the meatballs will fit in a single layer and be submerged in the sauce later on.) Cover the vegetables with cold water. Add 2 of the eggs for the *albóndigas* to hard-boil them. Bring to the boil over a medium heat, then decrease the heat to an active simmer. After 6 minutes, remove the eggs to a bowl of cold water. Continue cooking the vegetables for 15 minutes.

2. Cool and peel the eggs under cold running water and immediately plunge them into a small bowl of ice water so they don't develop a dark ring around the yolk.

3. Cool the vegetables in the liquid for another 20 minutes.

4. Use a slotted spoon to transfer the vegetables to a blender. Pulse on medium speed to chop coarsely. Add the garlic, cumin, coriander and stock and pulse again until the sauce is speckled with coriander – not too long or the tomatillo seeds will purée and make the sauce pasty.

5. Rinse the pan in which the vegetables were cooked, dry it and add the oil. Place over a medium heat and when the oil has heated, add the sauce and the salt. Cook, stirring occasionally, over a medium heat until slightly thickened, about 10 minutes. Remove from the heat if you're not ready to add the meatballs.

6. For the *albóndigas*, quarter the hard-boiled eggs lengthways, then cut across into 1cm pieces and set aside.

7. Pour the hot milk over the breadcrumbs in a mixing bowl and let stand 5 minutes without stirring. Add the minced beef, ham, onion, chopped mint, salt, pepper and the remaining (raw) egg. Use a rubber spatula to fold everything together evenly without overmixing. Fold in the chopped eggs last.

8. Reheat the sauce if necessary and while it's coming to the boil, divide the beef mixture into 12 equal parts; use moistened hands to roll them into 12 balls. Once the sauce is simmering again, gently slip the meatballs into the sauce and return to the boil. Adjust the heat so that the sauce just simmers and cook for 30 minutes.

9. Prepare a few hours in advance and reheat before serving. Leftovers are good but *albóndigas* are best on the day they're prepared.

10. Serve in soup plates topped with the coriander, onion and cheese, with a large spoonful of steamed rice on the side. The toppings aren't obligatory but are traditional.

Makes one large loaf, about 8 servings

180ml milk, plus a little more if needed

140g fresh bread (trimmed of any crisp crusts before weighing) in 1cm dice

2 tablespoons olive oil

1 large white onion, 170–225g, peeled and finely chopped

3 large cloves garlic, peeled and finely chopped

One 340g jar roasted peppers, drained, trimmed of black spots and seeds, finely chopped

570g turkey mince

140ml tomato passata

10g finely chopped flat-leaf parsley

30g Parmigiano Reggiano, finely grated

1 medium egg

Salt and freshly ground black pepper

Minced turkey can cook up so dry that I hesitated to try a meatloaf made from it until a friend told me that she adds puréed cooked aubergine to hers. Though I didn't follow her method exactly, it did prompt me to add roasted peppers and a lot of passata, which, teamed with plenty of soaked fresh bread, made a moist and tender meatloaf.

1. Set a rack in the middle level of the oven and preheat to 190°C/gas mark 5.

2. Heat the milk to a simmer, then pour over the bread in a large mixing bowl. Let soak, then toss around with a rubber spatula to see if all the bread is evenly moistened. If not, add a little more milk. Mash the bread and milk with a potato masher while still warm, being careful not to stir, which will make it gluey.

3. Combine the oil, onion and garlic in a saucepan with a lid and set on a medium heat. Once the onions start to sizzle, decrease the heat, cover the pan, and sweat until very soft, about 15 minutes. Increase the heat back to medium and add the peppers. Cook until most of the pepper juices have evaporated, stirring often.

4. Add the vegetables and minced turkey to the mashed bread bowl and use the potato masher again to mix. Stir in all the remaining ingredients.

5. Take about 4 tablespoons of the mixture and press into a patty. Cook it in a small oiled nonstick pan for a couple of minutes on each side, then taste for seasoning. Adjust as necessary.

6. Spread the mixture into an oiled 23 x 33 x 5cm tin and form a tall loaf. Bake until the loaf reads 65–70°C on an instant-read thermometer, 35–45 minutes. Serve immediately or cool, wrap and serve cold.

MAKING BREADCRUMBS

Born of the desire to use every crumb of precious bread so that none go to waste, here are the principal types:

Dry breadcrumbs – made from hard bread without removing the crusts, broken into small pieces and pulsed in the food processor. Sift the resulting crumbs through a fine-mesh sieve to eliminate large flakes. Store in an airtight container in the freezer. Dry breadcrumbs are mostly used for breading fried foods, in some stuffings, or for sprinkling on a dish, often with grated cheese and baked to a golden crust. (When used as a main ingredient for stuffing or as a topping, they may be more coarsely ground for texture.)

Panko or Japanese breadcrumbs – made from firm white bread that's torn apart by vertical blades with large saw teeth. Panko may be white or tan, depending on whether the crust is removed, and are very crisp and coarse textured. A decent imitation can be made by putting firm white bread through the largest grating blade on a food processor and then drying the crumbs on a swiss roll tin in a 150°C/gas mark 2 oven for 10 minutes. Cool and store as above.

Fresh breadcrumbs – made from fresh bread diced and pulsed in a food processor, removing the crusts for white breadcrumbs. Fresh breadcrumbs are often used as a moistening agent in meatloaf or meatballs, when gently folded with liquid.

After years of trial and error, I arrived at this version of meatloaf, and I make it all the time now. The soaked breadcrumbs make the meatloaf moist whether you serve it hot or cold.

1. Set a rack in the middle level of the oven and preheat to 190°C/gas mark 5.

2. Combine the oil and onion in a medium sauté pan and cook over a low heat until soft and translucent, about 15 minutes.

3. Put the breadcrumbs in a large mixing bowl and pour over the hot milk. Let stand until the milk has been absorbed and the mixture is cool. Don't mix or it might become gummy and elastic.

4. Add the meat, cooked onions, egg and passata or ketchup and fold rather than stir the ingredients together.

5. Add the remaining ingredients (use a little less salt if using pecorino Romano) and fold in. Spread the mixture in an oiled 23 x 33cm gratin or baking dish to form a tall loaf. Bake until the loaf reads 65–70°C on an instant-read thermometer, about 30–35 minutes.

6. Serve immediately with mashed potatoes or a green vegetable or cool, wrap and serve cold.

Makes one 30cm loaf, about 8 servings

2 tablespoons olive oil or vegetable oil, such as safflower or rapeseed

1 medium white onion, about 225g, peeled and finely chopped

85g fresh breadcrumbs (see box, page 36)

140ml milk, scalded

450g beef mince

1 medium egg

75ml passata (or ketchup for a more 'American' flavour)

1 large clove garlic, peeled and grated on a Microplane

5g chopped flat-leaf parsley

20g Parmigiano Reggiano or pecorino Romano, grated

½ teaspoon salt

¼ teaspoon freshly ground black pepper

(better than) mum's meatloaf

QUICK CHANGES

ITALIAN-AMERICAN MEATBALLS:
• Omit the oil, onion and passata. Form the mixture into 12 equal meatballs.
• Heat about 5mm of vegetable oil in a 15cm nonstick pan and brown the meatballs, turning them in the oil so that they colour on all sides.
• Heat 3 tablespoons olive oil in a large saucepan with a lid. Add 3 cloves garlic, smashed and peeled, and cook over a medium heat until light golden. Off heat, stir in 790g passata, 240ml water and ½ teaspoon salt. Add a sprig or two of basil if you have some. Add the meatballs and bring the sauce to the boil. Decrease the heat to a simmer and place the lid ajar on the pan. Cook the sauce until reduced and flavourful, about 1 ½ hours.
• For a better flavoured sauce, brown 225g spareribs or a small shoulder pork chop in the oil before adding the garlic.

sicilian pasta with breadcrumbs

Makes 4–6 starter servings

TOMATO AND ANCHOVY SAUCE

75ml olive oil

3 large cloves garlic, smashed and peeled

One 55g tin anchovy fillets in oil, drained and finely chopped

240ml passata

75ml water

Salt and freshly ground black pepper

2 tablespoons chopped flat-leaf parsley

TOASTED BREADCRUMBS

115g dry breadcrumbs (see box, page 36)

2 tablespoons olive oil

450g spaghettini or other pasta

QUICK CHANGES

PASTA CU' VRUCCULI ARRIMINATI/ PASTA WITH CAULIFLOWER MASH:

• Separate a 900g cauliflower into florets, discarding the leaves and inner core and add to a large pot of boiling water. Cook until very tender and remove with a slotted spoon, reserving the cooking water.
• Substitute a large onion, finely chopped, for the garlic and cook with the oil in a saucepan over a low heat until soft. Add the anchovies, omit the passata, water and parsley.
• Soak 1/4 teaspoon saffron threads in 4 tablespoons hot water and add to the pan after stirring in the cooked cauliflower. Cook over a low heat, stirring occasionally, until disintegrated, about 15 minutes.
• Stir in 4 tablespoons each toasted pine nuts and dried currants and salt and pepper to taste.
• Bring the cooking water back to a boil with salt, and cook 450g of tubular pasta. Drain and toss with the sauce and additional cooking water if necessary.
• Sprinkle the breadcrumbs generously over the top and serve.

Though I'm one quarter Sicilian, I never tasted this dish until I visited cousins there in 1974. Breadcrumbs toasted in a little olive oil were a substitute for the grated cheese some people couldn't afford to buy to sprinkle on pasta. To this day, bread is considered precious in Sicily, and none is ever discarded. Anchovies packed in olive oil make an adequate substitute for the salted anchovies used in Sicily, though if you're lucky enough to find salted anchovies, use them, as oil-packed anchovies lack their salty bite. I like to use spaghettini (thin spaghetti) for this dish, though regular spaghetti can be used.

1. For the sauce, combine the oil and garlic in a small saucepan and set over a low heat. Let the garlic colour to a light golden, 2–3 minutes.

2. Remove the pan from the heat and stir in the anchovies. Use a heatproof silicone spatula to mash the anchovies into the oil, without mashing the garlic. Continue stirring and mashing back on the heat until the anchovies have almost disintegrated.

3. Remove from the heat and stir in the passata and water. Season lightly with salt and pepper (keep in mind that the anchovies may be salty) and set back on a medium heat. Bring to the boil and decrease the heat so that it simmers gently for about 20 minutes, after which taste and adjust the seasoning and discard the garlic.

4. While the sauce is cooking, combine the breadcrumbs and oil in a medium nonstick sauté pan and place over a medium heat.

Stir constantly and as the breadcrumbs begin to colour, decrease the heat to prevent burning. Continue toasting the crumbs until they are a deep golden colour.

5. Cook the pasta *al dente* in a large pot of boiling salted water, remembering to stir the pasta after adding it to the water until it returns to the boil.

6. Meanwhile, reheat the sauce and stir in the parsley.

7. Dip out a cupful of the cooking water, then drain the pasta well in a colander and return it to its pot. Evenly stir in the sauce until the pasta is lightly coated. Add a little of the reserved water if it seems dry. Sprinkle in about two thirds of the breadcrumbs.

8. Serve the pasta in heated soup plates, sprinkling each portion with some of the remaining breadcrumbs.

Not like typical stuffed peppers with a meat or rice filling, these are baked with a sprinkling of pine nuts and capers, topped with seasoned breadcrumbs and drizzled with olive oil. They make a fine first course alongside other simple antipasti, or a great side dish with plain grilled or roasted meat or fish. These peppers are typical of the Italian region of Puglia, where Ann's family has its origins. For advance preparation, get everything ready and bake close to the time you intend to serve them, or bake the peppers early in the day for the evening. However, don't make these the day before or the breadcrumbs will lose their freshly toasted flavour.

1. Set a rack in the middle level of the oven and preheat to 190°C/gas mark 5. Evenly spread the tomatoes in the prepared baking dish.

2. Rinse the peppers and drain them. Halve or quarter the peppers, depending on their size, and pull away the stem and seed pod. Shake or brush away any stray seeds. Arrange the pepper pieces, skin side down, on the tomatoes. Sprinkle the pine nuts and capers on top.

3. Mix the breadcrumbs with the garlic and parsley and top each piece of pepper with about 1 tablespoon of the mixture. Drizzle the olive oil over the breadcrumb topping.

4. Bake the peppers until they are tender and the breadcrumbs are deep golden, about 30 minutes, checking occasionally to make sure the tomatoes are not drying out too much. If necessary, add 1–2 tablespoons of water, but be sure to place it directly in the pan to avoid wetting the breadcrumbs.

5. Cool the peppers and serve them warm or at room temperature.

ann nurse's baked stuffed peppers

Makes 4–6 servings

200g well drained tinned plum tomatoes, crushed

3 large red or yellow peppers, or a combination, about 675g

45g pine nuts

50g tiny capers, rinsed and drained

75g dry breadcrumbs (see box, page 36)

2 large cloves garlic, peeled and finely grated on a Microplane

3 tablespoons finely chopped flat-leaf parsley

3–4 tablespoons olive oil

One 23 x 33 x 5cm glass or metal baking dish, or a similar size gratin dish, brushed with olive oil

peperoni imbottiti

QUICK CHANGES

BAKED CLAMS OREGANATE: A mainstay of Italian-American restaurants, these baked clams are worth making at home, where you can be sure of the freshness of all the ingredients. • For 4 people you'll need 1–1 ½ dozen small clams, such as palourdes, no more than 3-4cm in diameter. • Open the clams and set them on a medium baking dish that can go to the table. • To the breadcrumb mixture in step 3 above, add 1 teaspoon dried oregano, and a pinch of cayenne pepper. Spoon the topping into the clam halves and gently press it down with a fingertip. • Drizzle on another tablespoon of olive oil and bake at 190°C/gas mark 5 on the top rack of the oven until the crumbs are nicely browned and the clams are tender, 10 to 15 minutes. • Serve immediately.

real wiener schnitzel, hotel imperial, vienna

Serves 4

125g plain flour

2 medium eggs, well whisked

115g dry breadcrumbs (see box, page 36)

Fine sea salt or table salt

4 x 140g slices veal rib eye, pounded paper thin, see below

340g clarified butter, see below

A far cry from my mother's Monday dinner breaded veal cutlets, a real *Wiener schnitzel* isn't easy to find, even in Vienna. Veal rib eye pounded paper thin, lightly breaded with flour, beaten egg, and dry breadcrumbs made from *Semmeln*, classic Viennese dinner rolls, it's then shallow fried in clarified butter. This classic dish is a mega indulgence for sure, but worth every calorie. On a recent visit to Vienna, I had an opportunity to see then executive chef Siegfried Kroepfl of the Hotel Imperial prepare what is reputed to be the best schnitzel in Vienna. Here's the recipe exactly as he prepared it, but the most practical choice is best-quality veal cut from the topside. The same size slices of pork, chicken breast, or thin fish fillets, such as plaice or lemon sole, can be substituted, but the fish won't need pounding.

MORE ABOUT CLARIFIED BUTTER

To clarify 450g of butter, heat it slowly over a low heat in a medium saucepan. When it has melted, let it stand off heat for 10 minutes. Use a spoon to skim off the foamy solids on the top. Pour off the clarified butter, leaving behind the watery residue in the pan, into a plastic container, cover and refrigerate. The butter may be used a second time after frying a batch of schnitzels; pass it through a fine-mesh sieve to eliminate any crumbs, then cover and refrigerate as above. Use within a month.

Best quality cold-pressed vegetable oil, such as safflower (my favourite), olive (not extra-virgin), or rapeseed, make fine substitutes for the butter.

1. Put the flour, eggs and breadcrumbs into three separate shallow bowls.

2. Lightly salt the meat on each side. Using a fork, place one of the schnitzels into the bowl of flour. Gently press down so that the flour adheres, then turn over and repeat.

3. Next dip the meat on both sides in the beaten egg.

4. Place the egg-coated schnitzel into the bowl of breadcrumbs and gently shake the bowl to coat the underside of the schnitzel. Turn it over and repeat with the second side. Avoid pressing the crumbs into the meat, which will make a hard coating.

5. Repeat with the remaining schnitzels, remembering to clean the breadcrumbs off the end of the fork between each schnitzel.

You may leave the schnitzels covered at a cool room temperature for 1–2 hours before cooking them.

6. When ready to cook, heat the clarified butter over a medium heat in a 23cm sauté pan to 160°C. One at a time, cook the schnitzels until golden on each side, less than 2 minutes per side – the meat is so thin it will easily cook through. Transfer the schnitzels to baking sheets lined with kitchen paper to drain.

7. Serve on warm dinner plates with a tossed salad or a potato salad with a simple oil and vinegar dressing. Drink an Austrian Riesling or Veltliner or a good quality beer.

Caesar Salad was created in 1924 by Italian-born chef Caesar Cardini at his restaurant in Tijuana, Mexico. Nothing more than a cos lettuce salad with garlicky toasted croûtons, dressed with garlic-scented olive oil, lemon juice, grated Parmesan cheese, a dash of Worcestershire sauce, and a partially cooked 'coddled' egg, the recipe has been modified in the intervening years to contain anchovies, crumbled bacon, and more recently strips of grilled chicken, fish or shellfish. Today, people are more concerned than ever before about consuming raw or partially cooked eggs, so you can substitute sugar-free mayonnaise for the egg.

Makes 4 servings as a starter or side dish

90ml extra-virgin olive oil

1 large clove garlic, crushed and peeled

110g garlic croûtons, see below

1 pasteurised egg in the shell, dropped into boiling water for 1 minute and cooled, or 2 tablespoons sugar-free mayonnaise

3 tablespoons freshly squeezed lemon juice, strained before measuring

Dash of Worcestershire sauce

Salt and freshly ground black pepper

30g Parmigiano Reggiano, finely grated

2 small heads cos lettuce, about 450g total, wilted leaves removed, cut into 2.5cm pieces, rinsed and spun dry

1. An hour before you intend to serve the salad, combine the oil and crushed garlic and let steep for 30 minutes; remove and discard the garlic.

2. Prepare the croûtons (see box).

3. Right before serving the salad, transfer the coddled egg or mayonnaise to the salad bowl and whisk in the lemon juice, Worcestershire sauce and salt and pepper to taste. Slowly whisk in the garlic oil so that the dressing thickens and becomes smooth, but don't worry if it separates a little.

4. Scatter the grated cheese over the dressing, add the cut lettuce and toss everything together with salad servers so that the greens are evenly coated with the dressing and cheese.

5. Add the croûtons, toss again and serve immediately on chilled plates.

MAKING CROÛTONS

The name croûtons means 'little crusts' in French. They were originally made from thin slices of bread cut into round or heart shapes, fried in butter or oil and used to garnish meat dishes served in a sauce, such as veal Marengo, an early 19th-century dish.

For soup croûtons, cut simply flavoured bread, such as Easiest Home-Baked Bread, page 28, into 1cm slices. Cut away the crusts then cut the bread into 1cm dice. For 110g of croûtons, place them on a swiss roll tin and toss with 3 tablespoons melted butter or olive oil. Bake at 180°C/gas mark 4 on the middle rack, stirring often, until deep golden, about 10 minutes. Transfer to a clean tin, spread out, and let cool. Cover loosely if not using immediately. These are best prepared the same day you're serving them, especially when made with butter.

For salad croûtons, the procedure is the same. Toast them plain, with olive oil, or if they are to be used in a Caesar salad, olive oil that has been steeped with garlic. Alternatively, if the bread is firm enough when you slice it, rub one side with a halved and lightly smashed clove of garlic before cubing.

endive salad with hot bacon vinaigrette

Makes 4 starter servings

40g croûtons made from crustless bread, cut into
   1cm cubes (see box, page 43)

170g bacon lardons

1 tablespoon finely chopped shallot

1 tablespoon Dijon mustard

3½ teaspoons red wine vinegar

Salt and freshly ground black pepper

5 tablespoons extra-virgin olive oil

1 medium head endive, tough outer leaves and
   stems removed, rinsed, dried, and cut into 5cm
   pieces, at room temperature

All variations of this popular salad descend from a common past – a rich Burgundian dish called salade Lyonnaise, made up of dandelion greens, diced hard-boiled or poached eggs, diced cooked pork (usually a pig's foot), mashed cooked herring, garlic croûtons, and diced bacon. A hot dressing made from the rendered bacon fat with vinegar, most likely to wilt the greens, is poured over. Today's version is made with frisée or endive, cooked diced bacon, croûtons and a vinegary dressing, sometimes incorporating hot bacon fat, with an optional poached egg.

My introduction to this type of salad occurred at the pioneering New York bistro Quatorze on West 14th Street, opened by Mark di Giulio and Peter Meltzer. Their version is simple, excellent, and easy to prepare – it pares down the original to endive with a hot bacon vinaigrette, smoky diced bacon and crisp croûtons.

1. Set a rack in the middle level of the oven and preheat to 190°C/gas mark 5.

2. Bake the croûtons in a small ovenproof sauté pan until dry and just beginning to colour, 8–10 minutes. Slide the croûtons into a small bowl and add the bacon lardons to the hot pan. Bake the bacon until it renders some of its fat, about 5 minutes.

3. Transfer the bacon lardons from the fat onto kitchen paper to drain and discard all but 3 tablespoons of the fat.

4. For the dressing, whisk the shallot, mustard, vinegar and a pinch each of salt and pepper in a small bowl. Whisk in the oil a little at a time until smooth. The recipe up until this point can be done early in the day and set aside at room temperature.

5. When you're ready to serve the salad, put the endive in a mixing bowl.

6. Reheat the bacon fat on a medium heat. Add the bacon lardons and cook, tossing or stirring occasionally, until they're lightly browned, about 3 or 4 minutes. Add the croûtons and cook, tossing or stirring, until they colour lightly. Use a slotted spoon to remove the croûtons and bacon and add them to the bowl of salad.

7. Place the pan back on a medium heat and add the dressing to the bacon fat left in the pan (it might splatter a little). Let it bubble up once and immediately pour over the croûtons, bacon and greens. Quickly toss and serve on room temperature plates.

chapter four

Slow-Rise Breads

If you have a patient nature, slow-rise breads will appeal to you. They're made from doughs that just need to be mixed together with a rubber spatula and left to rise at room temperature for 8–12 hours. After that, they're given a couple of turns, and you're off and running to shape your loaf, proof it and bake it.

The small amount of yeast used and the long rising time result in a dough that bakes up to a flavourful loaf. And unlike some slow-rise breads that are made from doughs so soft that they're a nightmare to handle, the doughs in this chapter have enough body to make shaping easy.

Slow-rise bread came into the spotlight several years ago, when food writer Mark Bittman did a story and recipe in *The New York Times* about New York baker Jim Lahey's bread, which is baked in a preheated and covered enamelled iron Dutch oven. Many adaptations have been published in bread books since that story appeared. When I spoke to Jim about it before starting this book, he would only acknowledge that he was flattered by the imitations of his method. I'm not providing that recipe here, mainly because *The New York Times* story is easy enough to find online, but I do include instructions for using a pizza stone to bake single loaves of the breads that follow.

The savoury bread puddings that follow the bread recipes are one of the most flavourful uses for leftover or stale bread of any kind. Bread puddings made from diced bread have all the ingredients evenly dispersed throughout the mixture, while those made from slices of bread are layered and are called *strata*. A pudding made from diced bread absorbs the custard more easily and is quickly ready for the oven; layers of sliced bread and other ingredients take longer to absorb the custard and are often chilled overnight to ensure even moistening. If you prefer a very crisp top crust, use firm bread, like the breads in this chapter. If you want a more gentle crunch, use a more tender bread, such as the sandwich breads in Chapter 5.

The main difference between slow-rise bread and other simple breads that are made with flour, water, yeast and salt lies in the fact that it needs only a little mixing; the long rising time develops all the gluten needed to make the dough smooth and elastic. It's among the easiest types of bread to make if you're careful to use plenty of flour on the work surface and your hands when shaping it, as the dough is soft and sticky.

Makes one round loaf, about 23cm in diameter

255g room-temperature tap water, about 24°C

½ teaspoon fine granulated active dried yeast or instant yeast

340g strong white bread flour

3 tablespoons chopped rosemary leaves, optional

1 teaspoon fine sea salt

One heavy baking sheet or pizza pan lined with sprayed or lightly oiled parchment paper, plus a spray bottle filled with warm water

QUICK CHANGES

EASIEST SLOW-RISE CIABATTA:
• Prepare Easiest Slow-Rise Bread to the end of step 5, preheating a baking stone at the same time.
• Pull the dough, without deflating it, to a rectangle about 15 x 20cm.
• Use an oiled bench scraper to cut it into two rectangles, each 15 x 10cm. Gently transfer the loaves to a piece of lightly oiled parchment paper that will fit your baking stone and cover with a flat-weave towel. Proof until the loaves puff, about 1 hour – they will not double in bulk.
• Spray with water and slide the loaves onto the stone. Resume the recipe at step 8. Once you get to step 9, the additional baking time should be 15–20 minutes.

1. Pour the water into a 3-litre or slightly larger mixing bowl and whisk in the yeast. Wait 30 seconds, then whisk again.

2. Combine the flour, rosemary, if using and salt and use a large rubber spatula to stir them into the liquid. Scrape the side of the bowl to make sure that no flour remains stuck there. Once the dough is a coherent mass, beat it for a few seconds.

3. Cover with clingfilm and let the dough ferment at room temperature for at least 8 hours, until more than doubled in bulk.

4. 2 hours before you are ready to form and bake the bread, use a plastic scraper to transfer the dough from the bowl to a well-floured work surface. See step 6, page 28, but let rest for 1 hour.

5. Set a rack in the middle level of the oven and preheat to 230°C/gas mark 8.

6. Use a scraper to invert the dough to a floured work surface and pull the sides of the dough in towards the centre to give the loaf a round shape, pinching the pulled-in pieces in place at the top. Invert the dough

USING A PIZZA STONE

Pizza or baking stones are a convenient tool to rig up a home oven to simulate baking directly on the hearth of a baker's oven. Made from a clay-stone composite, they come in a variety of sizes and shapes, but make sure to buy one that's about 5mm thick for maximum heat retention. Follow the manufacturer's directions for seasoning the stone, if required.

To bake any of the breads in this chapter on a pizza stone instead of a baking sheet, position on a rack below the middle level of the oven and preheat for at least 30 minutes at a temperature 20 degrees higher than the baking temperature required for the bread.

You can use a baker's peel or just a piece of stiff cardboard to transfer a risen loaf to the preheated stone. If you've never done this before, by all means practise the movement a few times while the stone is in place but before you've preheated the oven.

For added convenience, proof the loaf directly on a piece of lightly oiled parchment paper on the peel, cut to a size just a little larger all around than the loaf to minimise bits of burnt paper in the oven. Yes, the paper will probably burn, but that won't affect the taste of the bread. If you've proofed the loaf upside down in a banneton or cloth-lined basket, cover it with a piece of oiled paper, then with the peel, and invert, removing the banneton.

To slide the loaf onto the stone, position the far end of the peel at the far end of the stone. Angle the peel downward at 15–20 degrees and quickly jerk it away, leaving the loaf on the stone. If the recipe requires spraying the loaf with water while it's baking, make sure to use hot water and to aim for the loaf, as occasionally a stone will crack if sprayed.

You may also substitute a heavy-duty baking sheet or an overturned swiss roll tin for a pizza stone.

into a floured banneton (as in the photo) or a basket lined with a floured cloth and cover with a tea towel. Proof the loaf until it puffs, about 1 hour – it will not double in bulk.

7. Invert the paper-lined baking sheet onto the banetton and flip the banetton over onto the sheet and remove it. Use an X-Acto knife or a single-edge razor blade to cut a slash across the diameter of the loaf. Generously spray with water and place the pan in the oven.

8. Wait 5 minutes and spray again, then decrease the oven temperature to 220°C/gas mark 7. Bake the loaf until it is deep golden and the internal temperature reads 93°C on an instant read thermometer, 25–35 minutes.

9. Cool the loaf on a rack and keep loosely covered at room temperature on the day it's baked. Wrap and freeze for longer storage. Reheat at 180°C/gas mark 4 for 5 minutes and cool before serving.

olive bread from nice

Makes one 25-30cm loaf

375g room-temperature tap water, about 24°C

½ teaspoon fine granulated active dried yeast or instant yeast

500g strong white bread flour

1½ teaspoons fine sea salt

200g Niçoise olives, or other firm-textured black olives, pitted after weighing and coarsely chopped, see Note

One heavy baking sheet or pizza pan lined with sprayed or lightly oiled parchment paper, plus a spray bottle filled with warm water

Olives are a natural complement to bread, especially when they're baked inside it. Be sure to buy firm unpitted olives for this – pitted olives tend to be softer, and though buying them that way may save you time, the olives will disintegrate and add extra moisture to the dough.

1. Pour the water into a 3-litre or slightly larger mixing bowl and whisk in the yeast. Wait 30 seconds, then whisk again.

2. Combine the flour and salt and use a large rubber spatula to stir the flour mixture into the liquid. Scrape the side of the bowl to make sure that no flour remains stuck there. Once the dough is a coherent mass, beat it for a few seconds. Cover the bowl with clingfilm and let the dough ferment at room temperature for at least 8 hours. It will more than double in bulk.

3. A couple of hours before you are ready to form and bake the bread, use a plastic scraper to transfer the dough from the bowl to a well-floured work surface. Flour your hands and pull the dough into a long rectangle. Scatter the olives over half the length of the dough, then fold the other half of the dough over them. Gently press to stick the dough back together. Fold the two sides in to overlap at the middle, then roll the top towards you all the way to the end, swiss roll-style. Invert, flatten and repeat. Move the dough to a well-floured place and cover with a tea towel or sprayed or oiled clingfilm; let rest for 1 hour.

4. Set a rack in the middle level of the oven and preheat to 230°C/gas mark 8.

5. Use a scraper to invert the dough to a floured work surface and pull the sides of the dough in towards the centre to give the loaf a round shape, pinching the pulled-in pieces in place at the top. Invert the dough to a floured banneton or a basket lined with a floured cloth and cover it with a flat-weave tea towel. Proof the loaf until it puffs visibly, about 1 hour – it will not double in bulk.

6. Invert the paper-lined baking sheet onto the banetton and flip the banetton over onto the sheet and remove it. Use an X-Acto knife or a single-edge razor blade to cut a slash across the diameter of the loaf. Spray the loaf with water and place it in the oven.

7. Wait 5 minutes and spray again, then decrease the oven temperature to 220°C/gas mark 7.

8. Bake the loaf until it is deep golden and the internal temperature reads 93°C on an instant read thermometer, 30–40 minutes. Cool the loaf on a rack.

NOTE: Niçoise olives are too small to be pitted using a cherry or olive stoner. Smash the olives, a few at a time, with the side of a knife blade, then carefully pick through to separate them from the stones. If you can't find real Niçoise olives, substitute Kalamata olives or Moroccan oil-cured olives for them.

Many flavourful Italian and other European breads are made from white flour that doesn't have all the bran removed, resulting in a slightly darker crumb after baking. The heavy coating of sesame seeds on this bread recalls the bread from the Italian bakeries of my childhood. A mix of white and black sesame seeds, all poppy seeds, or no seeds at all would be equally good with this bread.

Makes one 25cm diameter round loaf

375g room-temperature tap water, about 24ºC

½ teaspoon fine granulated active dried yeast or instant yeast

400g strong white bread flour

100g wholemeal flour

1½ teaspoons fine sea salt

60g white (untoasted) sesame seeds

Maize meal for the baking sheet

One heavy baking sheet or pizza pan lined with sprayed or lightly oiled parchment, plus a spray bottle filled with warm water

1. Pour the water into a 3-litre or slightly larger mixing bowl and whisk in the yeast. Wait 30 seconds, then whisk again.

2. Combine the flours and salt and use a large rubber spatula to stir the flour mixture into the liquid. Scrape the side of the bowl to make sure that no flour remains stuck there. Once the dough is a coherent mass, beat it for a few seconds. Cover the bowl with clingfilm and let the dough ferment at room temperature for at least 8 hours. It will more than double in bulk.

3. A couple of hours before you are ready to form and bake the bread, use a plastic scraper to remove the dough from the bowl to a well-floured work surface. See step 6, page 28. Flour a small area on the work surface and set the dough on it, cover with a towel or sprayed or oiled clingfilm, and let rest for 1 hour.

4. Set a rack in the middle level of the oven and preheat to 230˚C/gas mark 8.

5. Use a scraper to invert the dough onto a floured work surface and pull the sides of the dough in towards the centre to give the loaf a round shape, pinching the pulled-in pieces in place at the top. Invert the dough to a floured banneton or a basket lined with a floured cloth and cover it with a flat-weave tea towel. Proof the loaf until it puffs visibly, about 1 hour – it will not double in bulk.

6. Invert the paper-lined baking sheet onto the banetton and flip the banetton over onto the sheet and remove it. Use an X-Acto knife or a single-edge razor blade to cut a slash across the diameter of the loaf. Spray with water and generously sprinkle with sesame seeds. Place in the oven.

7. Wait 5 minutes and spray again, then decrease the oven temperature to 220˚C/ gas mark 7.

8. Bake the loaf until it is deep golden and the internal temperature reads 93˚C on an instant read thermometer, 30–40 minutes. Cool the loaf on a rack.

Makes about 6 servings

4–6 medium poblano chilli peppers, about 675g, rinsed, halved, stems and seed pods removed

3 ears sweetcorn, husked

600ml whole milk

4 medium eggs

½ teaspoon salt

¼ teaspoon freshly ground black pepper

¼ teaspoon freshly grated nutmeg

55g unsalted butter, melted

4 medium spring onions, trimmed to 12.5cm long, green ends discarded, cut into 5mm pieces

15g coarsely chopped fresh coriander

225g Mexican *queso fresco* or sharp Cheddar, coarsely grated

6-8 x 1cm slices Easiest Slow-Rise Bread, page 48, or other mild-flavoured bread

One 2.5 litre gratin or other baking dish

MORE ABOUT STRATA

There are a few important points about making imaginative fillings for strata: All vegetables need to be cooked first so that they're tender and won't exude water into the filling. Stick to assertively flavoured vegetables like leeks, onions, broccoli, spinach, Swiss chard or asparagus. Avoid root vegetables like carrots, potatoes, and turnips, which soak up flavour without contributing much. Chopped herbs such as parsley or chives, or torn leaves of basil are great in moderation – 2–4 tablespoons are enough. A cupful of halved cherry tomatoes can be good, but if using larger tomatoes, bake them at 190°C/ gas mark 5 for about 30 minutes on a tin covered with oiled parchment paper to rid them of excess water. Don't overdo it: 300–400g of filling is plenty.

Strata, the plural of the Latin *stratum*, means layers. Breakfast strata is an easy and delicious breakfast or brunch main course. A baking dish holds two layers of bread slices with a filling between them. A savoury custard is poured over and the dish is covered and refrigerated overnight so that the custard fully penetrates. Next morning, all you have to do is bake it. Try to use a metal or enamelled iron baking dish that can go straight from the refrigerator to the oven. If all you have is a glass or porcelain dish, remove it from the refrigerator 1 hour before baking. Use any bread you like, and if it isn't really thick-crusted you don't even have to remove the crust. The important thing is to patch together a full, even layer of bread slices both under and over the filling. This recipe uses some classic Mexican flavours and ingredients, but breakfast strata is a very versatile dish, so see the box for other filling suggestions.

1. Set the chillies under the grill and cook until they start to form charred blisters, about 5 minutes. Use tongs to turn the chillies and cook for 5 minutes on the other side. Repeat, turning the chillies skin side up again and letting them char evenly.

2. Transfer the chilli halves to a bowl and cover with clingfilm; let steam for 5 minutes. Remove the charred skin from each chilli and cut them into 5mm strips. Set aside.

3. Bring a pan of water to the boil, salt it and add the sweetcorn. Return to the boil and cook for 5 minutes. Remove the corn and let cool. Stand an ear of corn upright and use a sharp knife to cut away the kernels. Over a bowl, use the back of the knife to scrape the cut surface for any remaining bits of corn.

4. Whisk the milk, eggs, salt, pepper and nutmeg together.

5. To assemble, brush the inside of the baking dish with some of the butter and arrange half the bread slices in an even layer, patching with any scraps or odd pieces if necessary. Sprinkle half the remaining butter on the bread.

6. Evenly pour about a quarter of the milk mixture over the bread slices. Scatter the sliced chillies, corn, spring onions, coriander and three quarters of the cheese over the soaked bread. Pour on another quarter of the milk mixture.

7. Cover with the remaining bread slices to form an even layer. Evenly pour the remaining milk mixture over the top layer of bread. Sprinkle with the remaining cheese and butter. Cover with clingfilm and refrigerate for at least 4 hours, or overnight.

8. About 30 minutes before you want to bake the strata, set a rack in the middle level of the oven and preheat to 180°C/gas mark 4.

9. Bake the strata until the top is well browned and the filling is set and no longer liquid, 60–70 minutes.

10. Cool for 5 minutes before serving directly from the baking dish.

Makes about 6 generous servings

300g cubed bread, such as Easiest Slow-Rise Bread, page 48, or Italian Sesame Loaf, page 51, with or without crusts

720ml whole milk

3 medium eggs

½ teaspoon fine sea salt or table salt

Freshly ground black pepper

Pinch of freshly grated nutmeg

140g coarsely grated sharp cheddar

340g grape or cherry tomatoes, halved

One 20–23cm gratin dish or other baking dish, well buttered

M aking a great bread pudding, either savoury or sweet, depends on two things: getting the cubes of bread sufficiently dry so that they easily soak up the liquid in the recipe and giving them time to do so by adding the liquid in stages. Like most savoury bread puddings, this is also an excellent side dish with simply grilled or roasted chicken or turkey.

1. Set a rack in the middle level of the oven and preheat to 180°C/gas mark 4.

2. Scatter the bread cubes on a swiss roll tin and bake for about 15 minutes to dry them.

3. Meanwhile, whisk the milk with the eggs, salt, pepper and nutmeg.

4. Put the warm bread cubes in a large mixing bowl and fold in half the milk mixture, followed by three-quarters of the cheese and all of the tomatoes. Scrape the mixture into the prepared baking dish. Pour over the rest of the milk mixture, then top with the remaining grated cheese. Let rest for 10 to 15 minutes before baking.

5. Bake the pudding until it is set and the top has browned nicely, 45–55 minutes.

6. Cool on a rack for 5 minutes, then serve hot from the baking dish.

QUICK CHANGES

Add-ins: thinly slice a 55-85g link of cooked Italian or other sausage or 2 links of smaller breakfast sausages and add along with the cheese and tomatoes in step 4; replace the sausage with 115g bacon cut into 5mm dice, cooked and drained.
• Add 3–4 tablespoons finely snipped chives and fold them into the bread cubes before adding the liquid. Replace the chives with or also add 3–4 tablespoons chopped flat-leaf parsley.
TOMATO AND BASIL BREAD PUDDING: Substitute 140g finely grated Parmigiano Reggiano for the Cheddar. Add 15g torn basil leaves with the tomatoes. Scatter 20g more grated Parmigiano Reggiano on top before baking.

*R*amequin, a speciality of the western French-speaking part of Switzerland, approaches constructing a bread pudding in an unusual way. Slices of bread and cheese, cut to the same size and thickness, are slanted and overlapped in a baking dish and a light custard mixture is poured over them. While this is usually made with a white sandwich bread like the ones in Chapter 5, I like using more porous breads, like the ones in this chapter.

1. Set a rack in the middle level of the oven and preheat to 190°C/gas mark 5.

2. In a rectangular dish, arrange 2 bread slices side by side at the far narrow end. Top each with a slice of cheese. Place 2 more slices of bread into the dish, about 4–5cm in from the edge so that they partially overlap the first slices. Top with cheese, then position the last two slices of bread the same way, topping with the slices of cheese. In an oval dish, start with 1 slice, then add 2, then add 2 more, then add 1 at the end, so that the arrangement of the slices follows the shape of the dish.

3. Whisk together the milk, eggs, salt, and nutmeg and pour half over the bread and cheese and let it soak in for 5 minutes. Pour in the remaining milk mixture.

4. Set the baking dish in a larger tin and add 1cm of hot water to the larger tin. Place in the oven and decrease the temperature to 180°C/gas mark 4. Bake until the cheese is melted and nicely browned and the custard is set, 35–45 minutes. Use a small spoon to lift some of the bread in the centre of the pudding to make sure the centre isn't still liquid. If it is, continue baking for 5–10 minutes longer and check again.

5. Cool on a rack for 5 minutes, then serve immediately with some bacon or sausage for brunch or a green salad for lunch.

swiss bread & cheese pudding

Makes 6 brunch or lunch servings

6 x 1cm slices Easiest Slow-Rise Bread, page 48, trimmed to 7.5 x 12.5cm

6 x 1cm slices Swiss Emmentaler or Gruyère cheese

600ml whole milk, scalded

3 medium eggs

¼ teaspoon fine sea salt and freshly ground black pepper

Pinch of freshly grated nutmeg

One 2–2.5 litre gratin or other baking dish, buttered, set into a larger tin for baking

ramequin

Green vegetables and leafy greens are perfect in a moist and tender bread pudding like this. Use this master recipe that combines cooked spinach and Roquefort, or another blue-veined cheese, as a model for the Quick Changes below. If you decide to branch out from the suggestions here, always make sure the vegetables are cooked so that they don't exude excess water into the pudding as raw vegetables might. You may also add sausage, bacon or herbs as suggested in the Quick Changes on page 54.

Makes about 6 generous servings

300g cubed bread, such as Easiest Slow-Rise Bread, page 48, or Italian Sesame Loaf, page 51, with or without crusts

280g frozen spinach, thawed or fresh spinach (see Note)

½ white onion, chopped

30g butter

120ml double cream (optional)

170g Roquefort or other blue-veined cheese, crumbled

720ml whole milk

3 medium eggs

½ teaspoon fine sea salt or table salt

Freshly ground black pepper

Pinch of freshly grated nutmeg

One 20-23cm gratin dish or other baking dish, well buttered

1. Set a rack in the middle level of the oven and preheat to 180°C/gas mark 4.

2. Scatter the bread cubes on a swiss roll tin and bake for about 15 minutes to dry them.

3. Meanwhile, wring the water out of the thawed spinach a handful at a time.

4. Cook the onion in the butter over a low heat in a medium sauté pan until it's soft and translucent. Stir in the spinach and cook until the spinach is no longer watery, about 5 minutes, stirring occasionally. Stir in the double cream if you're feeling indulgent and cool slightly. Add the Roquefort.

5. Whisk the milk with the eggs, salt, pepper and nutmeg.

6. Put the warm bread cubes in a large mixing bowl and fold in half the milk mixture, followed by the spinach mixture. Transfer to the prepared baking dish and pour over the rest of the milk mixture. Let the pudding rest for 10–15 minutes before baking.

7. Bake the pudding until it is set and the top has browned nicely, 45–55 minutes.

8. Cool on a rack for 5 minutes, then serve hot from the baking dish.

NOTE: To use fresh spinach, rinse 450g baby spinach and put it in a large saucepan over a high heat. Once the water on the spinach starts to give off a little steam, cover the pan and steam the spinach until it's wilted and cooked through, about 5 minutes, checking several times that it isn't boiling dry. Drain and cool, then squeeze out the water and chop.

QUICK CHANGES

ROASTED ASPARAGUS AND GRUYÈRE BREAD PUDDING:
• Trim 450g asparagus into 10cm lengths and soak for at least 20 minutes at a time in several changes of water to release any sand.
• Set a rack in the upper third of the oven and preheat to 230°C/gas mark 8.
• Drain the asparagus in a colander then roll them on kitchen paper to blot excess moisture. Arrange the asparagus on a swiss roll tin and add 1–2 tablespoons olive oil. Roll the asparagus around on the tin to coat evenly and bake, shaking the tin, so that they cook evenly, until cooked through and lightly charred, 10–15 minutes.
• Cool the asparagus and cut them into 5cm lengths.
• When assembling, substitute the asparagus for the spinach and 170g coarsely grated Swiss Gruyère for the Roquefort.

BROCCOLI AND CHEDDAR BREAD PUDDING:
• Cut a 675g head of broccoli into florets and cook them in boiling salted water until tender. Drain, cool and cut into smaller pieces if large.
• Substitute the cooked broccoli for the spinach and 170g coarsely grated sharp cheddar for the Roquefort.

spinach & roquefort bread pudding

chapter five

Tin-Baked Breads

Baking bread in a loaf tin is a practical way to get easy-to-cut squarish slices of bread ideal for toast and simple sandwiches. Though I love the Perfect White Tin Bread and all its variations in my last book, *BAKE!*, I wanted something a little different for the basic tin bread here, and I decided to add some eggs and a little more butter to the basic formula, which resulted in this book's recipe for Golden Sandwich Bread, with its sunny-coloured crumb. The bread is richer than a typical sandwich bread and has an almost brioche-like quality, though it's neither as rich nor as sweet as a typical brioche. I've also devised a new way to prepare both cinnamon swirl raisin bread and a couple of part wholemeal and mixed grain breads that really bring the distinctive flavour of wheat and other grains to the foreground in a simply prepared bread.

Rather than embark on another adventure, I decided to adapt bread genius Professor Calvel's formula for *pain de mie*, or Pullman sandwich bread. Baked in a special closed tin, the resulting bread makes perfectly symmetrical square slices, while the bread has a slightly dense texture that makes it perfect for use in sandwiches that require untoasted bread, such as the Italian *tramezzini* that begin the recipe section following the breads.

Before beginning to write the sandwich recipes in this chapter, I made a short research trip to a New York theatre district deli famous for its over-the-top sandwiches. A typical sandwich had over 12.5cm of corned beef piled between two 2cm-thick slices of rye bread – enough corned beef for three sandwiches! That brings me to my prime rule of sandwich making: don't overfill. Second rule: use thinly sliced bread.

The sandwiches in this chapter are simple and easy to prepare and are some of my favourites. Later chapters match more substantial and cooked or baked sandwiches with other breads, but in most of the sandwich recipes here, you can use any bread you like with your favourite filling.

golden sandwich bread

Makes two 23cm loaves

800g strong white bread flour

2 tablespoons sugar

170g room-temperature tap water, about 24°C

1 tablespoon/10g fine granulated active dried yeast or instant yeast

225g whole milk, scalded and cooled

3 medium eggs at room temperature

60g butter, cut into 8 pieces and softened

1 tablespoon fine sea salt

Two 23 x 12.5 x 7.5cm (900g) loaf tins, buttered and the bases lined with parchment paper

This is addictively good bread for toast, sandwiches and French toast, though it's also great just sliced and untoasted. Enriched with eggs and a small amount of butter, it's in the spirit of a brioche loaf, but much less rich. I've written the recipe to make two loaves since it's so easy to prepare. My recommendation is to use one loaf straight away and wrap and freeze the other for later use.

1. Combine the flour and sugar in a large bowl and set aside.

2. Pour the water into the bowl of an electric mixer and whisk in the yeast. Wait 5 minutes, then whisk again. Whisk in the cooled milk and eggs.

3. Use a large rubber spatula to stir the flour mixture into the liquid a little at a time, stirring to combine between additions.

4. Place the bowl on the mixer with the dough hook and scatter pieces of butter on the surface of the dough; mix on the lowest speed for 1 minute. Stop the mixer and let the dough rest for 15 minutes.

5. Increase the speed to medium, sprinkle in the salt, and beat the dough until it is smooth and elastic, for 2–3 minutes longer. Scrape the dough into an oiled bowl and turn it over so that the top is oiled. Cover with clingfilm and let ferment until almost doubled in bulk, about 45 minutes.

6. Invert the dough to a lightly floured work surface. Flatten the dough to a disc. Fold the two sides in to overlap at the middle, then roll the top towards you all the way to the end, swiss roll-style. Invert, flatten and repeat. Return the dough to the bowl (oil the bowl again if necessary), cover, and let ferment until fully doubled, 30–45 minutes.

7. Invert the dough to a floured work surface and shape it into a rough square. Use a bench scraper to cut the dough into 2 equal rectangles, each about 715g. Pull the narrow ends of 1 rectangle of dough outward to widen. From one of the wide ends fold the sides in about 2.5cm or so, then roll down from the top as for turning the dough. Drop the roll into one of the tins, seam side down. Repeat with the second loaf and tin.

8. Cover with oiled or sprayed clingfilm and let the loaves proof until they have risen about 1cm above the rim of the tin. Once they're close to the top of the tin, set a rack a notch below the middle level and preheat the oven to 200°C/gas mark 6.

9. Place the loaves in the oven and immediately reduce the temperature to 190°C/gas mark 5. Bake until well risen and deep golden, with an internal temperature of at least 93°C, 30–40 minutes.

10. Unmould the loaves and cool on a rack on their sides. Wrap and keep at room temperature, or double wrap and freeze.

cinnamon raisin swirl bread

Makes one 23cm loaf

400g strong white bread flour

2 tablespoons sugar

7g sachet fine granulated active dried yeast or instant yeast

170 grams room-temperature tap water, about 24°C

112g whole milk, scalded and cooled

30g unsalted butter, cut into 6 pieces and softened

1½ teaspoons fine sea salt

175g raisins

2½ teaspoons ground cinnamon

1 teaspoon cocoa powder (optional)

One 23 x 12.5 x 7.5cm (900g) loaf tin, buttered and the base lined with parchment paper

QUICK CHANGES

TWO LOAVES:
• Double all the ingredients except the yeast, which should be 1 tablespoon/10 grams.
• To form both loaves at the same time, press the raisin dough to a 40cm square and the cinnamon dough to a 20 x 40cm rectangle. Position, moisten and roll as at right, but cut into 2 equal lengths and drop into separate tins.
• Substitute sultanas or dried currants for the raisins, or use a combination. Dried cherries or cranberries would be fun, too.

I've loved raisin bread with an appetising-looking cinnamon swirl running through it since childhood, but my attempts to duplicate the cinnamon swirl of industrially made bread have always resulted in the baked bread having gaps around the cinnamon part. When I did a chocolate swirl bread for *BAKE!*, I decided to add the chocolate to a third of the dough, and this is exactly the technique I'm using here – the raisins are distributed throughout the white dough, and the cinnamon is added to a portion of dough left raisin-free to emphasise the pattern.

1. Combine the flour and sugar in a large bowl and set aside.

2. Pour the water into the bowl of an electric mixer and whisk in the yeast. Wait 5 minutes, then whisk again. Whisk in the cooled milk.

3. Use a large rubber spatula to stir in the flour mixture a little at a time, then distribute pieces of butter over the dough. Place the bowl on the mixer with the dough hook and mix on the lowest speed for 2 minutes, then let the dough rest for 15 minutes.

4. Increase the speed to medium and sprinkle in the salt. Beat the dough until it is smooth and elastic, 2–3 minutes. Remove about one third of the dough and set aside, covered, in a small oiled bowl.

5. Add the raisins to the dough remaining in the bowl. Mix on the lowest speed until the raisins are evenly distributed throughout the dough, about 2 minutes. Scrape the dough with the raisins into an oiled bowl and turn it over so that the top is oiled. Cover with clingfilm and let the dough ferment until almost doubled, about 45 minutes.

6. Place the reserved one third of the dough in the mixer bowl and repeat step 5, substituting the cinnamon and cocoa, if using, for the raisins. Return the cinnamon dough to its own small bowl after mixing.

7. Invert each dough to a lightly floured work surface. Flatten the dough to a disc. Fold the two sides in to overlap at the middle, then roll the top towards you, swiss roll-style. Invert, flatten, and repeat. Place the doughs in their separate bowls (oil the bowls again if necessary), cover, and let ferment until fully doubled, about 45 minutes.

8. Invert the raisin dough to a floured work surface and shape it into a 20cm square. Press or roll the dough to a 20 x 40cm rectangle. Press or roll the cinnamon dough to a 20cm square. Brush the surface of the raisin dough with water and position the cinnamon dough on it 2.5cm in from the 20cm end of the raisin dough closest to you. Brush the surface of the cinnamon dough with water. Fold the 2.5cm border of raisin dough over the cinnamon dough and roll away from you, swiss roll-style, until the dough is a thick cylinder. Drop the dough into the prepared tin, seam side down.

9. Cover with oiled or sprayed clingfilm and let the loaf proof until risen about 1cm above the rim of the tin. Once the loaf is close to the top of the tin, set a rack a notch below the middle level and preheat the oven to 200°C/gas mark 6.

10. Place the loaf in the oven and immediately reduce the temperature to 190°C/gas mark 5. Bake until the bread is well risen and deep golden and has an internal temperature of at least 93°C, 30–40 minutes.

11. Unmould the loaf and cool completely on a rack on its side to prevent it from falling. Wrap and keep at room temperature, or double wrap and freeze.

Once, when Nancy Nicholas and I were visiting our friend Maida Heatter in Miami Beach, Maida proudly brought forth this loaf for breakfast. Beautifully tan outside and golden within, it was flecked with spicy dots of crushed green peppercorns that perfectly complemented the cheddar flavour of the loaf. Maida toasted some and gave us bitter orange marmalade with it, and the combination was as delicious as it had initially seemed unusual.

1. Whisk the water and yeast together in the bowl of an electric mixer and whisk in the cooled milk and eggs.

2. Quickly combine the flour and sugar, and use a rubber spatula to stir the dry mixture into the liquid until all the flour has been absorbed. Distribute the butter in 5 or 6 pieces. Place the bowl on the mixer fitted with the dough hook and mix on the lowest speed for 2 minutes, then let the dough rest for 15 minutes.

3. Start the mixer on medium-low speed, sprinkle in the salt, and mix until the dough is smooth, 2–3 minutes, sprinkling in the cheese and peppercorns after 1 minute.

4. Scrape the dough into an oiled bowl and turn it over so that the top is oiled. Cover with clingfilm and let the dough ferment until more than doubled in size, 30 to 45 minutes.

5. Invert the dough to a floured work surface. Flatten the dough to a disc. Fold the two sides in to overlap at the middle, then roll the top towards you all the way to the end, swiss roll-style. Return to the bowl, cover, and allow it to ferment until fully doubled, 30–45 minutes.

6. Invert the dough to a floured surface and pull it into a rough 20cm square, deflating it as little as possible. Tightly roll the dough from the top towards you, swiss roll-style, pinching the dough at the end to seal. Drop the rolled dough seam side down into the prepared tin.

7. Cover the tin with oiled or sprayed clingfilm and let the loaf proof until risen about 2.5cm above the rim of the tin. Once it's close to the top of the tin, set a rack a notch below the middle level of the oven and preheat the oven to 200°C/gas mark 6.

8. Place the loaf in the oven and immediately reduce the temperature to 190°C/gas mark 5. Bake until well risen and deep golden, with an internal temperature of at least 93°C, 30–40 minutes.

9. Unmould and cool on a rack on its side to prevent falling. Wrap and keep at room temperature, or double wrap and freeze.

Makes one 23cm loaf

60g room-temperature tap water, about 24°C

7g sachet fine granulated active dried yeast or instant yeast

75g whole milk, scalded and cooled

2 medium eggs at room temperature

400g grams strong white bread flour

1 tablespoon sugar

45g unsalted butter

1 teaspoon fine sea salt

115g sharp Cheddar, coarsely grated

4 teaspoons green peppercorns packed in vinegar, drained and crushed

One 23 x 12.5 x 7.5cm (900g) loaf tin, buttered and the base lined with parchment paper

QUICK CHANGES

• Substitute a similar aged cheese such as Gruyère, Emmentaler, or Cantal. You could also try one of the many excellent local cheddars available in the UK.

• Green peppercorns packed in vinegar can be a bother to find but Asian stores carry inexpensive jars and cans of green peppercorns still on the branch packed in brine, which is what I use when I can't find the much more expensive French ones in vinegar. Or substitute an equal amount of coarsely ground black pepper.

maida's cheddar bread

Makes one 23cm loaf

WHOLEMEAL DOUGH

150g warm tap water, about 38°C

270g strong wholemeal bread flour

2 tablespoons moist light brown sugar

15g unsalted butter

WHITE DOUGH

150g room-temperature tap water, about 24°C

7g sachet fine granulated active dried yeast or instant yeast

180g strong white bread flour

1½ teaspoons fine sea salt

One 23 x 12.5 x 7.5cm (900g) loaf tin, buttered and the base lined with parchment paper

---

QUICK CHANGES

To make 2 loaves, double all the ingredients except the yeast, which should be 1 tablespoon /10 grams.

MULTIGRAIN SANDWICH BREAD: See below for dark and white dough ingredients and proportions. You can mix the whole grain flours in any proportion, keeping to 260–270 grams total and making the white dough with strong white bread flour.

MULTIGRAIN DOUGH

150g warm tap water

65g wholemeal flour

65g light or dark rye flour

65g white spelt flour

65g stoneground yellow maize meal

2 tablespoons honey

1½ teaspoons fine sea salt

15g unsalted butter

WHITE DOUGH

150g room-temperature tap water, about 24°C

7g sachet fine granulated active dried yeast or instant yeast

180g strong white bread flour

Getting the best texture possible in a wholemeal bread depends a lot on giving the ground bran in the flour time to absorb water and soften. In this recipe, I'm approaching the challenge by mixing the wholemeal flour with some warm water and letting the mixture rest for an hour before mixing the dough. At the same time, the white flour component of the dough is starting to ferment so that the process is speeded up a little once the two are combined. The quantities here are for a single loaf; see Quick Changes to increase to two loaves.

1. For the wholemeal dough, pour the water into the bowl of an electric mixer fitted with the dough hook and add the wholemeal flour, sugar, and butter. Use a rubber spatula to stir the ingredients to a rough dough, then mix on the lowest speed until smooth, about 2 minutes. Remove the bowl from the mixer, cover it with clingfilm, and rinse off the dough hook.

2. For the white dough, mix the water and yeast in a medium bowl and use a rubber spatula to stir in the flour. The dough will be a little dry, but keep mixing until all the flour is absorbed. Cover with clingfilm.

3. Let both doughs rest for 1 hour.

4. Scrape the white dough from its bowl over the wholemeal dough in the mixer bowl and mix on the lowest speed until the doughs are smoothly blended together, about 2 minutes. Sprinkle in the salt and increase the speed to low/medium and beat 2 minutes longer.

5. Scrape the dough into a lightly oiled bowl and turn it over so that the top is oiled. Cover with clingfilm and let rest for 30 minutes.

6. Scrape the dough to a floured surface. Flatten the dough to a disc. Fold the two sides in to overlap at the middle, then roll the top towards you all the way to the end, swiss roll-style. Invert, flatten and repeat. Return the dough to the bowl smooth (bottom) side upward, and let it rise until fully doubled, about 45 minutes longer, depending on the room temperature.

7. Invert the dough to a floured surface and without deflating it too much, pull it into a 20cm square. Tightly roll the dough towards you and place in the tin seam side down.

8. Cover with oiled or sprayed clingfilm and let the loaf proof until it has risen about 1cm above the rim of the tin. Once it's close to the top of the tin, set a rack a notch below the middle level and preheat the oven to 200°C/gas mark 6.

9. Place the loaf in the oven and immediately reduce the temperature to 190°C/gas mark 5. Bake until the bread is well risen and deep golden and has an internal temperature of at least 93°C, 30–40 minutes.

10. Unmould the loaf and cool on a rack on its side to prevent it from falling.

My friend Kyra Effren has been baking since she was old enough to hold a wooden spoon. This type of bread is wildly popular in South Africa, where Kyra grew up. The seed bread makes wonderful morning toast and is very happy under a coat of butter. This is more of a batter bread than the other recipes in this chapter and goes right into the tin after mixing.

1. In a small bowl, whisk the water and yeast together; set aside.

2. Combine the wholemeal flour, strong white bread flour, bran, seeds and salt in a large mixing bowl; stir well to mix.

3. Make a well in the centre of the dry ingredients and add the yeast mixture, honey and oil. Use a large rubber spatula to stir everything smoothly together. Cover the bowl and let the batter rest for 10 minutes.

4. Beat the batter for 1 minute to make it slightly smoother, then scrape it into the prepared tin and smooth the top. Cover with oiled or sprayed clingfilm and let rise until it reaches the top of the tin, about 1 hour.

5. About 30 minutes after you place the batter in the tin, set a rack in the middle level of the oven and preheat to 190°C/gas mark 5.

6. Once the batter is fully risen, bake the bread until it is firm and has an internal temperature of 93°C, about 45 minutes.

7. Unmould, set the loaf on its side on a rack, and cool completely. Wrap and keep until the next day before serving – both the texture and flavour improve with a day's rest.

Makes one 23cm loaf

280g warm tap water, about 38°C

1 tablespoon/10g fine granulated active dried yeast or instant yeast

300g strong wholemeal bread flour

65g strong white bread flour

4 tablespoons wheat or oat bran

45g sunflower seeds

30g white sesame seeds

2 tablespoons poppy seeds

2 teaspoons fine sea salt

75g honey or dark, thick, barley malt extract

2 tablespoons mild-flavoured vegetable oil, such as safflower or rapeseed

One 23 x 12.5 x 7.5cm (900g) loaf tin, oiled or sprayed with vegetable cooking spray

kyra's seed bread

french sandwich bread

Makes one 23cm loaf

200g whole milk, scalded and cooled

100g room-temperature tap water, about 24°C

7g sachet fine granulated active dried yeast or instant yeast

1 tablespoon sugar

470g strong white bread flour

40g unsalted butter, softened

1½ teaspoons fine sea salt

One 23 x 10 x 10cm covered Pullman tin or one 23 x 12.5 x 7.5cm loaf tin, brushed with soft butter and sprayed with vegetable cooking spray

---

QUICK CHANGES

These are the proportions for a 33 x 10 x 10cm Pullman tin:

300g whole milk, scalded and cooled

150g room-temperature tap water, about 24°C

1 tablespoon fine granulated active dried yeast or instant yeast

1½ tablespoons sugar

675g strong white bread flour

2¼ teaspoons fine sea salt

60g unsalted butter

Mie is French for the interior or crumb of a loaf of bread and this sandwich bread, or Pullman loaf, as it's sometimes called, has a fine white crumb perfect for delicate sandwiches and toast. To bake this, you'll need a special Pullman loaf tin that's straight sided and has a cover so that the dough bakes to a perfectly symmetrical shape. You can buy one at www.bakerybits.co.uk. If you'd like to try the bread before purchasing the special tin, it can also be baked in a standard loaf tin.

This is adapted from Professor Calvel's formula in his book, *Le Goût du Pain* (*The Flavour of Bread*/Editions Jerome Villette, 1990).

1. Whisk the water and yeast together in the bowl of an electric mixer, then whisk in the cooled milk and sugar.

2. Use a large rubber spatula to stir the flour into the liquid. Scrape the side of the bowl and continue mixing until no dry flour remains visible. Distribute the butter in 8 or 10 pieces on the dough.

3. Place the bowl on the mixer with the dough hook and beat on the lowest speed for 2 minutes. Stop the mixer and let the dough rest for 15 minutes.

4. Sprinkle in the salt and beat the dough on medium speed until it is smooth and elastic, about 5 minutes.

5. Scrape the dough into an oiled bowl, turn it over so that the top is oiled, and let the dough ferment until it is almost doubled in bulk, about 45 minutes.

6. Scrape the dough onto a floured surface. Flatten the dough to a disc. Fold the two sides in to overlap at the middle, then roll the top towards you all the way to the end, swiss roll-style. Invert, flatten and repeat. Return the dough to the bowl smooth (bottom) side upward, and let it rise until fully doubled, 30–45 minutes longer, depending on the room temperature.

7. Invert the dough to a floured work surface and divide it in half. One piece at a time, pull the dough to a rough rectangle and tightly roll it from the farthest long end towards you, swiss roll-style, pinching the end of the dough to seal. Leave the pieces of dough on the work surface seam side up and cover loosely with a cloth or oiled clingfilm; let rest for 20 minutes.

8. To form the loaf, place both pieces of dough 5mm away from each other on a floured work surface. Grasping one of the short ends with each hand, twist the dough in opposite directions to make an interlocked spiral.

9. Slide both hands, palms upward, under the twisted dough and invert it, seam side down, into the prepared tin. Slide the cover about ⅔ of the way across the top of the tin. Let the loaf proof until it is about 2.5cm away from the top of the tin.

10. Set a rack in the lower third of the oven and preheat to 200°C/gas mark 6.

11. Once the dough has risen so that it is only 1cm away from the top of the tin, slide the cover closed and place the tin in the oven. Decrease the temperature to 190°C/gas mark 5 and bake for 25 minutes.

12. Without removing the tin from the oven, use oven mitts to slide the cover off the tin. Continue baking until the internal temperature of the dough is over 93°C, 10–15 minutes longer.

13. Remove the loaf from the oven and unmould it onto a rack to cool. Wrap in clingfilm and keep at room temperature if using the same day or double wrap and freeze for longer storage.

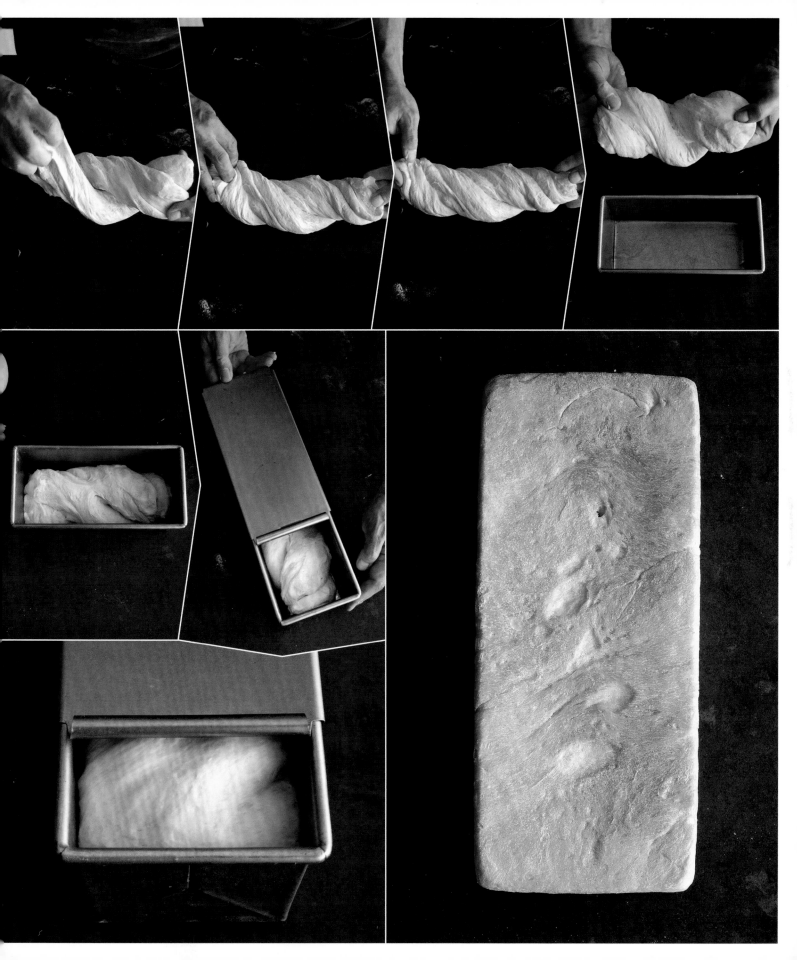

First made at the Caffè Mulassano in Turin in 1925, *tramezzini* were an Italianised version of British tea sandwiches. Made on white Pullman bread called *pan carré*, or square bread, in a very Turin combination of Italian and French, they were named by Italian poet Gabriele d'Annunzio. Because the word *sandwich* was difficult to pronounce in Italian, d'Annunzio invented the word *tramezzino*, which has overtones of both 'between' (*tra* in Italian) and 'half' (*mezzo*). In 1925, it was traditional in Italy (as it still is today) to stop for an after-work snack and a glass of wine or an aperitif on the way home, while fashionable ladies might entertain friends at home after shopping or a game of cards. *Tramezzini* fit right in. Today, when few people in large Italian cities return home for the main meal of the day in the early afternoon, *tramezzini* are often eaten as a light lunch.

This isn't really a recipe, but some instructions and suggestions for preparing *tramezzini*.

1. Stack 5mm slices of *Pain de Mie*, page 66, and use a sharp serrated knife to trim away the crusts.

2. Arrange the slices of bread sequentially, two at a time, facing each other.

3. Spread one side of each slice of bread with a very thin layer of softened butter or mayonnaise.

4. Evenly spread or stack the filling to the edge of half the slices of bread, being careful not to make the filling thicker in the centre. Each filling should be no thicker than one slice of bread. See opposite for suggested fillings.

5. Top with the second slices of bread. Cut the *tramezzini* diagonally and stack the triangular halves on a serving plate or a footed cake stand as they're displayed in Italy (see photograph).

6. For advance preparation, cover the *tramezzini* with clingfilm, a damp kitchen towel, and more clingfilm to keep them from drying out.

italian snack sandwiches

FILLING SUGGESTIONS

Mix **140g tinned tuna packed in olive oil**, drained, with **a tablespoon each of chopped parsley and chopped capers**; spread on 2 slices of bread and grind a little **black pepper** on the tuna. Top with **paper-thin slices of tomato, tender leaves of lettuce or a few leaves of rocket**, and 2 more slices of bread. If using **tomato**, keep it upward in the sandwich to prevent it from seeping into the bread.

Thinly sliced prosciutto or boiled ham topped with **thin slices of mozzarella or Swiss Gruyère**. Add **tomato** if using mozzarella or **thinly sliced non-sweet pickles** if using Gruyère.

Thinly sliced prosciutto topped with **chopped artichoke hearts preserved in oil**.

Thinly sliced mozzarella and **tomato**, sprinkled with **salt, pepper**, and some torn leaves of **fresh basil**.

Thinly sliced *mortadella*, thinly sliced mozzarella, roasted peppers that have been marinated in olive oil, salt, and a sliced clove of garlic for a couple of hours before using, and some torn leaves of **fresh basil**.

my father's tomato sandwich

I inherited my love of butter from my father. During my childhood, he only let loose with butter when we made these tomato sandwiches. Even though we lived in an inner-city neighbourhood, we always had a few tomato plants in our garden every summer. You don't need to have tomatoes growing at your doorstep to make this sandwich taste right, but you must use a perfectly ripe, height-of-the-season tomato.

Here are instructions for a single sandwich, since this is a perfect solitary treat. When you taste it maybe you'll smile impishly as my father did when he ate one, looking as though he had just been caught doing something naughty.

Soften **15g butter** and spread **two 1cm slices of untoasted Golden Sandwich Bread** with it. Rinse and cut away the stem end of **1 perfectly ripe medium tomato**, about 140g, and cut it into 5 or 6 slices. Arrange the tomato slices on one of the slices of buttered bread and lightly **salt and pepper**. Top with the remaining bread, butter side down, cut in half diagonally and enjoy immediately, preferably standing up in the kitchen right after you've brought home or picked the tomatoes.

QUICK CHANGES

BLT: This is another pleasure I shared with my father for a weekend lunch. It was for the two of us alone, since it contained a little from the tiny and frowned-upon jar of mayonnaise in our refrigerator to which my mother and her mother had such an aversion they wouldn't even touch the jar!

• Lightly toast 2 slices of Golden Sandwich Bread, page 60, or *Pain de Mie*, page 66, and generously spread with mayonnaise.
• Top one slice with a leaf or two of rinsed and dried leaf lettuce or tender outer leaves of iceberg lettuce.
• Add 2–3 5mm slices of tomato; salt and pepper lightly.
• Top with 3–4 slices of freshly cooked bacon, preferably still warm, and the remaining slice of bread, mayonnaise side down.
• Cut diagonally and enjoy immediately.

NEO-CLUB SANDWICH:
• Add a thin layer of sliced, cooked chicken breast, page 71, between the tomato and bacon, above.
• A classic club sandwich has 3 slices of bread and the layer above the bacon, lettuce, and tomato one is identical, substituting the sliced chicken for the bacon. Here I'm omitting the third slice of bread.

MAKING SANDWICHES

Sandwiches as simple as the ones here need a little 'glue' to keep them together; that's usually a thin layer of mayonnaise or butter on the bread. Take it easy, though I have to admit that I sometimes overdo it with the butter myself. Butter or mayonnaise lightly flavoured with some fresh herbs, such as chives, parsley or tarragon, or with some freshly ground pepper or a little sweet Hungarian paprika, can beautifully complement simple sandwich fillings. I love both mustard and Russian dressing in certain sandwiches, but condiments like those are meant to be spread on the filling, not on the bread, whose delicate flavour would be overpowered by them.

To me, a chicken sandwich is the height of delicacy. Lightly toasted and still-warm best quality bread, a little butter or mayonnaise, and perfectly cooked and seasoned chicken – nothing else need interfere. In this version, the chicken breast is quickly cooked with rosemary, olive oil and a touch of garlic, then finished in the oven until just cooked through and still moist and juicy. After a few minutes' rest, the chicken is thinly sliced and piled onto the bread. I like the rosemary version best warm and the tarragon version that follows it better after the chicken is completely cooled.

Makes 2 sandwiches

2 small skinless and boneless chicken breast halves, about 225g total

Salt and freshly ground black pepper

2 tablespoons finely chopped rosemary leaves (a spice grinder does this to perfection)

1 tablespoon olive or vegetable oil such as safflower

2 cloves garlic, smashed and peeled

4 slices Golden Sandwich Bread, page 60, or any other bread of your choice

30g unsalted butter, softened

1. Set a rack in the middle level of the oven and preheat to 180°C/gas mark 4.

2. Use kitchen paper to dry the chicken breasts and season them all over with salt and pepper. Sprinkle both sides of each breast with the rosemary, pressing it on.

3. Place a small sauté pan over a medium-high heat and add the oil. Slide the 2 breast halves into the pan and cook for 1 minute.

4. Add the garlic, reduce the heat to medium and cook for 1 further minute.

5. Use tongs to turn the chicken pieces in the pan and cook for 1 minute longer. Turn the garlic too, if it's colouring too much on the first side and beginning to burn.

6. Put the pan in the oven and cook until the chicken is just fully cooked through, another 3–4 minutes, or until its interior temperature

is 74°C on an instant-read thermometer. Transfer the chicken to a plate and let it cool for 5 minutes while you toast the bread.

7. Once the bread is ready, use a thin, sharp slicing knife to cut the chicken lengthways on a slant to make 3 or 4 thin slices.

8. Butter the slices of still-warm toast, divide the chicken slices evenly between 2 of the slices, and top with the remaining slices of toast, buttered side down. Cut diagonally and serve immediately with a salad of sliced tomatoes, simply dressed with salt, pepper, olive oil and a few torn basil leaves.

QUICK CHANGES

TARRAGON CHICKEN:
• Substitute chopped fresh tarragon for the rosemary.
• Use vegetable oil or a combination of vegetable oil and butter in place of the olive oil and omit the garlic.
• Squeeze the juice of a quarter of a small lemon over the chicken before placing in the oven.
• Cool completely before slicing and making the sandwiches.

LARGER CHICKEN BREASTS:
• Cook exactly the same way – just increase the seasonings proportionately. They'll cook longer in the oven, so be sure to check the temperature as in step 6 to make sure they're fully cooked.
• If you want to cook some chicken this way for a more elaborate sandwich, such as the Neo-Club Sandwich opposite, or if you want to add a favourite spread or condiment to the sandwich, then omit the herbs and garlic, but keep the lemon juice.

EXTREMELY MOIST CHICKEN:
• Stir 2 tablespoons fine sea salt with 120ml hot water in a medium bowl until the salt is dissolved.
• Add 480ml cold water and the raw chicken breasts and place a small plate on the surface of the liquid to keep the chicken submerged. Cover and chill for 1 hour before cooking.

TIN-BAKED BREADS

71

Makes 1 sandwich or more

FRED MORIN'S GREEN TOMATO CHUTNEY

900g green tomatoes, thinly sliced

1 tablespoon pickling, or other additive-free salt

4 tablespoons granulated sugar

4 tablespoons light brown sugar

1 teaspoon ground turmeric

120ml apple cider vinegar

2 dried red Thai chillies, Mexican *chillies de arbol*, or ¼ teaspoon cayenne pepper

2 tablespoons mustard seeds

ANN NURSE'S DIVINE BAKED HAM

One 5.5–9kg brined and smoked ham

45g whole cloves

720ml pineapple juice

450g dark brown sugar

470ml dark corn syrup (available at some supermarkets or online) or golden syrup.

2 slices Golden Sandwich Bread, page 60, or 1 Albert Kumin's Kaiser Roll, page 80, split

15g butter, softened

ABOUT TOASTING

Years ago it was common to toast sliced sandwich bread only on one side, and the toasted side would become the outside of the sandwich – you get the toasty flavour and a bit of crunch from the toasted side, but the inside of the sandwich remains soft. Set an oven rack a notch away from the highest level and preheat the grill to high. Place the bread slices on a baking sheet into the oven and don't walk away – it will take only a few seconds to toast the top of the bread. Transfer the toasted bread to a rack, toasted side down, to cool before assembling your sandwiches.

Though a ham sandwich m[...] isn't bad, the best is made [...] York, my friend Ann Nurse[...] ham, although she imports her ha[...] baked ham for a party, the leftove[...] great sandwiches, especially with [...] my friend Fred Morin, the chef-ow[...] restaurant in Montreal.

1. For the chutney, toss the tomato slices [...] a bowl with the pickling salt. Transfer to a non-reactive colander, set the colander o[...] the bowl, and let drain for 2 hours.

2. Rinse the tomato slices under cold running water and a handful at a time, twi[...] them in a tea towel to extract as much moisture as possible.

3. In a medium non-reactive saucepan stir together the sugars with the turmeric. Stir in the apple cider vinegar and bring to the boil. Add the tomatoes and the chillies or cayenne pepper. Bring to the boil over a medium heat, then reduce the heat and simmer, stirring occasionally, for 15 minutes, adding 4 tablespoons water if the chutney is dry. Add the mustard seeds and cook until the mixture has thickened, but not until all the liquid has evaporated, 5–10 minutes. If the chutney overcooks it will solidify as it cools. Test the chutney by placing a few tablespoons on a chilled plate in the refrigerator until completely cooled to make sure it doesn't solidify; if it does, add 4 tablespoons water and bring back to the boil.

4. Remove the whole chillies if used. Pack in 2 sterilised 250ml containers, cool to room temperature, press clingfilm against the surface of the chutney and cover the containers. Refrigerate and use within a couple of weeks.

and sides of the ham. Stud all over with cloves at the points of the little diamonds. Pour the pineapple juice over the ham and bake for 1½ hours, basting with the juice in the tin every 20 minutes.

6. Remove the ham from the oven and set on the hob. One handful at a time, pack the brown sugar all over the top and sides of the ham. Pour the corn syrup over the sugar. Return to the oven and bake, basting every 10 minutes, until the ham is beautifully glazed to a deep brown colour, about 1 further hour, or for a total of 25 minutes per kg. Cool the ham on its rack in the tin for 30 minutes, then transfer it to a serving plate for carving.

7. For a single sandwich, lightly toast 2 slices of sandwich bread or split a Kaiser roll and let cool slightly. Spread the cut surfaces sparingly with softened butter. Top with 3–4 5mm slices of freshly baked ham. Spread with 1½ tablespoons green tomato chutney and top with the second slice of bread or roll. Cut in half and serve with more chutney on the side if you wish.

Makes enough for 4 sandwiches

6 medium eggs

4 tablespoons mayonnaise, bought or home-made, or more to taste

2 tablespoons finely chopped spring onions or shallots

2 tablespoons chopped flat-leaf parsley

Salt and freshly ground black pepper

1 tablespoon lemon juice, strained before measuring

1–2 teaspoons Dijon mustard, optional

½ teaspoon Hungarian sweet paprika

8 slices Part Wholemeal or Multigrain Sandwich Bread, page 64, or Kyra's Seed Bread, page 65, toasted or untoasted

1 small bunch watercress or baby rocket, rinsed, dried and stemmed, or ¼ iceberg lettuce, shredded

Sliced tomato, optional

QUICK CHANGES

• Replace the paprika with 2 teaspoons curry powder, a popular seasoning for egg salad.

• If you want some crunch, add 50g finely diced interior rib of celery, or some chopped toasted walnuts or pecans.

Ida Constanos, the mother of my friend-since-birth Jeanette Pagnoni, would often make a Friday dinner of tuna and egg salads, coleslaw and potato salad. Jeanette's younger brother, Peter, would announce, 'Mommy's making egg shell salad for dinner.' The version below meets with rave reviews whenever I make it, but I'm careful about the shells. If you want to serve some coleslaw with the sandwiches, see the recipe on page 98.

1. To cook the eggs, put them in a saucepan where they'll fit in a single layer and cover them by several centimetres of cold water. Place on a medium heat and bring to the full rolling boil. Set a timer and cook the eggs for exactly 5 minutes so that the very centres of the yolks are still slightly soft. Put a bowl in the sink and use a slotted spoon to transfer the eggs to the bowl. Let cold water run over the eggs as you use the back of the spoon to gently smash the shell of each one in several places, then add about 2 cups of ice cubes and enough water to cover the eggs in the bowl.

2. Remove and peel the eggs one at a time and set aside. Rinse the peeled eggs under running water and return them to the bowl of ice water until they're fully cold. Transfer to a dry bowl, cover with clingfilm and refrigerate until needed.

3. When you're ready to make the salad, whisk together the mayonnaise, spring onions, parsley, salt, pepper, lemon juice, mustard (if using) and paprika in a medium mixing bowl. Coarsely chop the eggs and add to the bowl, then gently fold everything together.

4. Divide the salad evenly among 4 of the slices of bread, spreading it flat, then top with the greens and tomato slices, if using. Cover with the remaining bread and cut in half diagonally.

Makes about 560g filling, enough for 4–6 sandwiches

450g skinned and boned cooked chicken meat, coarsely diced

3 spring onions, white and half the green, about 55g, coarsely chopped

2 interior ribs celery, about 55g, coarsely chopped

2 tablespoons chopped flat-leaf parsley

Salt and freshly ground black pepper to taste

1 tablespoon lemon juice, strained before measuring

115g mayonnaise, bought or home-made

8 slices Kyra's Seed Bread, page 65, Part Wholemeal or Multigrain Sandwich Bread, page 64, toasted or untoasted

1 small bunch watercress or baby rocket, rinsed, dried, and stemmed, or ¼ iceberg lettuce, shredded, optional

Sliced tomato, optional

The first time I tasted a coffee-shop chicken salad sandwich as a teenager, I was hooked. If I don't have some leftover roasted chicken, I poach chicken thighs (see below) and use them instead. Chicken salad is a perfect sandwich filling, but it can be frustrating when chunks of chicken fall out of the sandwich, a little problem I remedy by pulsing all the ingredients in the food processor for a couple of seconds before adding the seasonings and mayonnaise. While there's nothing unusual or innovative about this chicken salad, preparing it with chicken that hasn't been boiled to death is a real improvement on most versions.

1. Put the chicken, spring onions and celery in a bowl as you cut them and use a rubber spatula to mix. Pulse the mixture half a dozen times in a food processor until finely chopped but not puréed. Scrape back into the bowl.

2. Add the parsley and salt and pepper and stir in; taste for seasoning and adjust if necessary. Sprinkle on the lemon juice and fold in the mayonnaise. Cover and refrigerate if not using immediately for up to 48 hours.

3. Divide the salad evenly among 4 of the slices of bread, spreading it flat, then top with the greens and tomato slices, if using. Cover with the remaining bread and cut in half diagonally. If you want to serve some coleslaw with the sandwiches, see the recipe on page 98.

poached chicken with a bonus

Makes about 450g cooked chicken and about 1½ litres broth

1.1kg bone-in chicken thighs

1 large or 2 small carrots, rinsed and peeled

2 large exterior ribs celery, trimmed and rinsed

½ large white onion (about 115g) or 1 large leek, split and rinsed

1 plum tomato, halved if fresh, or 2 from a tin, well drained

3 sprigs flat-leaf parsley

3 sprigs thyme

2 small bay leaves

2.5 litres cold water

1 teaspoon salt

One 6-litre stockpot or enamelled iron Dutch oven with a cover

Poaching chicken for chicken or other salads keeps it moist and flavourful. I always use bone-in chicken thighs for this, but of course you may use an equivalent amount of bone-in breasts. The yield in usable meat will be greater with breasts, but the tradeoff is that the bonus broth will be much less flavourful.

1. Put the chicken in a large pot and add the vegetables and herbs. Pour in the water and give it a good stir, then stir in the salt. Place over a high heat until the liquid approaches the boil, then reduce the heat to delay the boiling for a few minutes while you use a slotted spoon or ladle to skim the foam that accumulates on the surface.

2. Keeping the heat at medium, let the liquid come to the boil. Reduce the heat so that the liquid simmers actively. Cook the chicken until it is tender and cooked through, 20 to 30 minutes, depending on the size of the thighs. Use a slotted spoon to transfer one to a cutting board and cut right over the bone to see if it's sufficiently cooked.

3. Once the chicken is cooked, use a slotted spoon to remove all the thighs to a cutting board and let cool for a few minutes. Let the broth continue to simmer.

4. Using a knife and fork, pull away the skin and separate the meat from the bones, being careful to cut away the little nibs of cartilage that cling to the meat at the ends of the bones. Return the skin, bones and pieces of cartilage to the stock and let it simmer gently for 1 further hour.

5. Place the chicken meat in a plastic container or a bowl, covered tightly with a lid or clingfilm, and refrigerate for up to 2 days. Strain the stock through a fine-meshed sieve and let cool for a few minutes at room temperature. Don't worry about removing the fat from the stock – it will rise to the top and is easier to remove after the stock has chilled. Pack the stock into plastic containers and refrigerate for up to 5 days, or freeze for later use.

A speciality of the Swiss canton called Vaud, a malakoff is a dome of a cheese mixture that sits atop a disc of bread. After frying, the outer crust and the bread become golden and crisp, while the cheese mixture inside becomes melted and creamy – a little like a fondue in a crust.

My first malakoff tasting occurred in 2004 at Thierry Saxe's Café au Bon Vin in Chardonne. His recipe is a closely guarded secret, so this one is adapted from Marianne Kaltenbach's *Aus Schweizer Kuechen* (From Swiss Kitchens). Double the recipe if you like, but you only need to increase the oil to 1 litre. Use a slightly wider pan so that you'll be able to fry 4 malakoffs at a time.

Use a knife and fork to eat the malakoffs and pair with a cool, dry white wine. At the Café au Bon Vin, they serve a platter of house-cured sliced meats like prosciutto and dried sausage as a first course before and a simple frozen dessert or sorbet afterward.

Makes 8 malakoffs or 4 servings

Eight 1cm-thick slices Golden Sandwich Bread, page 60, or *Pain de Mie*, page 66

CHEESE MIXTURE

2 tablespoons plain flour

¼ teaspoon each fine sea salt and freshly ground black pepper

⅛ teaspoon finely grated nutmeg

400g Swiss Gruyère, finely grated

2 medium eggs

1 small clove garlic, grated on a Microplane

1 tablespoon Kirsch or dry white wine

1 medium egg white, beaten with a fork until liquid

720ml mild vegetable oil, such as safflower or rapeseed

French cornichons and pickled cocktail onions for serving

One swiss roll tin lined with parchment paper for drying the bread discs; one 3-litre enamelled iron or other deep 23cm pan or a wok for frying; plus one swiss roll tin covered with kitchen paper for draining

1. Set a rack in the middle level of the oven and preheat to 180°C/gas mark 4.

2. Use a plain 7.5cm biscuit cutter to cut an even disc from each of the bread slices. Arrange the discs on the prepared tin and bake them until dry but not toasted, about 15 minutes. Cool the bread discs on the tin.

3. For the cheese mixture, stir the flour, salt, pepper and nutmeg together in a medium mixing bowl. Add the cheese and use your hands, fingers splayed apart, to toss the cheese and flour mixture together until evenly mixed.

4. In another bowl, whisk the eggs, garlic, and Kirsch together and use a rubber spatula to scrape the egg mixture over the cheese and flour. Fold the liquid and cheese together to form a stiff paste.

5. Divide the cheese mixture into 8 equal pieces. Generously brush one of the bread discs with egg white. Roll one piece into a ball between the palms of your hands and place on top of the bread disc. Press to adhere, then shape into a half sphere. Place back on the tin and repeat with the remaining bread discs and cheese mixture.

6. For advance preparation, cover and refrigerate, but fry them on the same day or they may dry out. Bring back to room temperature 1 hour before frying.

7. When you are ready to serve the malakoffs, have heated plates and the pickles and onions ready. Heat the oil in your chosen pan to 180°C, as measured by a deep-fry/candy thermometer. Place 2 or 3 malakoffs in the oil, bread side down, to seal the cheese to the bread immediately. Fry for 1 minute, then turn over and continue frying until the malakoffs are a deep golden brown, about 2 minutes longer on each side.

8. Use a slotted spoon or skimmer to lift them to drain for a minute, then serve immediately.

9. Repeat until all the malakoffs have been fried, serving them with the cornichons and onions as soon as they are ready.

chapter six

Rolls & Individual Breads

Though they were probably first prepared to grace the tables of the aristocracy, today rolls and other individual breads are easily available and among the most popular breads all over the world. Millions of rolls are produced daily just to hold burgers, and when you add all the bagels, muffins, Kaiser rolls and hot dog rolls, it amounts to a staggering quantity.

Since they need to be formed individually, rolls are a bit of extra work compared to making a single loaf of bread, but you gain back some time because they proof and bake relatively quickly.

It was difficult to narrow down the selection of rolls in this chapter, some of which were dictated by the sandwiches that follow the roll recipes. I was especially happy when my teacher and former chef Albert Kumin shared the formula – 90 dozen strong – for the Kaiser rolls that were made for Windows on the World (where I worked for many years) and the rest of the World Trade Center restaurant complex. Other favourites here are the Mexican rolls known as *teleras*, which are soft ovals with tops grooved to keep them flat while baking, used for the sandwiches called *tortas* in Mexico.

albert kumin's kaiser rolls

Makes 8 rolls

225g room-temperature tap water, about 24°C

1 tablespoon fine granulated active dried yeast or instant yeast

2¼ teaspoons sugar

1 teaspoon malt syrup or honey

2 medium egg yolks

2 tablespoons mild vegetable oil, such as safflower or rapeseed

475g strong white bread flour

1½ teaspoons fine sea salt

Poppy seeds or sesame seeds for sprinkling, optional

Two baking sheets or swiss roll tins lined with parchment paper

Every day thousands of New Yorkers stop at delis and coffee carts on their way to work and pick up 'a buttered roll and a coffee, regular' – a Kaiser roll split and thickly spread with butter and a coffee with milk and sugar added. My teacher Albert Kumin recently shared this recipe with me, of which 300 dozen or so rolls were prepared daily for Windows on the World and the many restaurants and other food outlets in the World Trade Center. I earned my stripes as a pastry chef running the pastry department of the restaurant, but in those early days, Albert was always available by phone 108 floors below, and so I was never really alone. Memories of that time are now forever tinged with sadness after the senseless destruction of the Twin Towers and the lives of almost all the restaurant staff in 2001.

1. Whisk the water and yeast together in the bowl of an electric mixer; wait 1 minute, then whisk again. Whisk in the sugar, malt syrup, egg yolks and oil.

2. Use a large rubber spatula to stir in the flour. Place the bowl on the mixer fitted with the dough hook and mix on the lowest speed for 2 minutes. Stop the mixer and let the dough rest for 15 minutes.

3. Start the mixer again on the lowest speed and sprinkle in the salt. Increase the speed to medium and beat the dough until it is smooth and elastic, about 3 or 4 more minutes.

4. Scrape the dough into an oiled bowl and turn it so that the top is oiled. Cover the bowl with clingfilm and let the dough ferment until it is almost doubled in bulk, about 45 minutes.

5. Invert the dough onto a lightly floured work surface and, without deflating it too much, divide it into 8 equal pieces of about 96g each. Use a scale to get them exactly the right size.

6. Flour a board or baking sheet and set it near the work surface. To round each piece of dough, move one to a flour-free place in front of you. Cup your right hand over the piece of dough so that the top of your palm just beyond your fingers is touching the dough. Press the piece of dough and move your hand in a circular motion at the same time. If you're pressing hard enough you'll be able to feel the dough turning into a sphere. Repeat with the remaining pieces of dough. (See the video on my website for a demonstration of rounding.) Invert them, rounded side downward, to the prepared tin. Cover loosely with a piece of sprayed or oiled clingfilm and let the rolls rest for 10 minutes.

7. To shape, take one of the rolls from the tin and invert it so that it's right side up again. Use the palm of your hand to gently flatten to a disc. Lightly flour the tops of all the rolls and, one at a time, gently press with a Kaiser roll stamp (see Note below), twisting it about 3mm and pressing down harder at the same time, but without pressing all the way through to the bottom of the roll. Invert the roll to a floured cloth and proof the rolls until doubled in bulk, 30-40 minutes. After about 15 minutes, set racks in the upper and lower thirds of the oven and preheat to 220°C/gas mark 7.

8. Once the rolls are fully proofed, carefully invert them, 4 to each tin, so that the stamped side is upward. Spray with water and sprinkle with poppy or sesame seeds if you wish. Place the tins in the oven, wait 1 minute, then spray the rolls again.

9. Reduce the heat to 200°C/gas mark 6 and bake the rolls until well risen and golden, 20–25 minutes. Once the rolls are fully risen and starting to colour, about halfway through the baking time, turn the tins back to front and move the tin on the upper rack to the lower one and vice versa.

10. Cool the rolls on a rack and use them the day they are baked, or wrap, bag, and freeze for longer storage. Reheat the defrosted rolls at 180°C/gas mark 4 for 3 minutes and cool before serving.

NOTE: You can purchase a Kaiser roll stamp at www.bakerybits.co.uk

Based on an old Swiss recipe for milk-based rolls called *Weggli* in Swiss German, these are my favourites for a burger or hot dog. They're soft-textured but not mushy and have a hint of sweetness from the milk and malt syrup. Sprinkle the burger buns with sesame seeds if you like, or leave them plain. This is a two-step dough: First you make a simple sponge that ferments for about an hour – this only takes a few minutes to put together. After you mix the sponge, prepare all the other ingredients so you can complete the dough as soon as the sponge is ready.

Makes 10 rolls

SPONGE

200g milk, scalded and cooled to 35°C

1 tablespoon fine granulated active dried yeast or instant yeast

200g strong white bread flour

DOUGH

200g milk, scalded and cooled to 35°C

2 teaspoons malt syrup or honey

370g strong white bread flour

2 teaspoons fine sea salt

75g unsalted butter, softened

Milk, for brushing

White sesame seeds, optional

Two baking sheets or swiss roll tins lined with parchment paper

1. For the sponge, pour the milk into the bowl of an electric mixer and whisk in the yeast. Wait 1 minute and whisk again. Use a rubber spatula to stir the flour into the milk, stirring and scraping the sides of the bowl until no dry flour remains – the sponge will be fairly firm. Cover the bowl with clingfilm and let the sponge ferment until it has more than doubled in bulk, about 1 hour.

2. For the dough, use the rubber spatula to stir the milk and malt syrup into the sponge, followed by the flour. Place the bowl on the mixer fitted with the dough hook and mix on the lowest speed for 2 minutes, then let the dough rest for 15 minutes.

3. Sprinkle in the salt and mix the dough on medium speed until it is smoother, 2–3 minutes more. Beat in the butter in 3 separate additions, continuing to beat until the dough is smooth, elastic and shiny. Scrape into an oiled bowl and turn the dough over so that the top is oiled. Cover with clingfilm and let the dough ferment until it starts to puff, about 30 minutes.

4. Scrape the dough onto a lightly floured surface. Flatten to a disc and fold the two sides in to overlap at the middle, then roll the top towards you, swiss roll-style. Invert,

flatten and repeat. Return the dough to the bowl, seam side down, cover, and let ferment until fully doubled, 30–45 minutes.

5. To form burger buns, slide the dough to a floured surface and form into a rough square without deflating it. Cut into 10 equal pieces of 100–105g each. Round each piece as in step 6, page 80, then invert to a well-floured tea towel. Cover with oiled clingfilm and let proof until almost doubled, about 30 minutes. Halfway through, set racks in the upper and lower thirds of the oven and preheat to 200°C/gas mark 6.

6. Invert the buns to the prepared tins, spacing them at least 7.5cm apart all around, and gently press to deflate each to 1cm thick. Brush with milk and sprinkle with the sesame seeds, if using. Place in the oven and decrease the temperature to 190°C/gas mark 5. Bake the buns until well risen and deep golden, 20-25 minutes. Once the buns are fully risen and starting to colour, about halfway through baking, turn the tins back to front and move the tin on the upper rack to the lower one and vice versa.

7. Cool the buns on a rack and use them the day they are baked, or wrap, bag and freeze

for longer storage. Reheat defrosted buns at 180°C/gas mark 4 for 3 minutes and cool before serving. Only cut the buns in half horizontally just before using them.

8. For hot dog rolls, after rounding the dough in step 5, only let them rest on the floured towel for 10 minutes. Take one of the rolls and use the palm of your hand to roll it into a cylinder about 15cm long. Invert back to the floured towel and proof until almost doubled, about 30 minutes. Invert to tins, deflate and brush with milk as in step 6. Normally hot dog rolls are not sprinkled with sesame seeds. Bake, cool and store as for the burger buns. Just before using, cut the rolls lengthways three-quarters of the way through.

mexican
sandwich rolls

Makes 8 rolls

340g cool tap water, about 21°C

7g sachet fine granulated active dried yeast or
    instant yeast

225g whole milk, scalded and cooled

800g strong white bread flour

2 tablespoons sugar

1 tablespoon fine sea salt

Maize meal for the tin

One heavy baking sheet or swiss roll tin sprinkled
    with maize meal, plus a spray bottle filled with
    warm water, and one 1cm-diameter dowel

hese are the rolls that *tortas*, Mexican sandwiches, are made on. They're split and reheated in the oven, or split and the cut sides buttered and quickly toasted on a griddle. Their light texture and thin crust make it easier to bite through the large amounts of filling common in tortas.

1. Whisk the water and yeast together in the bowl of an electric mixer. Whisk in the cooled milk. Add the flour and sugar and stir. Place the bowl on the mixer with the dough hook attachment and beat on the lowest speed until a rough dough forms, about 3 minutes, then let the dough rest for 15 minutes.

2. Sprinkle in the salt and beat the dough on medium speed until smooth and elastic, about 3 minutes.

3. Scrape the dough into an oiled bowl and cover it with a piece of oiled clingfilm. Let the dough rise until it's more than doubled in bulk, about 2 hours.

4. Scrape the dough onto a floured work surface. Flour the dough and your hands and flatten the dough to a disc. Fold the two sides in to overlap at the middle, then roll the top towards you all the way to the end, swiss roll-style. Invert, flatten and repeat; scrape it back into the bowl. Cover the dough and let it rest another 30 minutes.

5. Flour the work surface and use a scraper to invert and move the dough onto it. Gently ease the dough, without deflating it too much, into a 20cm square. Use an oiled scraper to cut the square into 8 equal pieces, each about 120g. Round each piece of dough (see step 6, page 80), placing it upside down on a flour-dusted tea towel. If the dough is very sticky, flour the palm of your hand, not the dough. Cover with another towel or oiled or sprayed clingfilm and let the rolls rest for 10 minutes.

6. To form the *teleras*, place a piece of dough rounded side upward on a lightly floured surface and use the palm of your hand to gently flatten it. Generously flour the surface of the roll and use a 1cm diameter dowel to mark 2 parallel lines in the top of the roll in its length. Each line should be a little less than one-third of the way in from the side. Use the dowel to roll back and forth and make a 5mm wide trench in each of the marked places. Repeat with the remaining pieces of dough. Arrange 4 rolls on each of the prepared pans, spacing them well apart, and cover them again. Let the rolls proof until they're about 50% larger than their original size. Once the *teleras* have started to puff, set racks in the upper and lower thirds of the oven and preheat to 230°C/gas mark 8.

7. Once the rolls have fully risen, place the tins in the oven and decrease the heat to 200°C/gas mark 6. Bake until well risen and golden, 20–25 minutes. Once the rolls are fully risen and starting to colour, about halfway through the baking time, turn the tins back to front and move the tin on the upper rack to the lower one and vice versa.

8. Cool the rolls on a rack and use them the day they are baked, or wrap, bag and freeze for longer storage. Reheat the defrosted rolls at 180°C/gas mark 4 for 3 minutes and cool before serving.

QUICK CHANGES

SUB ROLLS: For subs, heros, grinders, or whatever they call them where you live, divide the dough into 6 equal pieces, each about 235g. Shape as for the baguettes on page 109, but don't taper the ends of the loaves; roll them only to a 30cm length. Place two of the loaves on each tin. Proof as above and slash the loaves as for the baguettes. Bake, cool and store as above.

My first bagel recipe more than 20 years ago yielded a very dense and firm bagel that while authentic, is not to everyone's taste. Generations of Americans have grown up with fluffy bagels from supermarket bakeries and expect a fairly tender bagel. This recipe, as its name implies, produces a bagel that's neither light as a roll nor challengingly chewy. To get a moderately chewy texture, you have to use high gluten flour; malt syrup is also essential both in the dough and in the water for poaching the bagels before they're baked. Thanks to my friend Sim Cass, resident bread expert at the Institute of Culinary Education, for sharing his recipe.

Makes 7 large bagels

DOUGH

285g room temperature tap water, about 24°C

1½ teaspoons malt syrup

7g sachet fine granulated active dried yeast or instant yeast

400g high-gluten flour or strong white bread flour

60g plain flour

1 teaspoon fine sea salt

POACHING AND FINISHING

4 litres water

3 tablespoons malt syrup

Poppy seeds and/or white sesame seeds for finishing, optional, in shallow bowls

Two baking sheets or swiss roll tins lined with lightly oiled or sprayed parchment paper or foil

1. Whisk the water, malt syrup and yeast together in the bowl of an electric mixer. Wait a minute and whisk again. Use a large rubber spatula to stir in both flours.

2. Place the bowl on the mixer fitted with the dough hook and mix on the lowest speed until all the flour has been absorbed, about 2 minutes, then let rest for 10 minutes.

3. Sprinkle in the salt and mix on low speed until the dough is smooth and elastic, 5–6 minutes longer – this dough is quite firm. Invert the dough to a lightly floured work surface and knead briefly by hand.

4. Place the dough in an oiled bowl and turn it over so that the top is oiled. Cover the bowl with clingfilm and let the dough ferment until doubled in bulk, about an hour.

5. Slide the dough from the bowl to an unfloured work surface and roll it to a thick sausage shape. Use a bench scraper to mark, then cut, the dough into 7 equal pieces, each about 110g (use a scale to get them exact). To form a bagel, press a piece of dough into a rough square and fold the top down to the centre and press it in place, then roll towards you to the other end and seal the edge in place, pressing with the heel of your hand. Repeat with the remaining pieces of dough, covering them with a tea towel or clingfilm.

6. Have a small bowl of water handy. Starting with the first piece formed, roll it to a 25cm length, gently pointing the ends. Use your fingertips to moisten the ends, then overlap them by an inch to form a circle. Insert your hand into the circle and roll your palm back and forth over the juncture to seal it. Place the bagels well apart on the prepared tins as they are formed, keeping them covered with oiled or sprayed clingfilm. Let the bagels proof until they have risen about 50% over their original size.

7. Set racks in the upper and lower thirds of the oven and preheat to 190°C/gas mark 5 (if your oven has a convection setting, use it at 180°C/gas mark 4). Bring the water to the boil in a large pan and have a skimmer and a rack set on a swiss roll tin on the hob.

8. Stir the malt syrup into the boiling water. Use the skimmer to lower 2–3 bagels into the water, one at a time, and let them poach for about 10 seconds on each side. Lift the bagels from the water and drain for a few seconds over the pot. If you want to encrust a bagel with seeds, immediately invert it into the bowl of seeds, leave it for a couple of seconds, then gently transfer back to one of the tins. Continue until all the bagels have been poached and returned to the tins.

9. Bake the bagels until they are well risen, deep golden and firm, about 20 minutes. Once the bagels are fully risen and starting to colour, about halfway through the baking time, turn the tins back to front and move the tin on the upper rack to the lower one and vice versa.

10. Cool the bagels on a rack and use them the day they are baked, or wrap, bag and freeze for longer storage. Reheat the defrosted bagels at 180°C/gas mark 4 for 3 minutes and cool before serving.

turkish sesame rings

Makes six 15cm rings

DOUGH

250g room-temperature tap water, about 24°C

7g sachet fine granulated active dried yeast or instant yeast

2 teaspoons sugar or pomegranate molasses

450g strong white bread flour

1½ teaspoons fine sea salt

2 litres room-temperature tap water

2 tablespoons pomegranate molasses or black treacle

140g white sesame seeds

One large or two smaller swiss roll tins lined with parchment paper

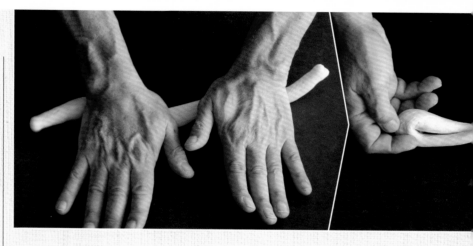

A *simit* – an individual ring-shaped bread – looks a little like a bagel, but it's coated all over with sesame seeds. Also, like bagels, *simits* are dipped into warm water containing molasses. In the recipe here, I've used pomegranate molasses (available from some supermarkets or online), but ordinary molasses will do just as well. The dough is easy to prepare; forming a *simit* takes a little practice (use a ruler) but it's not really difficult. A big thank you to author, food stylist, and blogger Cenk Sonmezsoy (www.cafefernando.com), who sent me a steady stream of emails from Istanbul to guide me through my *simit*-making efforts.

1. Whisk the water and yeast together in the bowl of an electric mixer. Wait 30 seconds and then whisk in the sugar.

2. Use a rubber spatula to stir the flour into the liquid. Attach the dough hook and beat for 2 minutes on the lowest speed. Stop the mixer and let the dough rest for 10 minutes.

3. Start the mixer again on medium speed and sprinkle in the salt. Mix until the dough is smoother and elastic, about 2 minutes longer. Cover the bowl with oiled or sprayed clingfilm and let the dough ferment until it is doubled in bulk, about 1 hour.

4. Invert the dough to a lightly floured work surface and pull it into a rough square. Use a bench scraper to divide the dough into 6 equal pieces, about 120g each. Round each piece and transfer them to a floured work surface; cover with oiled or sprayed clingfilm and let rest for 10 minutes.

5. Right after rounding the dough, set a rack in the lower third of the oven and preheat to 200°C/gas mark 6. Stir the water and molasses for finishing together and have a large skimmer ready; put the sesame seeds in a shallow bowl.

6. Pre-form the strands that will become the *simits* by inverting one of the rounded pieces of dough to the work surface and gently deflating it to a thick disc. Roll the dough once towards you from the far end and press to seal. Flatten and repeat once or twice more, pinching the seam closed when you get to the end. Repeat with the remaining pieces of dough.

7. To form the rings, roll one of the pieces of dough under the palms of your hands to a strand 45cm long. Fold the strand in the middle to make a hairpin shape, pinch the ends closed, and give the double strand 3 or 4 twists, turning in opposite directions from both ends at the same time. Give the twisted strand a gentle press, then roll it back to 45cm long, slightly tapering the last 1cm or so. Join the ends at the thinner areas to avoid leaving a bulge and set aside, covered, on another tin or cutting board. Repeat with the remaining pieces of dough. Let the formed *simits* rest, covered, for 10 minutes.

8. To dip and encrust the *simits* with the sesame seeds, put the tin or board of formed *simits* on your left, followed by, in order, the bowl of molasses water, the sesame seeds and the prepared baking tin. One at a time, slide a *simit* into the molasses water and press down with the skimmer to submerge it completely. Turn it so that the bottom is upward, lift it from the liquid, and let it drain for a few seconds. Slide the *simit* into the sesame seeds and press the seeds against the outside and into the side of the opening. Turn the *simit* over to encrust the bottom. Slide both hands under the *simit* and transfer it to the prepared tin. Repeat with the remaining *simits*.

9. Bake the *simits* until they are deep golden, about 10 minutes, then turn them over so that the bottoms colour well too, 5–10 minutes more.

10. Cool on a rack and serve soon after baking. For longer storage, wrap individually and freeze. Defrost and bake at 190°C/gas mark 5 for 3–4 minutes and cool before serving.

muffins

Makes twelve 9cm muffins

340g room-temperature tap water, about 24°C

1 tablespoon fine granulated active dried yeast or instant yeast

1 tablespoon malt syrup or honey

540g strong white bread flour

2 teaspoons fine sea salt

60g unsalted butter, softened

Maize meal for the tins

Two baking sheets or swiss roll tins dusted with maize meal, plus a griddle or non-stick sauté pan

Home-made muffins have better flavour and texture than the industrially made variety. You'll need a 9cm plain round biscuit cutter to form them and a griddle or wide non-stick sauté pan for baking. Cutting the muffins generates scraps of dough; some are useful for testing the temperature of the griddle. I like to freeze the rest. When I bake another batch of muffins I defrost the dough and bring it to room temperature before adding it to the new batch – the 'old dough' contributes a superior texture and flavour to the muffins. See page 24 for more on 'old dough.'

1. Whisk the water and yeast together in the bowl of an electric mixer, then whisk in the malt syrup. Use a rubber spatula to stir in the flour.

2. Place the bowl on the mixer fitted with the dough hook and distribute pieces of the butter on the dough; mix on lowest speed until the dough looks moist and soft, about 2 minutes. Stop the mixer and let the dough rest for 15 minutes.

3. Sprinkle in the salt and mix on low speed until the dough is smooth and elastic, 5–6 minutes longer – this dough is quite soft.

4. Scrape the dough into an oiled bowl and turn it over so that the top is oiled. Cover the bowl with clingfilm and let the dough ferment until it increases about 50% over its original size, about 30 minutes.

5. Invert the dough to a floured work surface and flatten to a disc. Fold the two sides in to overlap at the middle, then roll the top towards you all the way to the end, swiss roll-style. Invert, flatten and repeat. Return the dough to the bowl, seam side down, cover again and let the dough ferment until fully doubled, about 30 minutes longer.

6. Slide the dough from the bowl to a floured work surface and press it into a square about 1cm thick. Slide the dough to a flour-dusted baking sheet or the back of a swiss roll tin, cover it with clingfilm and refrigerate it for 30 minutes.

7. Slide the dough from the tin to a floured work surface and gently roll it to a 5mm thickness. Use a floured biscuit cutter to form the muffins – cut straight down without twisting, as doing so will ruin the side of the muffin and prevent it from rising straight sided. Place the formed muffins a couple of centimetres apart on the prepared tins and dust the tops with more maize meal. Save some of the scraps on a plate or separate tin and reserve the rest of the scraps for a future batch of muffins, as explained above. Let the muffins proof until puffy and almost doubled, about 45 minutes.

8. About 10 minutes before the muffins are fully proofed, start to heat the griddle over a medium heat. After about 3 minutes, test the temperature with one of the dough scraps – it should take about 3 minutes to begin to rise and colour very lightly on the bottom. Increase the heat if the dough isn't taking on much colour after 3 minutes and decrease it if it's getting too dark. Once you've adjusted the heat, bake as many muffins as will comfortably fit on the griddle, leaving about 2.5cm between them. Bake the muffins for 5 minutes on each side, adjusting the heat if necessary if they are colouring too quickly. Cool the muffins on a rack and continue baking and cooling the remaining muffins.

9. Store the muffins loosely covered if you're serving them the same day, or wrap, bag and freeze for longer storage. Defrost before attempting to split.

10. Use a fork to split the muffins you're going to serve and toast them. Serve with butter and your favourite jam or marmalade. A toasted muffin also makes a great roll for a thin burger.

These large rolls are used exclusively to make the famous New Orleans *muffuletta* sandwich (see page 101). Filled with a mix of sliced deli meats and cheeses topped with a garlicky marinated olive and vegetable salad, the sandwich is a speciality of Central Grocery, an Italian food store in the city's famous French Quarter. The name derives from the roll itself, traditionally made in Sicily from an all durum-flour dough. This version has no durum flour in it, but is still a great base for the sandwich. The large size makes it practical for other types of sandwiches, since they can easily be cut into wedges to serve.

Makes three to four 23–25cm round rolls

510g room-temperature tap water, about 24°C

7g sachet fine granulated active dried yeast or instant yeast

2 tablespoons olive oil

810g strong white bread flour

2 teaspoons fine sea salt

90g white sesame seeds for topping

Two baking sheets or swiss roll tins lined with parchment paper or foil

1. Pour the water into the bowl of an electric mixer and whisk in the yeast. Wait 30 seconds and whisk again. Whisk in the oil.

2. Use a large rubber spatula to stir the flour into the mixer bowl a little at a time until you've used all the flour. Make sure all the flour is mixed into the liquid and there isn't any clinging to the side of the bowl.

3. Attach the dough hook. Mix on the lowest speed until the dough comes together around the hook, 1–2 minutes. Stop the mixer and pull the dough away from the hook; let rest for 15 minutes.

4. Sprinkle in the salt and increase the speed to low/medium and mix until the dough is smooth and elastic, 2–3 minutes.

5. Scrape the dough into an oiled bowl and turn it over so that the top is oiled. Cover with clingfilm and let the dough ferment until it starts to puff, about 30 minutes.

6. Scrape the dough to a floured work surface, flour your hands, and pull the dough into a rough rectangle. Fold the two sides in to overlap at the middle, then roll the top towards you, swiss roll-style. Invert the dough back to the bowl and cover again. Let the dough ferment until it has fully doubled in bulk, about 30 minutes.

7. To shape the rolls, use a flexible plastic scraper to slide the dough from the bowl, right side up, to a floured work surface; try to keep from deflating the dough. Divide the dough into 3 equal pieces, each about 335g (for a thinner roll, divide the dough into 4 pieces, each about 250g). Round each piece of dough by pushing against the bottom of the dough all around with the sides of your hands held palms upward. The dough will quickly form an even sphere. Place the rolls on the prepared tins and cover them with flat-weave tea towels or pieces of sprayed or oiled clingfilm. Let the rolls proof until they start to puff, about 30 minutes.

8. Set racks in the upper and lower thirds of the oven and preheat to 230°C/gas mark 8.

9. Once the rolls have proofed to about 50% larger than their original size, flour the palms of your hands and gently press each to flatten it to about 2.5cm thick. Generously spray the rolls with water and sprinkle heavily with sesame seeds.

10. Decrease the heat to 220°C/gas mark 7 and bake the rolls until well risen and golden, with an internal temperature of over 93°C, 25–30 minutes. Once the rolls are fully risen and starting to colour, about halfway through the baking time, turn the tins back to front and move the tin on the upper rack to the lower one and vice versa.

11. Cool the rolls on a rack and use them the day they are baked, or wrap, bag and freeze for longer storage. Reheat the defrosted rolls at 180°C/gas mark 4 for 3 minutes and cool before serving.

Makes 10 rolls or soft pretzels

DOUGH

225g room-temperature tap water about 24ºC

7g sachet fine granulated active dried yeast or instant yeast

5 teaspoons vegetable oil, such as safflower or rapeseed

400g strong white bread flour

1½ teaspoons fine sea salt

DIPPING SOLUTION

2 litres warm tap water, about 38°C

2 tablespoons malt syrup

180g bicarbonate of soda

2 baking sheets or swiss roll tins lined with oiled parchment paper or foil plus another tin covered with a rack for draining

I fell in love with these delicious dark brown rolls as soon as I arrived in Switzerland for the first time in 1973. Made from the same dough used for soft pretzels, the dark crust is obtained by dipping the fully proofed rolls into a 4% solution of lye and water. I know it sounds shocking, but every pretzel, soft or hard, in the world is made exactly the same way. Food-grade lye is available from online sources, but it's caustic enough to burn your skin badly, and it could be fatal. Consequently I'm not giving instructions here. A decent approximation of the dark crust can be obtained by dipping the rolls in an innocuous solution of water, malt syrup and bicarbonate of soda.

Normally they're refrigerated overnight before being dipped and baked, but here I've given instructions to proof them at room temperature after forming and to dip and bake them straight after.

1. Whisk the water and yeast together in the bowl of an electric mixer; wait 30 seconds and whisk again, then whisk in the oil. Use a rubber spatula to thoroughly stir in the flour. Place the bowl on the mixer fitted with the dough hook and mix on the lowest speed for 2 minutes, then let rest for 10 minutes.

2. Mix on medium speed, sprinkling in the salt, until the dough is smooth and elastic, 2–3 minutes. Cover the bowl and let the dough ferment for 30 minutes.

3. Scrape the dough to a lightly floured work surface and flatten to a disc. Fold the two sides in to overlap at the middle, then roll the top towards you all the way to the end, swiss roll-style. Invert, flatten and repeat. Let the dough ferment until fully doubled in bulk, about 30–45 minutes longer.

4. Slide the dough, seam side down, to a floured place on the work surface and use the palms of your hands to flatten it. Use a bench scraper to divide the dough into 10 pieces, each about 65g. To round each piece of dough, move one to a flour-free place in front of you. Cup your right hand over the piece of dough so that the top of your palm just beyond your fingers is touching the dough. Press the piece of dough and move your hand in a circular motion at the same time. If you're pressing hard enough you'll be able to feel the dough turning into a sphere. (See the video on my website for a demonstration of rounding.) Repeat with the remaining pieces of dough and set the rounded pieces of dough on a lightly floured area of the work surface. Cover again with a tea towel or clingfilm and let them rest for 15 minutes.

5. Stir the water, malt syrup and bicarbonate of soda together in a shallow bowl. Place a rack over a swiss roll tin and have a skimmer ready for dipping the rolls.

6. To form the rolls, take one of the rounded pieces of dough and invert it on a floured surface. Press with the palm of your hand to flatten, then pull to a triangular shape. Use a rolling pin to roll it to an isosceles triangle with a base of about 9cm and about 20cm long. If the dough resists, set aside and form the other pieces, then go back and re-roll them to the right size. To form a roll, pull the base of the triangle to about 10cm and roll towards the point, pulling on the point at the same time. End with the point on the bottom. Arrange the rolls on one of the prepared pans and let them proof until they start to puff, about 20 minutes.

7. Once all the rolls are formed, set racks in the upper and lower thirds of the oven and preheat to 200°C/gas mark 6.

8. Place the tin of proofed rolls to your left, the bowl of dipping solution to the right of the rolls, and the rack-covered tin to the right of the dipping solution. Gently slide one of the rolls, seam side up, into the dipping solution, then use the skimmer to turn it right side up and place it on the rack to drain. Leave the rolls on the rack until they have dried.

9. Lightly spray or oil parchment paper on the baking tins and carefully transfer the dried rolls to the prepared tins. Use a single-edge razor or X-Acto knife to make a 6.5cm cut in the top of each roll.

10. Place the tins in the oven, and decrease the heat to 190°C/gas mark 5. Bake the rolls until they are well risen and dark golden, 20–25 minutes. Once the rolls are fully risen and starting to colour, about halfway through the baking time, turn the tins back to front and move the tin on the upper rack to the lower one and vice versa.

11. Cool the rolls on a rack and use them the day they are baked, or wrap, bag and freeze for longer storage. Reheat the defrosted rolls at 180°C/gas mark 4 for 3 minutes and cool before serving.

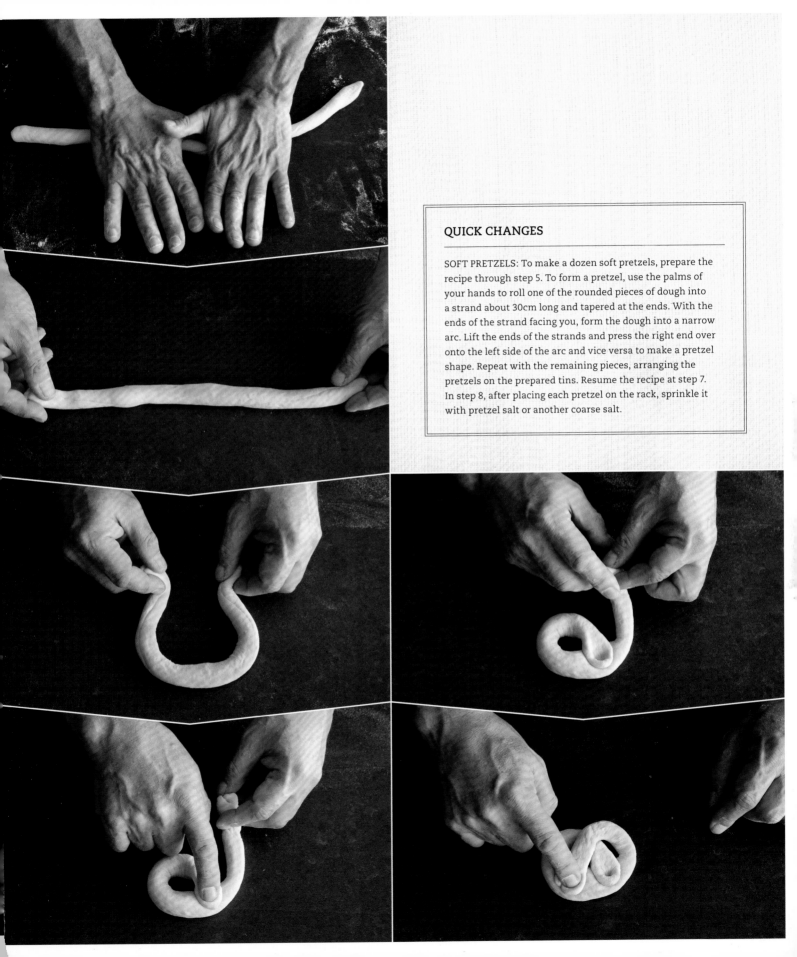

QUICK CHANGES

SOFT PRETZELS: To make a dozen soft pretzels, prepare the
recipe through step 5. To form a pretzel, use the palms of
your hands to roll one of the rounded pieces of dough into
a strand about 30cm long and tapered at the ends. With the
ends of the strand facing you, form the dough into a narrow
arc. Lift the ends of the strands and press the right end over
onto the left side of the arc and vice versa to make a pretzel
shape. Repeat with the remaining pieces, arranging the
pretzels on the prepared tins. Resume the recipe at step 7.
In step 8, after placing each pretzel on the rack, sprinkle it
with pretzel salt or another coarse salt.

Makes 4 burgers

1 kg freshly minced beef

Salt and freshly ground black pepper

4 thin slices white onion

4 leaves iceberg lettuce, rinsed and dried

4 Burger Buns, page 81

Your favourite burger condiments, such as mustard, ketchup, or others

I often go to Missouri for book signings organised by Tim Brennan, owner of Cravings, a great bakery café in Webster Groves, just outside St. Louis. During one of my first visits Tim suggested a burger for lunch. I'm never one to refuse a burger, so off we went to O'Connell's, a friendly Irish bar. The burger was – and still is – exceptional. Thick, moist, tender and juicy, and perfectly cooked medium rare, just the way I like it. The owner, Jack Parker, happily shared the secret of his great burgers. The meat is minced chuck steak, with a ratio of 80% lean to 20% fat. According to Jack, compressing the meat and eliminating air pockets is what keeps the burger juicy. Cooked under a standard restaurant kitchen grill with the flame above, they're just slightly charred on the outside.

1. Preheat an oven grill or an outdoor grill.

2. Divide the meat into 4 equal 250g portions. Roll each into a ball and drop it from a height of about 60 centimetres to the work surface 3 or 4 times. Then flatten the portions of meat by vigorously passing them back and forth between the palms of your hands 8–10 times each.

3. Grill the burgers about 3 minutes on each side for medium rare, 55°C on an instant-read thermometer.

4. Serve immediately on a split burger bun. Salt and pepper lightly, then top each with a slice of onion and a leaf of lettuce.

QUICK CHANGES

DAGWOOD BURGER **>>**: Dagwood Bumstead, the comic strip character who was fond of making towering sandwiches, would probably approve of the way I like to garnish a home-made burger. Spread the bottom half of the bun with mayonnaise and top with a lettuce leaf and 3–4 slices of pickle. (See page 92 for a pickle recipe). Top with the burger, salt and pepper, a slice of cheese, a slice of onion, a slice of tomato and another lettuce leaf. Any ketchup or mustard should go under the onion. Or substitute onion marmalade, page 137, for the raw onion.

PATTY MELT: A diner staple that's quickly disappearing from menus, a patty melt is a fun change of pace from the standard. After forming the burgers, shape each into a square. While the burgers are cooking, toast some sliced sandwich bread. One minute after you turn the burgers, quickly salt and pepper them, and then top each with a 30g slice of your favourite cheese – I like Swiss Gruyère or sharp Cheddar. Serve between 2 slices of toast.

with quick spicy pickle spears

Makes enough for 8 sandwiches, plus a bonus of leftovers

8 Kaiser Rolls, page 80, freshly made and split

Slow Roasted Brisket, still warm and thinly sliced, see below

Prepared horseradish, deli mustard, and/or Russian dressing, page 157

Quick Spicy Pickle Spears, see below

I've been a fan of the Second Avenue Deli since I started living in New York City in 1978. Abe Lebewohl started a tiny luncheonette on the corner of Second Avenue and East 10th Street in 1954, and it prospered and expanded. After Abe's tragic murder/robbery in 1996, his family kept the deli alive. Today it's still prospering, albeit in a new location on East 33rd Street and a recently opened branch on the Upper East Side – and there's no other place like it.

Slow-cooked beef brisket makes a tender and flavourful sandwich, especially on a Kaiser roll. Since it's not practical to cook an entire brisket at home, I've scaled this down for a smaller piece of beef easily available in most butcher shops and supermarkets. It's best prepared for a party when you know you'll be able to serve the brisket freshly cooked without having to reheat it. You can also serve – or substitute – warm, thinly sliced corned beef or pastrami.

SECOND AVENUE DELI SLOW-ROASTED BRISKET

Dry off **2.3kg second cut beef brisket**, season with **salt and pepper,** and place on a rack in a roasting tin. Set a rack in the lower third of the oven and preheat to 230°C/gas mark 8. Trim the stem and root ends from **4 large onions**; peel and quarter them. Peel and cut **2 carrots** into 5cm chunks; rinse and cut **3 large ribs of celery** the same way. Have **6–8 unpeeled cloves of garlic** and **3–4 large bay leaves** ready. Place the roasting tin in the oven and cook for 15 minutes to start colouring the meat on the outside. Reduce the heat to 180°C/gas mark 4 without opening the oven and wait another 15 minutes. Add the onions, carrots, celery, garlic and bay leaves to the tin around the meat and roast for 30 minutes, checking after a few minutes to make sure the vegetables aren't burning. If after 45 minutes liquid isn't starting to accumulate in the tin, add 120ml water. Continue roasting,

basting every 10 minutes or so with the juices in the pan, until the meat is cooked through, tender, and has an internal temperature of 85°C, another 2 hours. The total cooking time is about 3 hours. Transfer the meat to a cutting board, cover it loosely with aluminium foil to keep warm, and wait about 15 minutes before slicing and making the sandwiches. You can make some quick pan gravy by adding a cup of water to the tin and letting it reduce until flavourful and syrupy over a high heat. Put any leftover sliced meat in a shallow bowl and strain the gravy over it. Cool, cover and refrigerate and reheat slowly in the gravy within a day or two.

QUICK SPICY PICKLE SPEARS

Sterilise a half litre canning jar and its two-piece cover in boiling water for a few minutes, then remove from the heat and leave in the water. Bring **120ml water, 150ml distilled white vinegar**, and **½**

teaspoon salt to the boil; pour into a bowl and refrigerate to cool completely. Rinse and trim the ends from **2 cucumbers, just about 450g or a little less**. Peel or not as you wish. Halve them lengthways and cut each half into 4–6 spears. Use tongs to lift the jar from the hot water and let any water inside drain back into the pan. Stand the jar on a folded tea towel and cool for a few seconds. Stand the pickle spears upright in the jar, adding **2 cloves of garlic**, peeled and halved, a couple of washed **sprigs of dill** if you like, and **1–2 small dried Thai chillies or Mexican *chillies de arbol*.** Pour the cooled brine into the jar to within 5mm of the top. Remove the lid and ring from the water and use tongs to put the lid in place. Cool the ring until you can comfortably handle it, then screw it tightly in place. Cool completely, then refrigerate. Wait a week before trying the pickles, and use them within a month of making them. Do not store these at room temperature or they'll spoil quickly.

Possibly the most interesting sandwiches in the world, Mexican *tortas* combine boldly seasoned elements in a way that achieves both complexity and a certain delicacy. A *torta* is usually constructed on a *telera* roll, but there are dozens of regional variations on the bread. This recipe is from my very dear friend Roberto Santibañez, chef/owner of Fonda in the East Village in Manhattan and in Park Slope in Brooklyn, New York. Friendship aside, my critical side knows that he cooks the best Mexican food outside Mexico, bar none.

Makes 4 tortas

4 *Teleras*, page 82, or other rolls of your choice

30g unsalted butter, softened to spreading consistency

8 tablespoons refried black beans, see below

Half the *carnitas*, see below, warm but not red hot

4 paper-thin slices white or red onion, peeled but left intact

4 slices pickled jalapeños, or more or less to taste, see Note below

1 ripe Hass avocado, quartered, peeled, and each quarter cut across into 1cm slices

2 tablespoons mayonnaise, Mexican crema, or crème fraiche

1. Split the rolls and butter. Lightly toast the buttered sides on a griddle, in a large sauté pan over a medium heat or under the grill.

2. Spread the bottom halves of each roll with 2 tablespoons refried beans. Spread a quarter of the *carnitas* on each. Top with the slices of onion, the pickled jalapeños, and the avocado.

3. Spread the top halves of each roll with mayonnaise or crema and press lightly on the *torta* to adhere. Tortas are not usually cut in half before being served but this gringo recommends you do so to make eating a little easier. Serve immediately.

NOTE: The pickled jalapeños can be replaced with 1 tablespoon chipotle chillies in adobo sauce. Pulse the whole tin of chillies and sauce in a food processor, pack into a plastic container, press clingfilm against the surface, and refrigerate.

REFRIED BLACK BEANS
Combine **1 tablespoon olive or mild vegetable oil**, such as safflower or rapeseed, **1 tablespoon finely grated white onion** (it's okay if it's mainly liquid), and **½ small clove garlic**, finely grated, in a medium saucepan. Set over a low heat and cook until the aroma of the garlic is evident and the onion and garlic are starting to colour a little. Off heat, stir in **420g tinned black beans** and their liquid. Stir in **¼ teaspoon ground toasted chipotle chilli** or other ground hot pepper

and **¼ teaspoon crumbled dried oregano leaves**, preferably Mexican. Increase the heat slightly to bring to the boil, then decrease again and start using a potato masher to turn the beans to a purée. Regulate the heat so that the beans simmer gently and cook, stirring frequently, until they thicken slightly. Stir in **salt** to taste – they shouldn't be too salty. Cool the beans and scrape them into a plastic container for storage. Bring to room temperature before using.

CARNITAS
Combine **900g boneless pork shoulder** with some fat on the meat, cut into 4cm pieces, with **720ml water, 140g thinly sliced white onion, 4 tablespoons vegetable oil, 2 tablespoons orange juice, 8 peeled cloves garlic, 3 medium bay leaves** and **1 teaspoon each dried oregano**, crumbled, and **fine sea salt** in a 3- to 4-litre enamelled iron Dutch oven. Bring to the boil over a medium heat, skimming as necessary, then reduce the heat to an active simmer. Cook until the water evaporates, the pork is very tender and it starts to fry in its rendered fat, about 1 ½ hours. Transfer to a gratin dish or other baking dish and bake the pork and fat at 230°C/gas mark 8 until it colours deeply, about 20 minutes. Cool to just warm. For advance preparation, cool, cover, and refrigerate. Reheat and cool to lukewarm before using.

QUICK CHANGES

TORTA DE ALBÓNDIGAS: For a single sandwich, after spreading the bottom half of the *telera* with the beans, top with 2 of the *albondigas* and some of their sauce on page 34 – they should be warm but not hot. Sprinkle with coriander, onion and cheese as in the *albóndigas* recipe. Top with avocado if you wish, then spread the top half of the roll with mayonnaise or crema.

TORTA DE PECHUGA: For a single sandwich, cook a chicken breast as in Rosemary Chicken Sandwiches, page 71. Slice if you wish, but in Mexico it would be used whole. Assemble the sandwich as at left, but sprinkle with 1 tablespoon of crumbled *queso fresco*.

TORTA DE MILANESA: Bread and fry in vegetable oil some thin 85g pork or chicken cutlets as in *Wiener Schnitzel*, page 42. Assemble like the *Torta de Pechuga*, above.

My favourite establishment in the Newark neighbourhood where I grew up was Blasi's Great Big Hole in the Wall, a hot dog joint a couple of blocks from where we lived. The name wasn't a fantasy: There was a bar next door and the owners of Blasi's and of Campesi's bar broke a rough opening in the common wall of the two businesses so the food could be passed directly into the bar. An 'Italian' hot dog smothered with fried onions and peppers, served on a roll that was shaped like a hunk of baguette, was the most popular item.

I loved it when my mother added some sausage to her weekly meat sauce for pasta. After cooking in the sauce for a couple of hours the sausage was tender, flavourful, and all the pesky lumps of fat had melted. So I've merged Blasi's fried peppers and onions and a bit of tomato to create tender braised sausage links for this sandwich.

Makes 3–6 sandwiches, depending how much you fill them

3 red peppers (about 675g), cut into 1cm strips

1 tablespoon extra-virgin olive oil, plus extra

Salt

1 large white onion, thinly sliced

6 links (about 450g) sweet Italian sausage

100g well-drained and chopped tinned Italian plum tomatoes

120ml water

3–6 Sub Rolls (page 82, Quick Changes)

1. Set a rack in the middle level of the oven and preheat to 200°C/gas mark 6. Toss the peppers with the oil and a sprinkling of salt in a 23 x 33 x 5cm baking dish or small roasting tin and bake for about 20 minutes, stirring often.

2. Remove the tin from the oven and stir in the onions. Return to the oven for another 20 minutes, again stirring often.

3. Meanwhile, brown the sausages in a few drops of olive oil in a non-stick sauté pan.

4. Remove the peppers and onions from the oven (leave the oven on) and stir in the tomatoes and water. Salt lightly and add the sausages, embedding them in the liquid. Bring to the boil over a medium heat, tightly cover the tin with aluminium foil and return to the oven. Decrease the oven temperature to 180°C/gas mark 4 and bake until the sausage is tender and the liquid very reduced, about 1 hour. After half an hour, remove the tin from the oven and make sure

the liquid isn't evaporating too quickly. If it is, add 60–75ml more water.

5. For advance preparation, you can make the braised sausages a couple of days earlier, then cool and refrigerate them. Reheat them in a shallow sauté pan over a low heat before serving.

6. Once the sausages are ready, cut the sub rolls into the same length as one or two links of sausage. Split them lengthways but leave the halves attached on one side and heat them at 180°C/gas mark 4 for 3 minutes to crisp the crust. Stuff each roll as you like.

QUICK CHANGES

SPICY SAUSAGE AND PEPPERS:
• Rinse then halve 6 long green hot peppers lengthways; use a teaspoon to scrape away the seed pods and any stray seeds. Cut the peppers into 5cm lengths.
• Add along with the onions, because the peppers' flesh is much thinner than an ordinary green pepper's and they will burn if added earlier.

MEATBALL HERO:
• Substitute the Italian meatballs cooked in tomato sauce, a variation of the meatloaf on page 37.
• Halve the meatballs before filling the sandwich for easier eating.

Makes 4 sandwiches

CRAB CAKES

1 pound crabmeat, see Note below right

1 medium egg

4 tablespoons mayonnaise

1 teaspoon lemon juice

Dash of Worcestershire sauce

¼ teaspoon ground celery seed, see Note below

¼ teaspoon salt

¼ teaspoon dry mustard

Large pinch of ground white pepper

5 tablespoons fresh breadcrumbs

1 tablespoon finely chopped green pepper

1 tablespoon finely chopped red pepper or roasted red pepper from a jar

One swiss roll tin lined with oiled or sprayed foil

SANDWICHES

4 Albert Kumin's Kaiser Rolls, page 80, or Hamburger Buns, page 81, split and lightly toasted on the cut sides

4 outer leaves of iceberg lettuce, rinsed and dried

Mayonnaise or tartar sauce, optional

Coleslaw, see opposite, optional

NOTE: In Baltimore, normally Old Bay seasoning, a blend of 18 herbs and spices, is used.

Every time I go to Baltimore, I ask the first few people I meet where to get the best crab cakes. After *BAKE!* was published I spent a weekend in Baltimore, arranged by my friend, food writer and restaurant reviewer Dara Bunjon, to promote the book. I asked in advance if we could go for crab cakes as soon as I arrived. Dara drove me out to the suburbs and took me to a big diner-style restaurant, the G&M, home of the grilled crab cake – a new twist for me. They were moist, tender and flavourful, with big chunks of extremely fresh crab. Later, I asked Dara if she had any ideas about how they were seasoned and made. She dropped everything and sent me a newly created recipe and a photo of the results within a day. Thank you, Miss Baltimore!

1. Unpack the crabmeat to a large plate and pick through for bits of shell and cartilage without breaking the meat apart too much. Cover and refrigerate until needed.

2. Whisk the egg and mayonnaise together in a medium mixing bowl and whisk in the lemon juice and Worcestershire sauce. Scatter in the celery seed, salt, mustard and pepper and whisk until smooth.

3. Sprinkle with the breadcrumbs, green and red peppers and the crabmeat. Use a large rubber spatula to fold everything together gently but thoroughly.

4. Divide the mixture into 4 equal parts and use slightly moistened hands to form patties the same diameter as your rolls. Cover and chill if not serving immediately.

5. Preheat the grill and set a rack one notch below the highest one. Arrange the crab cakes on the prepared tin and grill them until golden on top, about 8 minutes, turning the tin back to front once about halfway through. Use a wide flexible metal spatula to turn the crab cakes and grill them on the other side, about 5 minutes longer.

6. Let the crab cakes cool for a minute or so while you toast the rolls.

7. Place a leaf of the lettuce on the bottom half of the roll, top with a crab cake and the top of the roll. Serve immediately.

NOTE: Crabmeat designated as 'claw' is dark in colour and is not usually used to make crab cakes; it's the least expensive type of crabmeat. Jumbo or lump crabmeat is made up of single muscles that control the crab's 'arms' and is the most expensive type. What you want for a crab cake is the middle quality; it comes mostly from the central body cavity of a crab, and may be labelled 'special,' 'backfin,' or just 'crabmeat' and is a combination of small pieces and broken pieces of lump. Pasteurised fresh or tinned crabmeat is a very good substitute.

MY FAVOURITE COLESLAW

Shred **a small, about 675g, head of green cabbage** and place in a large bowl. Add **3 spring onions**, rinsed, trimmed, and white and light green parts finely sliced, **¼ each of a large green and red pepper and a peeled carrot**, all grated on the largest holes of a box grater. In a separate bowl whisk together **120ml apple cider vinegar, 1 teaspoon salt, 1–2 teaspoons sugar** to taste, **115g soured cream**, and **115g mayonnaise**. Fold the dressing into the vegetables, mixing well; cover and refrigerate until ready to serve. Check the seasoning before serving and correct with a little more salt or sugar as necessary.

If there's such a thing as a world-class sandwich, this is it. A *muffuletta* from Central Grocery is so good that it should be considered a crime to leave New Orleans without enjoying one. The olive salad derives from the Sicilian tradition of marinating still slightly bitter newly brined olives in oil, vinegar, garlic and other seasonings, including chopped celery, to sweeten and flavour them.

The olive salad recipe here is based on a family recipe from my friend Gerard Bertolino, who is from Gretna, Louisiana, right outside New Orleans. His version omits the carrots and cauliflower used in Central Grocery's, but the flavour is incredibly similar. I've scaled back the quantities so you'll have enough for a couple of *muffulettas*, but you can make more if you like; it will keep refrigerated for a month or so.

1. First make the olive salad. Combine all the ingredients except the oil, garlic and vinegar in a large bowl.

2. Combine the oil and garlic and stir in the vinegar. Pour over the salad and use a rubber spatula to fold everything together. Let stand for 1 hour at room temperature, folding again 3 or 4 times to develop flavour. Taste and correct the seasoning with more salt, pepper, and vinegar.

3. For advance preparation, pack into a plastic container or canning jar. Add more oil to cover all the ingredients if necessary. Cover the container and refrigerate until needed. Bring the amount you need to room temperature before using.

4. When the olive salad is ready, spread on the bottom half of the roll and leave it to soak in for a few minutes. Arrange the sliced meats and provolone in separate layers over the salad and cover with the top half of the roll.

5. Cut the *muffuletta* in quarters and serve. It needs no accompaniment.

NOTE: At Central Grocery, the olive salad is placed on top of the sliced meats and cheese. I like it underneath because it makes the sandwich easier to cut and eat.

OLIVE SALAD

Makes about 450g

125g large pimento-stuffed olives, coarsely chopped

60ml brine from the jar of olives

50g pitted Greek olives, such as Kalamata, coarsely chopped

3 short interior stalks celery with leaves, cut into 5mm dice

50g tiny capers in brine, drained and rinsed

3 small pickled *peperoncini* or other mildly spicy pickled peppers, halved, seeded and chopped

Salt (just a small sprinkle) and freshly ground black pepper

2 tablespoons finely chopped flat-leaf parsley

1 tablespoon dried oregano, preferably Sicilian

75ml olive oil

2 small cloves garlic, peeled and finely grated

2 tablespoons red wine vinegar

MUFFULETTA

Makes one large sandwich, 2–4 servings

1 New Orleans Sicilian Sesame Roll, page 87, split horizontally

225g Olive Salad, including some of the liquid from the jar, see above

140g thinly sliced boiled ham

140g thinly sliced *mortadella*

140g thinly sliced Genoa salami

140g thinly sliced loaf-style provolone cheese

IL SOLITO

Makes 1 panino

1 ciabatta roll, page 106

55g *prosciutto Toscano*, sliced paper thin, see Note below

2 tablespoons black olive tapenade, bought or home-made, see below

55g fresh mild sheep's milk cheese, crumbled, see Note below

6 cherry or grape tomatoes, or more depending on the size, halved

NOTE: Prosciutto Toscano can be sourced online from www.gastronomica.co.uk. Alternatively, use prosciutto di Parma or a domestic brand. A mild goat's cheese such as Montrachet or a domestic brand is a good substitute for fresh sheep's milk cheese.

I n Italy a *panino* (the singular) means roll. Today it has come to mean any one of a wide variety of sandwiches made on rolls, sliced firm textured bread, or even focaccia. Alessandro Frassica, owner of ´ino, a panino shop in Florence, told me that most of his panini are made on ciabatta rolls, though focaccia (page 160) and *Pane Sciocco*, the Tuscan salt-free bread (page 113), are also popular. Alessandro shared the recipe for his most popular panino, 'Il Solito' (the usual).

1. Split the roll horizontally and heat briefly, without toasting, in the oven.

2. Place a layer of prosciutto on the bottom half of the roll and spread the tapenade on it. Sprinkle on the cheese, then the halved tomatoes, cut side up.

3. Cover with the top of the roll and gently press. Cut in half across the centre and serve immediately.

TAPENADE

Stone **225g black olives** and mix in the bowl of a food processor with just the **drained anchovies from a 55g tin** (save the oil) and **80g well-drained capers**. Pulse the ingredients at 1-second intervals to make a chunky purée. Making 5-second pulses with one hand and pouring with the other, first add the oil from the tin of anchovies, followed by **60ml more olive oil**, each a teaspoon at a time – the idea is to get the tapenade ingredients to emulsify with the oil. Old Provençal cookbooks suggest adding a teaspoon of Dijon mustard, which is optional.

SUGGESTIONS FOR FILLING PANINI

The following is a list of meats and fish, cheeses, dressings, vegetables and greens for contemporary Italian panini. Mix and match at will or think up your own combinations but avoid pairing multiple salty or smoked elements – one of those is enough for any panino.

Breads: These are mentioned above. If you want to use focaccia, make sure to keep it on the soft side when you bake it and go easy on the salt for topping it.

Meats and fish: Thinly sliced prosciutto, cooked ham, salami, peeled dried sausage, rare roast beef, *mortadella*, sweet or hot *capicola* or *soppressata*, smoked salmon, anchovies or sardine fillets packed in oil, rings of fried calamari, flaked tuna in olive oil, cold sliced chicken breast or thin slices of country pâté.

Cheeses: Thinly sliced Fontina, Gruyère, Emmentaler, aged Gouda, provolone, fresh or smoked mozzarella or *burrata*, crumbled Gorgonzola or other blue-veined cheese, shavings of Parmigiano-Reggiano or pecorino Romano, crumbled fresh goat's or sheep's milk cheese, freshly made ricotta or *ricotta salata*.

Dressings and spreads: Extra-virgin olive oil, drops of best quality aged balsamic vinegar, tapenade (see opposite), freshly made basil pesto, Dijon mustard, or softened unsalted butter.

Vegetables and greens: Leaf lettuce; rocket; outer leaves of iceberg lettuce; grilled or roasted thinly sliced vegetables such as aubergine or courgettes; roasted and peeled red, yellow or green peppers dressed with olive oil, salt, and grated garlic; sun-dried tomatoes soaked in hot water, drained, and dressed with olive oil; sliced fresh summer tomatoes; halved cherry or grape tomatoes.

During the three summer seasons I spent working at the Sporting Club in Monte Carlo in the mid-seventies, we didn't start work until 3 p.m. We young cooks would spend the morning on the beach in front of our residence hotel or at the nearby *Plage du Larvotto*, Monte Carlo's fancy public beach. Dinner was provided at work, so most of us would save money by having a mid-morning combination of breakfast and lunch, and more often than not it was a *pan bagnat* that in those days cost about a dollar. A little like a salade niçoise on a roll, a good *pan bagnat* is oily and moist and quite perfect for a casual lunch or picnic. Though it's a little large, the New Orleans Sicilian Sesame Roll, minus its coating of sesame seeds, is perfect for a *pan bagnat*.

1. Split the roll and generously brush the cut sides with extra-virgin olive oil.

2. Starting on the bottom of the roll, evenly arrange half the anchovies. Cover with slices of tomato, sweet onion and pepper.

3. Scatter the olives on top. Add a few torn leaves of basil, though it's not traditional. Cover with the top of the roll and press well to adhere. Cut into quarters to serve.

Makes 1 sandwich

1 New Orleans Sicilian Sesame Roll, page 87

Extra-virgin olive oil for brushing

One 55g tin anchovies, well drained

½ ripe summer tomato, sliced thinly

½ sweet onion, sliced paper thin

½ sweet red or yellow pepper, sliced thinly

25g pitted niçoise olives

Fresh basil leaves, torn

pan bagnat de monaco

chapter seven

Yeast-Based Two-Step Breads

Right after *BAKE!* was published, a friend phoned to alert me that there was a mistake in one of the chapters: 'I've just started reading a chapter called Two-Step Breads, and all the recipes have seven or eight steps in them. Is this right?' I explained that the steps referred to are the two different doughs that are used to make the bread. The first is a pre-ferment of flour, water and yeast, usually made the day or a few hours before, while the second incorporates the pre-ferment into mixing the final dough. This chapter, too, is devoted to 'two-step breads', but there are a few more steps needed to get to a final baked bread.

All the pre-ferments here are of a type that's called a poolish (poo-LEASH), a fairly liquid pre-ferment made from flour, water and a small amount of yeast. It takes about five minutes to prepare, can be mixed by hand, and just needs to ferment until you're ready to make the final dough. Using a poolish adds enzymes to a newly mixed dough, which condition the dough to make it smoother and easier to handle. They also help the yeast digest the natural sugars in the flour more efficiently and contribute flavour and texture normally only acquired by a long fermentation time for the whole dough.

Though it's possible to make a poolish with a variety of different amounts of water in relation to the weight of the flour, I like to use equal parts of each. A thin poolish is easy to mix into the other dough ingredients.

The breads in this chapter are varied – from a typical French-style baguette to a Sicilian all durum-flour bread that utilises a durum-flour poolish.

Makes 2 large loaves or 8-12 rolls

POOLISH

100g room-temperature tap water, about 24°C

Pinch of fine granulated active dried yeast or instant yeast

100g strong white bread flour

DOUGH

300g room-temperature tap water, about 24°C

½ teaspoon fine granulated active dried yeast or instant yeast

300g strong white bread flour

100g plain flour

1½ teaspoons fine sea salt

One baking sheet or swiss roll tin lined with parchment paper

---

QUICK CHANGES

CIABATTA ROLLS: These are great for sandwiches, as well as for serving as individual dinner rolls.
• In step 6, after dividing the dough into 2 rectangles, cut each across again at 7.5cm intervals (oil the bench scraper again if it starts to stick to the dough) to make 8 rectangular rolls.
• To make thinner rolls, gently stretch the rectangles of dough on the work surface to about 45cm in length, then cut across at 7.5cm intervals to make 12 rolls.
• Use a wide spatula to transfer the rolls to the tin, spacing them at least 5cm apart all around.
• Resume the recipe at the end of step 7, when you cover the dough and preheat the oven.
• Check the internal temperature of the rolls after 15 minutes of baking to make sure they don't get too dry.

Ciabatta means 'slipper' and although the name refers to the fairly flat rectangular form of the bread, it's also pretty slippery because the dough is so soft. It is manageable, yet it still requires care and attention when handling. Keep a bowl of dusting flour and a bench scraper nearby when you're working with the dough and above all, stay calm – it's just a piece of dough, after all. The addition of plain flour weakens the bread flour and makes a less elastic dough that bakes a better ciabatta.

1. For the poolish, whisk the water and yeast together in a medium mixing bowl and stir in the flour until smooth. Cover with clingfilm and let ferment at room temperature until very risen and bubbly, about 12 hours. If it's warm in the room, let the poolish ferment for 2–3 hours, then refrigerate for the remaining time. Remove from the fridge 1 hour before using it.

2. For the dough, whisk the water and yeast together in the bowl of an electric mixer and use a large rubber spatula to stir in the poolish. Stir in the flours and place the bowl on the mixer fitted with the paddle attachment. Beat on lowest speed until the dough looks smooth, about 2 minutes. Stop and let the dough rest for 15 minutes.

3. Start the mixer again on low/medium speed, sprinkle in the salt, and beat the dough until more elastic but still quite loose, about 2 minutes. Scrape the dough into a lightly oiled bowl; lightly oil the palm of your hand and gently press it against the top of the dough to oil it. Cover with clingfilm and let the dough ferment until it starts to puff, about 30 minutes.

4. Scrape the dough onto a generously floured surface and use an oiled bench scraper: flatten the dough to a disc, fold the two sides in to overlap at the middle, then roll the top towards you swiss roll-style. Rinse, dry, and oil the bowl again and return the dough to the bowl, seam side down, lightly oiling the top again. Cover with clingfilm and let the dough rest for 30 minutes.

5. Repeat step 4.

6. To shape the loaves, scrape the dough from the bowl smooth side up to a generously floured work surface. Without deflating it too much, pull the dough into a rough rectangle about 30cm long and 20cm wide. Use an oiled bench scraper to cut the dough in half to make two 10 x 30cm rectangles. Flour the palms of your hands and slide them under the narrow sides of one of the loaves and quickly transfer it to one side of the prepared tin, gently stretching it to the full length of the tin as you do. Repeat with the second piece of dough. The loaves should each be about 4cm in from the side of the tin with about 7.5cm between them. Cover the loaves with a tea towel or oiled clingfilm and let proof until very puffy, about 30–60 minutes.

7. Soon after you cover the loaves, set a rack in the middle level of the oven, remove the racks above and below it, and preheat to 260°C/gas mark 10. Place a cast iron frying pan or other heavy pan directly on the floor of the oven. Have a tray of ice cubes ready.

8. Uncover the loaves, place them in the oven, and quickly throw 6–8 ice cubes into the frying pan. Reduce the temperature to 220°C/gas mark 7 and bake the loaves until well risen and deep golden, with an internal temperature of over 93°C, 20–25 minutes.

9. Cool the loaves on a rack and use the same day, or double wrap and freeze. After defrosting, bake the bread at 180°C/gas mark 4 for 3 minutes, then cool before serving.

Conquering the baguette is a little like running your first race – you can't necessarily do it without some training first. Mixing the dough is easy – it's no more difficult than any of the other bread recipes in this book. Handling it is a little more challenging, because the dough is soft, but once you give the dough a couple of turns it's more elastic and easier to handle. But shaping a baguette, proofing it to just the right degree and slashing the top of the loaf all require care, or the baguette won't have a good texture, flavour or appearance.

Thanks to the Internet, you can watch Professor Calvel shape a baguette several times himself. On my website there's a link to the 1971 *French Chef* episode when Julia Child visited Calvel at his school in Paris. If you try Julia's one-step baguette recipe, weigh out 450g of flour – don't scoop it up with measuring cups as she does or you'll get far too much flour, as proven by the dry dough she demonstrates.

Makes two 38–43cm baguettes

POOLISH

60g room-temperature tap water, about 24°C

¼ teaspoon fine granulated active dried yeast or instant yeast

60g strong white bread flour

DOUGH

125g room-temperature tap water, about 24°C

½ teaspoon fine granulated active dried yeast or instant yeast

½ teaspoon malt syrup

240g strong white bread flour

1¼ teaspoons fine sea salt

One *couche* or a flat-weave tea towel dusted with flour on a baking sheet or the back of a swiss roll tin and one heavy baking sheet or pizza stone for baking

PART I: THE DOUGH

1. For the poolish, whisk the water and yeast together in a small bowl; wait 30 seconds, then whisk again. Use a small rubber spatula to stir in the flour. Cover with clingfilm and let ferment at room temperature until more than doubled in bulk, about 4 hours. Alternatively, let the poolish start to ferment until it rises visibly at room temperature and refrigerate it until the next day, a maximum of 16 hours. If you have refrigerated the poolish, bring it to room temperature before mixing the dough.

2. For the dough, whisk the water and yeast together in the bowl of an electric mixer; wait 30 seconds and whisk again. Whisk in the malt syrup. Use a small rubber spatula to stir in the poolish; once it's thoroughly mixed in, stir in the flour. Place the bowl on the mixer and attach the dough hook. Mix on low speed until the dough comes together somewhat, about 2 minutes – it will be quite soft. Stop the mixer and let the dough rest for 15 minutes.

3. Start the mixer again on medium speed and sprinkle in the salt. Mix until the dough is smoother and more elastic, 2–3 minutes. Scrape the dough into an oiled bowl and turn it so that the top is oiled. Cover the bowl with clingfilm and let the dough ferment until it increases about 50% over its original size.

4. Invert the dough, smooth top side down, onto a floured work surface. Flatten the dough to a disc. Fold the two sides in to overlap at the middle, then roll the top towards you all the way to the end, swiss roll-style. Invert, flatten and repeat. Return the dough to the bowl, seam side down and cover again. Let the dough ferment until it doubles in bulk, about 1 hour. *Continued*

professor calvel's baguette

PART II: FORMING THE BAGUETTES

1. Invert the dough, smooth side down, onto a lightly floured work surface and use a bench scraper to divide it into 2 equal pieces, each just under 250g. Fold each over to make quarter circle shapes.

2. Cover one of the pieces of dough. Use the palm of your hand to flatten the other piece gently and pull it into a rough square shape. Fold the top of the square down over the middle section and the bottom third upward about 2.5cm short of the top.

3. Use the palm of your hand to flatten the rectangle of dough and use the side of one hand, karate-chop style, to flatten a trench down the length of the dough. Fold the top down to the trench and use your fingertips to seal it in place. Fold over again and use the heel of your hand to seal the end of the dough to the cylinder formed.

4. Starting in the middle of the cylinder, roll with each hand, palms downward, to evenly elongate the cylinder of dough and make it about 38cm long. Slightly point the ends as you finish rolling. Lift the formed baguette seam side up to one side of the middle of the prepared cloth-covered tin. Pinch up the cloth about 3 inches away from the baguette and then bring it up next to the loaf to form a wall.

5. Form the second baguette and place it on the other side of the cloth wall. Lightly dust the tops of the 2 baguettes with flour and fold the outside of the cloth on either side to cover the baguettes.

6. Set a rack in the middle level of the oven and place your pizza stone or baking sheet on it. Remove the racks under it and place a small roasting tin for water on the bottom of the oven. Preheat to 245°C/gas mark 9.

PART III: PROOFING AND SLASHING

1. Let the baguettes proof until they are almost doubled in bulk, about 30 minutes – they should be visibly puffed but not too inflated.

2. Sprinkle a peel or a piece of stiff cardboard with maize meal or line with a piece of parchment paper the size of your pizza stone or baking sheet.

3. Place it next to the outside of one of the baguettes and lift the cloth on the other side of it to flip it onto the cardboard. Slide the baguette to the peel, leaving room for the other baguette.

4. Repeat with the other baguette.

5. Use an X-Acto knife or single-edge razor blade to make 3 or 4 long slashes along the length of the baguette, holding the blade almost parallel to the top of the loaf.

PART IV: BAKING AND COOLING

1. Quickly open the oven and slide the baguettes from the peel to the stone or baking sheet.

2. Quickly open the oven again and, averting your face, pour a couple of cups of water onto the tin or a cup of ice cubes into the frying pan. Wait 5 minutes and decrease the oven temperature to 200°C/gas mark 6.

3. Bake the baguettes until they are well risen and deep golden and their internal temperature is about 93°C, 20–25 minutes longer.

4. Cool the loaves on a rack. If the crust softens before you serve the baguettes, reheat them at 180°C for 3–4 minutes and cool on a rack to crisp the crust.

QUICK CHANGES

BOULES:
• Make 1 large or 2 smaller boules, step 5, page 130.

FICELLES:
• Divide the dough into 3 to 4 pieces, each about 165g, and form, proof, slash and bake as at left.
• The ficelles should be done 15–20 minutes after decreasing the temperature in step 2 of Baking.

BATARDS:
• After dividing the dough into 2 pieces, gently flatten each and pull on the sides all around, folding the pulled areas over to the centre. Cover and let rest for 5 minutes.
• Flatten to a disc and fold the top third down and seal in place, then fold again using the heel of your hand to seal the edge in place. Gently roll over, keeping the centre thicker, until the loaf is about 30cm long.
• Repeat with the second piece of dough. All the rest of the steps are exactly the same as at left.

professor calvel's baguette

sicilian remilled semolina bread

Makes one 23–25cm round loaf

ALL-DURUM POOLISH

75g room-temperature tap water, about 24°C

¼ teaspoon fine granulated active dried yeast or instant yeast

75g durum flour (see Note below)

ALL-DURUM DOUGH

225g room-temperature tap water, about 24°C

1 teaspoon fine granulated active dried yeast or instant yeast

360g durum flour

1½ teaspoons fine sea salt

90g sesame seeds for finishing

One heavy baking sheet or pizza pan dusted with maize meal, plus a spray bottle filled with warm water

Note: Durum flour can be sourced online if you can't find it in the supermarket. See page 10 for an explanation of the confusion between durum flour and semolina flour.

QUICK CHANGES

Form the dough into 2 batard shapes, page 109; the loaves will take 5–10 minutes less to bake.

The bright yellow crumb of this bread comes from 100% durum flour in the dough. Since semolina is coarsely ground durum wheat that looks like maize meal, the bread's name refers to the re-milling of coarse semolina into flour. Until recently in Sicily, much of this type of bread was made in the home and taken to a communal oven to be baked. A home baker knew nothing of poolish, but achieved similar results by saving a piece of dough and storing it wrapped in a cool place until the next batch of dough was prepared with it a few days later. The recipe here uses a poolish with similar results.

1. For the poolish, whisk the water and yeast together in a small bowl. Stir in the flour smoothly. Cover with clingfilm and let ferment at room temperature until more than doubled in bulk, about 4 hours.

2. For the dough, pour the water into the bowl of an electric mixer and whisk in the yeast; wait 30 seconds and whisk again. Use a rubber spatula to stir in the poolish.

3. Combine the flour and salt and use the spatula to stir this into the mixer bowl a little at a time. Make sure all the flour is mixed into the liquid.

4. Place the bowl on the mixer and attach the dough hook. Mix on the lowest speed until the dough comes together around the hook, 1–2 minutes. Stop the mixer and pull the dough away from the hook; let the dough rest for 15 minutes.

5. Increase the mixer speed to low/medium and mix until the dough is smooth and elastic, 2–3 minutes. Scrape the dough into an oiled bowl and turn it over so that the top is oiled. Cover with clingfilm. Let it ferment until it starts to puff, about 30 minutes.

6. Scrape the dough onto a floured work surface and with floured hands, pull into a rough rectangle. Fold the two sides in to overlap at the middle, then roll the top towards you swiss roll-style. Invert, flatten and repeat. Return the dough to the bowl, cover, and let ferment until fully doubled in bulk, about 30 minutes.

7. To shape the dough into a loaf, use a flexible plastic scraper to slide it from the bowl, smooth side up, to a floured work surface without deflating the dough. Round the loaf by pushing against the bottom of the dough all around with the sides of your hands held palms upward. It will quickly form an even sphere.

8. Place the dough on the prepared tin and loosely cover it with a flat-weave tea towel or piece of sprayed or oiled clingfilm. Let rest until it starts to puff again, about 30 minutes. As soon as you cover the loaf, set a rack in the middle level of the oven and preheat to 230°C/gas mark 8.

9. Once the dough has proofed to about 50% larger than its original size, flour the palms of your hands and gently press to flatten it to about 2.5cm thick. Use an X-Acto knife or single-edge razor blade to cut 3 or 4 3mm-deep slashes across the loaf, then 3 or 4 more at a 45-degree angle to the first ones. Spray the loaf with water and sprinkle generously with sesame seeds.

10. Place in the oven and wait 5 minutes, then open the oven and spray the loaf again; reduce the temperature to 220°C/gas mark 7. Bake until well risen and deep golden, with an internal temperature of 93°C, about 20–25 minutes.

11. Cool the loaf on a rack and serve on the day it's baked. Double wrap and freeze for longer storage. Defrost, reheat at 180°C/gas mark 4 for 3 minutes, and cool before serving.

A ficelle, or thin baguette (ficelle means 'string' in French), is a great variation on a standard baguette that emphasises crust over internal crumb. These are shaped the same way as Professor Calvel's baguettes; just pick up that recipe at Part II step 2, forming the baguettes, on page 109, but bear in mind that you'll have four instead of two loaves, which is why I've given instructions below for proofing and baking them on tins rather than the standard way.

1. For the poolish, whisk the water and yeast together in a small bowl. Stir in the flour smoothly. Cover with clingfilm and let ferment at room temperature until more than doubled in bulk, about 4 hours.

2. For the dough, whisk the water and yeast together in the bowl of an electric mixer; wait 30 seconds and whisk again. Use a large rubber spatula to stir in the poolish until it is fully mixed with the water. Mix the bread and wholemeal flours together and evenly stir into the poolish and water.

3. Place the bowl on the mixer fitted with the dough hook and mix on the lowest speed for 2 minutes. Stop the mixer and let the dough rest for 15 minutes.

4. Start the mixer again on medium speed and sprinkle in the salt. Mix until the dough is smoother and elastic, about 2–3 minutes longer. Scrape the dough into an oiled bowl and turn it over so that the top is oiled. Cover with clingfilm and let the dough ferment until it just starts to puff, about 30 minutes.

5. Scrape the dough onto a floured surface. Flatten the dough to a disc. Fold the two sides in to overlap at the middle, then roll the top towards you all the way to the end, swiss roll-style. Invert, flatten and repeat. Place the dough back in the bowl, seam side down, and cover. Let the dough ferment until it is fully doubled, about 45 minutes longer.

6. To form the ficelles, invert the dough to a lightly floured surface and divide it into 4 equal pieces, each about 175g. Fold each piece of dough over on itself to make it half as long, and cover 3 pieces of the dough. To shape into a ficelle, start at Part II, step 2, on page 109 and shape as for the baguettes. Repeat with the remaining pieces of dough.

7. Transfer the formed loaves to the prepared tins, dust them lightly with flour, and cover again. Let the loaves proof until they are fully doubled in size, 30–45 minutes. Once they have started to puff, set a rack in the middle level of the oven and preheat to 230°C/gas mark 8.

8. Once fully proofed, use a single-edge razor or X-Acto knife held at a 45-degree angle to the loaf and slash the tops of the loaves 3 or 4 times in the length. Place the tin in the oven and immediately reduce the temperature to 220°C/gas mark 7. Bake the loaves until they are well risen, deeply coloured and have an internal temperature over 93°C, about 20 minutes.

9. Cool the loaves on a rack and serve them the same day. Double wrap and freeze for longer storage. Defrost, reheat at 180°C/gas mark 4 for 3 minutes, and cool before serving.

Makes 4 thin loaves

POOLISH

60g room-temperature tap water, about 24°C

Pinch of fine granulated active dried yeast or instant yeast

60g strong white bread flour

DOUGH

225g room-temperature tap water, about 75°F

1 teaspoon fine granulated active dried yeast or instant yeast

180g strong white bread flour

180g strong wholemeal bread flour

1½ teaspoons fine sea salt

Maize meal for the tin

Two baking sheets or swiss roll tins dusted with maize meal

wholemeal ficelles

The tradition of preparing salt-free bread in Tuscany doubtless developed at a time when there was an acute shortage of salt, after which people became accustomed to the bland flavour of *pane sciocco* (SHOW-ko). It's amusing that *sciocco* also means foolish or 'good for nothing' in Italian. This is the bread traditionally used for *panzanella*, Tuscan bread and tomato salad, and *pappa al pomodoro*, Tuscan bread and tomato soup. Also popular for panini, salt-free bread marries well with the salty cured meats that are often used in panini fillings.

This type of bread is normally prepared using a firmer Italian style pre-ferment called a *biga*. I find that a poolish does the job just as well.

1. For the poolish, whisk the water and yeast together in a small bowl. Stir in the flour until smooth. Cover with clingfilm and let ferment at room temperature until more than doubled in bulk, about 4 hours.

2. For the dough, pour the water into the bowl of an electric mixer and whisk in the yeast; wait 30 seconds and whisk again. Whisk in the malt syrup, if using. Use a rubber spatula to stir in the poolish, followed by the flour. Make sure all the flour is mixed and there isn't any on the sides of the bowl.

3. Place the bowl on the mixer and attach the dough hook. Mix on the lowest speed until the dough comes together around the dough hook, 1–2 minutes. Stop the mixer and pull the dough away from the hook; let the dough rest for 10 minutes.

4. Increase the mixer speed to low/medium and mix until the dough is smoother and more elastic, about 2–3 minutes.

5. Scrape the dough into an oiled bowl and turn it over so that the top is oiled. Cover the bowl with clingfilm and let the dough ferment until it starts to puff, about 30 minutes.

6. Scrape the dough to a floured work surface, flour your hands, and pull the dough into a rough rectangle. Fold the two sides in to overlap at the middle, then roll the top towards you, swiss roll-style. Invert, flatten and repeat. Let the dough ferment until it has fully doubled in bulk, about 30 minutes longer.

7. To shape the dough into a loaf, use a flexible plastic scraper to slide it from the bowl, right side up, to a floured work surface; try to keep from deflating the dough. Round the loaf by pushing against the bottom of the dough all around with the sides of your hands held palms upward. The dough will quickly form an even sphere. Place the dough on the prepared tin and cover it loosely with a flat-weave tea towel or piece of sprayed or oiled clingfilm. Let the dough rest until it starts to puff again, about 30 minutes. As soon as you cover the loaf, set a rack in the middle level of the oven and preheat to 230°C/gas mark 8.

8. Once the dough is proofed to about 50% larger than its original size, flour the palms of your hands and gently press to flatten it to about 2.5cm thick. Use an X-Acto knife or single-edge razor blade to cut a slash across the diameter of the loaf and then generously spray it with water. Place the tin in the oven.

9. Wait 5 minutes, open the oven and spray the loaf again, then reduce the oven temperature to 220°C/gas mark 7.

10. Bake the loaf until it is well risen and deep golden and the internal temperature reads 93°C on an instant-read thermometer, 20–25 minutes.

11. Cool the loaf on a rack and serve on the day it's baked. Double wrap and freeze for longer storage. Defrost, reheat at 180°C/gas mark 4 for 3 minutes, and cool before serving.

salt-free tuscan bread

Makes one 23–25cm round loaf

POOLISH

75g room-temperature tap water, about 24°C

¼ teaspoon fine granulated active dried yeast or instant yeast

75g strong white bread flour

DOUGH

225g room-temperature tap water, about 24°C

1 teaspoon fine granulated active dried yeast or instant yeast

1 teaspoon malt syrup, optional

360g strong white bread flour

One heavy baking sheet or pizza pan dusted with maize meal, plus a spray bottle filled with warm water

ABOUT SALT IN BREAD DOUGH

Aside from flavour, salt makes several other important contributions to bread dough. Initially it helps to control the action of the yeast and eventually helps to ensure a good crust colour. In the *Pane Sciocco*, the yeast action is controlled by using a relatively small amount, while the crust colour is improved by spraying the loaf before and during the initial stage of baking, melting some of the sugars on the surface and improving what might otherwise be an excessively pale crust.

cold spanish tomato & bread soup from cordoba

Makes 6–8 servings

SALMOREJO

900g perfectly ripe summer tomatoes, rinsed, stem ends cut away and diced

210g crustless firm white bread, such as Tuscan bread, page 113, or baguette, page 107, cut into 1cm cubes and left to dry for several hours at room temperature

1 large clove garlic, finely grated

2 teaspoons kosher salt or Maldon sea salt

120ml Spanish olive oil or other mild olive oil

1½ tablespoons sherry vinegar

GARNISHES

2 hard-boiled eggs, page 74, coarsely chopped

55g Spanish Serrano ham or prosciutto, thinly sliced and cut into 5mm dice

More olive oil for drizzling

In the heart of Andalusia, where gazpacho originated, Cordoba is home to gazpacho's thicker ancestor, *salmorejo*. A simple mixture of tomatoes, seasonings and moistened bread, *salmorejo* is usually garnished with chopped hard-boiled egg, thin dice of Spanish Serrano ham and a drizzle of olive oil. As in any dish of such simplicity, much depends on the quality of the ingredients. *Salmorejo* only has the right flavour when made with perfectly red and ripe summer tomatoes. This recipe is from my dear friend, writer and blogger Sandy Leonard. He tasted the soup in Cordoba and managed to pry the recipe out of the restaurant's chef before finishing his meal.

1. Put the tomatoes in the container of a blender.

2. Put the bread in a shallow bowl and sprinkle with about 120ml water. Wait a few minutes for the water to soak in, then gently squeeze the bread to extract excess water and add the moistened bread to the blender container.

3. Muddle the garlic and salt together and scrape into the blender.

4. Start the blender on low speed and gradually increase the speed until the mixture is finely puréed. Stop the blender and taste for salt, adding a little more if necessary.

5. Start the blender again on medium speed and drizzle in the oil in a thin stream, followed by the vinegar. Taste again and add a little more vinegar if you like. Check the consistency with a spoon: It should be no thicker than natural yogurt that's been stirred up. If it's thicker, add a little cold water to thin it out. *Salmorejo* isn't a thin soup, but it shouldn't be overly thick.

6. Pour the soup into a large bowl, cover with clingfilm, and chill for at least 2 hours before serving.

7. To serve, ladle the soup into chilled bowls and let guests help themselves to the garnishes, sprinkling them on the surface of the soup.

ABOUT BREAD SOUPS

Originally developed so that not even a crumb of precious bread should be wasted, bread soups are mostly made with slices of stale bread left over after a meal, especially in cultures where the standard loaf is a large round one that stays fresh for several days. Bread is used in two different ways in soups: a relatively small amount of stale bread may be soaked and added to a soup that's puréed to bind it. In other soups, notably the onion panade and the Portuguese bread soup here, the bread pretty much soaks up all the liquid, turning the soup into something like a very moist bread pudding. The recipes in this chapter include instructions for drying fresh bread if needed.

One of Washington D.C.'s most popular restaurants, Ris, is the creation of Ris Lacoste. Ris told me that she had learned the unusual method for this incredible onion soup from Chef Fernand Chambrette at La Varenne in Paris. It involves slowly cooking sliced onions, then cooking whole onions in a pan lined with butter and sugar until the bottom of the pan is covered, in Ris's words, 'with a caramelised molasses-like tar.' As delicious as it is unusual, the soup is frequently cited as the best in D.C. Since both methods for cooking the onions require several hours, it's best to make the soup the day before you serve it. Instead of using the typical individual crocks for onion soup, this recipe calls for serving it from a large pan. Choose a 4- to 5-litre enamelled iron Dutch oven that can go direct to the table from the oven.

1. To cook the sliced onions, melt the butter in a large pan over a medium heat. Stir in the onions until they're coated with butter, decrease the heat to low and cook, stirring occasionally. Watch carefully, so that the onions become soft and a delicate caramel colour; the process takes just about 2 hours.

2. Right after you start cooking the sliced onions, melt the butter for the onion caramel on a low heat in a small non-stick sauté pan. Stir in the sugar and add the whole onions. Let the sugar start to melt, then decrease the heat to low and continue cooking, occasionally turning the onions, until they are cooked through and the sugar and butter have caramelised to a deep brown. If the heat is low enough the process should take about 1½ hours.

3. Once the sliced onions are cooked, increase the heat to medium and add the sherry, using a wooden spoon to scrape any caramelised bits of onion from the bottom of the pan. Remove from the heat.

4. Once the whole onions are cooked, remove them from the pan and let cool. Pour off and discard any butter that has separated out and scrape the remaining caramel into the pan of sliced onions. Cool and finely chop the whole onions and add them to the pan.

5. To make the soup, add the stock and herbs to the pan and bring to the boil.

Decrease the heat so that the soup just simmers and cook for about 20 minutes. Season with salt and pepper and remove the thyme and bay leaves. For advance preparation, cool the soup and refrigerate, covered, until an hour or so before you're ready to serve it.

6. To serve, preheat the oven to 180°C/gas mark 4 and set a rack in the upper third. Brush the baguette slices with melted butter and place them on a small baking sheet. Bake until toasted and dry, about 15 minutes, keeping an eye on them so they don't burn. Cool them on the pan.

7. Preheat the grill, moving the rack to the middle of the oven. Reheat the soup to boiling in the pan you're serving it in. Float the toasted baguette slices on the surface of the soup covering it entirely; top with the sliced cheese and sprinkle the grated cheese over the slices. Place the pan under the grill and let the cheese melt and become bubbly, about 3 minutes.

8. Set the pan on the hob and slide a wide spatula between the side of the pan and the raft of baguette slices; gently lift and add in the port.

9. Serve immediately, using a large spoon to cut away and lift some of the toasted baguette into heated soup plates and ladling the soup around the bread.

Makes about 3 litres soup, about 8 servings

SLICED ONIONS

45g unsalted butter

900g large Spanish onions, peeled, halved and thinly sliced from stem to root end

3 tablespoons dry sherry, such as Amontillado

ONION CARAMEL

85g unsalted butter

3 tablespoons sugar

4 medium Spanish onions, about 675g, peeled but left whole

SOUP

1.4 litres beef stock

1.4 litres veal stock

3 branches fresh thyme

3 small bay leaves

Salt and freshly ground black pepper

8–12 large (about 9mm-thick) diagonal slices baguette, page 107, depending on the diameter of the pan for serving

30g unsalted butter, melted

8 thin slices Swiss Gruyère, about 115g

115g coarsely grated Swiss Gruyère

4 tablespoons ruby port

QUICK CHANGES

INDIVIDUAL CROCKS:
To serve the soup in individual oven-proof bowls, set the crocks on a swiss roll tin and ladle the hot soup into them. Preheat the grill, and top each crock with the bread and cheese as in step 7. Add 1½ teaspoons of port to each crock.

acquacotta

tuscan mushroom, tomato & bread soup

Makes 4 generous servings

3 tablespoons olive oil

2 small cloves garlic, smashed and peeled

450g cultivated mushrooms such as cremini, rinsed, bases of stems trimmed away, and sliced 1cm thick

150g well drained tinned Italian plum tomatoes, coarsely chopped

1.15 litres water

Salt and freshly ground black pepper

3 medium eggs

25g finely grated Parmigiano Reggiano

Four 1cm-thick slices Tuscan Bread, page 113, or another firm-textured white bread, halved and slowly toasted until dry

It wouldn't be the least exaggeration to say that there are hundreds of variations of this simple soup – which is Italian for 'cooked water' – many of which are nothing more than bread, water, a little olive oil and some herbs. This one, from the coastal Maremma part of Tuscany, is normally made with porcini mushrooms, perhaps still possible in Italy, but elsewhere an expensive solution to using up some stale bread. If you choose to omit the mushrooms altogether, double the amount of tomatoes.

1. Combine the oil and garlic in a deep saucepan and set over a medium heat. Let the garlic start to sizzle and take on some colour, turning it over so that it colours evenly, then add the sliced mushrooms. Toss or stir, decrease the heat a little and cook until the mushrooms start to wilt, about 10 minutes, tossing or stirring occasionally.

2. Add the tomatoes, bring to the boil, then decrease the heat so that the vegetables just simmer and cook until the tomatoes are no longer watery and the mushrooms are fully cooked through, about 10 minutes.

3. Stir in the water and bring the soup to the boil. Salt lightly (the cheese added later is salty), grind in some pepper and cook at a steady simmer until the soup is flavourful and slightly reduced, about 10 minutes. For advance preparation, remove from the heat, but serve within a few hours.

4. When you're ready to serve the soup, return it to the boil and remove from the heat.

5. Whisk the eggs and cheese together in a large bowl and set the bread slices in heated soup plates.

6. Whisk a couple of ladlefuls of the soup into the egg mixture, then stir in the rest of the soup in a stream. Quickly ladle the hot soup over the bread and serve immediately.

One of things that surprised me when I started work in Switzerland in 1973 was cheese salad. Strange to me or not, we had several varieties on the lunch menu at the hotel and *Kaesesalat* became part of my repertoire right away. Since then I order one occasionally while visiting Switzerland, but never tried making my own until I recently tasted a great version made by my friend Erika Lieben, a native of Basel who lives there and in New York. I liked Erika's salad so much I asked for the recipe, and this is an adaptation of it.

1. For the salad, combine all the ingredients except the croûtons and chives in a mixing bowl and fold together.

2. For the dressing, whisk the vinegar, horseradish, mustard, salt and pepper in a small bowl. Whisk in the oil gradually to make a smooth dressing. Stir in the spring onions and chervil and fold into the salad.

3. Right before serving, fold the salad together again and tip the bowl to drain it of any excess dressing. Fold in the croûtons and scrape the salad into a serving bowl or onto individual plates. Sprinkle with the chives.

Makes 4 starter servings

SALAD

170g Swiss Gruyère, cut into thin slices and then into 9mm squares

170g Swiss Emmentaler, cut into thin slices and then into 9mm squares

1 bunch radishes, rinsed, trimmed, and thinly sliced

75g diced spicy pickle spears, page 92, or French cornichons

100g diced red pepper

50g toasted croûtons, page 43, made from baguette, page 107, or another firm bread

1 tablespoon finely snipped chives

DRESSING

4 tablespoons white wine vinegar

2 teaspoons prepared horseradish

2 teaspoons Dijon mustard

Salt and freshly ground black pepper

75ml sunflower or nut oil

2 tablespoons finely cut spring onions

1 tablespoon chervil leaves or chopped flat-leaf parsley

swiss cheese salad

ABOUT BREAD SALADS

Bread and tomatoes or other vegetables, cheese or seafood are natural combinations. The Apulian bread salad on page 123 uses the common technique of slightly moistening stale bread before mixing it with the salad's other ingredients. While it's traditional, I much prefer the method of moistening the bread with the juice of a freshly grated tomato that appears in that recipe's Quick Changes. The other bread salads here use crisp croûtons – one with cheese and the other with shrimp. You can also modify the bread and tomato salad the same way, but even if toasted, the bread should be softened considerably or it just doesn't taste right.

Any tomato salad depends on one thing: perfectly ripe, height-of-summer tomatoes. Cherry or grape tomatoes might be fine in a tossed salad during the winter, but just don't have either the strength of flavour or the moisture for a salad like *cialedda*. Like the famous Tuscan bread salad, *panzanella*, the bread here is moistened with a little water first. Letting the salad stand for an hour or so both develops the flavour and further moistens the bread, so it's perfect to prepare in advance to serve to guests. The recipe comes from my dear friend Ann Amandolara Nurse, whose family comes from the area near Bari in Apulia.

bread & tomato salad from apulia

Makes 6–8 servings

200g firm-textured bread such as Tuscan Bread, page 113, Baguette, page 107, or *Pain au Levain*, page 130, cut into 1cm dice

120ml cold tap water

900g ripe tomatoes, stemmed and diced

1 medium red onion, peeled, halved, and thinly sliced from root to stem end

30g pitted Gaeta olives, quartered

2 teaspoons dried oregano

120ml extra-virgin olive oil

Salt

1. If the bread is very fresh, spread out the cubes on a couple of swiss roll tins and let them dry at room temperature for half a day. Or bake the bread cubes at 150°C/gas mark 2 until dry but not toasted, about 15 minutes, stirring them up once or twice while they're baking and cooling before using.

2. Place the bread cubes in a large mixing bowl and sprinkle with the water, using a large rubber spatula to fold it through and moisten all the bread. Let the bread rest for 10 minutes while you prepare the remaining ingredients.

3. Add the tomatoes, onion and olives. Use a large rubber spatula to fold everything together.

4. Sprinkle with the oregano, oil and salt, and fold again. Taste for seasoning and adjust if necessary. Cover the bowl with clingfilm and let the salad rest at a cool room temperature until you're ready to serve it, but no more than a couple of hours.

5. When you're ready to serve the salad, mound it on a flat serving plate. This is excellent as a first course, with a selection of antipasti, or as an accompaniment to simply cooked meat or fish.

QUICK CHANGES

• Substitute a handful of torn basil leaves for the oregano.
• Marcella Hazan has a great trick for moistening the bread for a similar salad in one of her books: she halves a large tomato and grates the cut side over the largest openings of a box grater over the bread. Grate the tomato half as though you're grating a piece of cheese and you'll just wind up with the skin in your hand after the tomato pulp is grated.

flemish salad of tiny shrimp & croutons

Makes 4 starter servings

30g unsalted butter

40g 5mm croûtons made from Tuscan Bread, page 113, Sicilian Semolina Bread, page 110, or *Pain de Mie*, page 66

3 tablespoons mayonnaise, preferably home-made

½ teaspoon Dijon mustard or more to taste

340g tiny peeled and cooked shrimp

12 small leaves roundhead or other tender lettuce, rinsed and dried

30g baby rocket leaves, rinsed and dried

2 teaspoons olive oil

Pinch each of sea salt and freshly ground black pepper

12 cherry or grape tomatoes, as tiny as possible, halved

2 tablespoons diced sun-dried tomatoes

2 tablespoons diced pitted Kalamata olives

35g tiny frozen peas, cooked, rinsed and chilled

3 hard-boiled eggs, page 74, quartered

Belgian chef Vincent Florizoone's restaurant, Grand Cabaret, is in Nieuwpoort, a coastal town close to the French border. Along that stretch of the North Sea's coast, fishermen use horse-drawn nets to trawl for tiny shrimp. I had a chance to meet Vincent when he was visiting New York; I asked him about the shrimp, and he agreed to send me a recipe using them. His shrimp salad recipe is a creation worthy of a multi-starred chef. I had to simplify the recipe, so I wrote it, tested it, then sent it along to Vincent for his approval. I'm glad to say that we're still friends even though I dissected and re-imagined his recipe.

1. For the croûtons, melt the butter in a small sauté pan over a medium heat. Once the foam on the butter begins to subside, decrease the heat and let the butter colour slightly. Add the croûtons, toss or gently stir to evenly coat with the butter, and cook, tossing or stirring until they're a light golden colour, about 3–5 minutes. Spread the croûtons on a plate covered with kitchen paper to drain and cool.

2. Whisk the mayonnaise and mustard together in a medium bowl and gently fold in the shrimp. Cover and refrigerate until you're ready to serve the salad.

3. Be sure that all the other ingredients are ready and cut before you start to assemble the salads.

4. Right before serving the salad, arrange the lettuce leaves in the centre of 4 salad or luncheon plates, root ends meeting in the centre and dividing the plates into thirds. Quickly toss the rocket with the oil, salt and pepper and arrange in the very centre of the plates.

5. Quickly fold the cherry tomatoes and croûtons into the shrimp salad and mound over the rocket on each plate.

6. Sprinkle each salad with a quarter each of the sun-dried tomatoes, olives and peas. Arrange a quarter of a hard-boiled egg on each of the lettuce leaves. Serve immediately before the croûtons start to soften.

chapter eight

Sourdough Breads

It's almost incredible that such simple processes as creating a sourdough starter and using it to make bread should be the focus of so much misinformation. Loony instructions, such as leaving the flour exposed to outside air so it can gather wild yeasts (and a whole lot more, I'm afraid), using yeast to get a starter going (then it's a sponge or poolish, not a sourdough), and adding vinegar to a dough to emphasise the sour flavour (save it for a salad) will all get results, but not necessarily a true sourdough starter or bread.

Though the use of sourdoughs for leavening bread is ancient, sourdough baking today is entrenched in several geographical areas. Because pioneers and travellers to California during the Gold Rush in the mid-nineteenth century frequently brought starters with them, San Francisco is an important centre of sourdough use, to the extent that the variety of organism that's unique to the Bay Area gained the scientific name of *Lactobacillus sanfranciscensis*. *Pain au levain*, French for sourdough bread, is making a comeback in France, where at one time it was the most commonly made bread. Access to high-speed mixing machines and highly refined flour after World War II turned everyone's attention away from the classic French dense country-style sourdough bread to the flimsy baguettes that were popular for a while. A less well-known centre of sourdough use is Milan, in the northern part of Italy. Industrial manufacturers of *panettone* favour sourdough over yeast because of the better keeping qualities it imparts. The fourth big centre of sourdough use is Germany and Scandinavia, where rye bread is a staple because rye grows easily in colder climates hostile to wheat. Since rye flour needs an acidic environment in order to develop any gluten at all, sourdough and rye bread are a natural combination. Rye and other wholegrain breads, including some that use sourdough, are in the next chapter.

SOURDOUGH STARTER

100g organic dark rye flour

100g distilled water or spring water

¼ teaspoon malt syrup, preferably organic

Pinch of additive free salt, such as pure sea salt

FEEDING THE STARTER

100g strong white bread flour or plain flour

100g distilled water or spring water

Making a sourdough starter isn't difficult, complicated or time consuming. It's similar to the method used by Professor Calvel, who combined dark rye and white flours to cultivate the initial fermentation. You'll be amazed at how easily it works. A sourdough results from the fermentation of natural yeasts in flour. The flour's yeast doesn't act alone; it lives in a state of symbiosis (this just means that they can't get along without each other) with *Lactobacilli* bacteria that contribute the sour flavour to the starter. *Lactobacilli* are everywhere and they are also responsible for turning milk into yogurt and are present in many types of cheese.

When you're going to start a sourdough, it's important that all your vessels and utensils be scrupulously clean. This helps to prevent contamination with other organisms that might be harmful to the developing yeasts right at the beginning of fermentation. After your sourdough starter is fully fermented, the yeasts and other beneficial organisms are strong enough to resist contamination from unwanted sources.

I like to use organic dark rye flour and distilled water for a new sourdough. Again, there's no reason to risk contamination, especially from chlorine that might be present in tap water expressly to kill natural organisms. Organic rye flour ferments more easily than white flour does, but once the starter begins to ferment actively, I switch to white flour. Aside from that, all you need to do is follow the instructions carefully and as with all other baking processes, look for the signs that your starter is ready to proceed to the next step instead of slavishly following a time schedule. Your efforts will be rewarded by having a living starter you can easily maintain and use for years to come.

Step 1: PROPOGATING A NEW SOURDOUGH STARTER

Wash one 2-litre glass or stainless steel bowl, one 1-litre bowl, one large metal soup spoon for stirring and scraping, measuring spoons and one liquid measuring cup in hot soapy water, rinse and drain until dry. Into the larger bowl put starter ingredients.

Stir well (it will be sticky, not a dough) and scrape into the smaller bowl. (Changing bowls eliminates what's stuck to the side of the bowl, which might turn moldy.) Cover with clingfilm, label with the date and time, and wait for signs of increased bulk, which will take place in 24–48 hours. When it's warmer in the kitchen, the initial mixture will ferment quickly. Professor Calvel wrote that the ideal temperature for beginning a starter is 27°C, though the temperature may go as low as 22°C. Any lower than that might make the starter spoil before it starts to ferment.

Step 2: FEEDING THE STARTER

Once your starter has visibly increased in bulk, you'll need to feed it. Leaving the starter in the smaller bowl, gradually stir in the water until smooth. Stir in the flour a little at a time, to make a soft dough. Scrape into a freshly washed large bowl, cover with clingfilm, and let the starter ferment until visibly increased in bulk, about 6–12 hours. Once the starter has increased 2–3 times over its original bulk, it needs to be fed within 12 hours.

Step 3: CONTINUING TO FEED THE STARTER

Measure 100g of your risen starter into a clean bowl and repeat step 2. Discard the remaining starter or feed 100g of it too as a backup or to give away. Let the starter ferment until it almost triples in bulk, 4–12 hours, then stir down, cover, and leave at room temperature. Feed the starter again within 12 hours.

Step 4: REPEAT STEPS

Repeat step 3 with one or both starters, discarding the extra starter from each. At this point the starter is strong enough to switch to tap water.

Once the starter is actively bubbling, smells pleasantly sour, and is easily increasing in bulk after feeding, you can start baking with it.

Continue feeding it every 12 hours until the fourth or fifth day. Once the starter has gone to the fifth day you can feed it once a day.

That's the whole process.

Step 5: REFRIGERATING THE STARTER

If you don't intend to use the starter for baking right away, wait until it has risen about halfway after feeding and refrigerate it. Once the starter has been refrigerated you'll need to feed it about every 5 days by repeating step 3 before you use it in a recipe. Either let the starter come to room temperature before you feed it or use warm water (no more than 38°C) to increase its temperature. I like to feed a starter that has been refrigerated at least 2 or 3 times before baking with it.

USING THE REFRIGERATED STARTER FOR BAKING: Once the refrigerated starter has been fed several times and is actively bubbling, measure out the quantity you need for the recipe you're preparing. To continue to maintain the starter, feed and cover 100g of the remaining starter as in step 3, let it rise halfway again, and refrigerate again as in step 5.

LONG-TERM MAINTENANCE: Feed the starter as in step 5, letting it rise halfway before refrigerating again.

FREEZING THE STARTER: Some sources condemn freezing a sourdough starter but I've had good luck with it. Defrost the starter at room temperature and proceed as for refrigerated starter in step 5.

If you intend to be away for more than a couple of weeks, freezing is your only alternative unless you have a friend who is willing to babysit your starter. Unless you intend to bake with your starter the minute you return, consider cultivating a new starter – it will be ready to use in just a few days.

NOTE: *Recipes that use this starter in the following two chapters always begin with a starter recently fed in the end of step 4 or 5, above, then a levain or sponge made from the starter. Think of the starter as the yeast added to the sponge in the recipe.*

ALTERNATIVES: If you do an Internet search of 'buy sourdough starter' you'll come up with quite a few choices. Some reputable baking supply companies sell semi-liquid starter for a reasonable price. Follow the instructions that come with the starter or feed as in step 2, above. Beware of anything that comes in powdered form, because many of those so-called starters are merely ground dehydrated pre-ferments made from yeast and flavouring.

ADDING YEAST: Never add yeast to a sourdough starter, though on occasion you may add a small amount of yeast to a dough that's leavened with sourdough. See individual recipes for amounts.

ABOUT SOURDOUGH BREADS

Breads made from a natural sourdough have a full, rounded flavour that emphasises the inherent wheaty sweetness of the flour used. Like slow-rise breads, sourdough mixtures, whether sponges or complete doughs, can't be rushed; the nature of your own starter and the temperature of the dough and room all come into play. Letting sponges and doughs ferment slowly assures a fine flavour and the best texture in the finished bread. The San Francisco-style bread in this chapter mimics the action of the particular organism found in the Bay Area's sourdough and has the characteristic tang associated with that bread.

french-style sourdough bread

Makes 1 large boule-shaped loaf

LEVAIN (SOURDOUGH SPONGE)

100g sourdough starter, page 128, fed twice in the previous 24 hours

100g room-temperature tap water, about 24°C

100g strong white bread flour

DOUGH

All the *levain*, above

150g room-temperature tap water, about 24°C

½ teaspoon fine granulated active dried yeast or instant yeast, optional

300g strong white bread flour

1½ teaspoons fine sea salt

One well-floured banneton or cloth-lined basket, plus a heated pizza stone or baking tin

---

QUICK CHANGES

• Use the same dough to make 2 batards, page 109, or 3 thin baguettes, page 107. They need to be proofed in cloth like the baguettes; follow the instructions on page 109.
• In the dough, substitute 65g light rye flour for an equal amount of the white flour, an old-fashioned French variation of *pain au levain*.
• Substitute wholemeal flour for half of the bread flour.

Preparing an adaptation of French *pain au levain* requires some advance planning. Beginning with a starter that you've already maintained for a while, it needs to go through at least two preliminary stages of fermentation. Depending on the temperature of the room, it can take up to 24 hours from the first feeding of the active starter to the baked bread. Most of the time is concentrated in the mixing, shaping, proofing and baking of the final dough. The final proofing time of the formed loaf is much longer than for doughs leavened with yeast. To gain a little time you may add a small amount of optional yeast in the recipe below. This dough benefits from being proofed in a basket or banneton to ensure a symmetrical shape.

1. For the *levain*, stir the starter and water together in a small bowl. Use a medium rubber spatula to stir in the flour a little at a time. Cover the bowl and let the *levain* ferment until it doubles in size, 4–6 hours, depending on the temperature of the room.

2. To make the dough, use a medium rubber spatula to mix the water with the *levain* in the bowl of an electric mixer. If using the yeast, whisk it into the water before stirring in the *levain*. Stir in the flour to form a dough, making sure to incorporate any flour that clings to the side of the bowl. Place the bowl on the mixer and attach the dough hook. Beat on the lowest speed until the dough starts to become smooth and elastic, about 3 minutes. Stop the mixer and let the dough rest for 15 minutes.

3. Start the mixer on low-medium speed and beat again, sprinkling in the salt, until the dough is smoother and more elastic, about 3–4 minutes. After mixing, the dough should have a temperature of 24°C–26°C.

4. Scrape the dough into an oiled bowl and turn it so that the top is oiled. Cover with clingfilm and let the dough ferment until it rises about 50% above its original volume, 1–2 hours.

5. To form the loaf as a boule, invert the dough to a floured work surface and fold the top, bottom, and sides of the dough toward the centre. Turn the dough over, cover it with a tea towel or clingfilm, and let it rest for 10 minutes. Uncover the dough and round the loaf by pushing against the bottom of the dough all around with the sides of your hands held palms upward.

The dough will quickly form an even sphere. Drop the dough, smooth top side down, into the prepared banneton or basket. Cover with oiled or sprayed clingfilm and let proof until doubled in bulk, 3–4 hours (sooner if you added yeast), depending on the temperature of the room.

6. Once the loaf is almost proofed, set a rack in the middle level of the oven and set a pizza stone or heavy baking sheet on it. Remove any racks under it and preheat to 230°C/gas mark 8. Place a small roasting tin or a cast iron frying pan on the very bottom of the oven.

7. Once the oven is ready, sprinkle the top of the risen loaf with maize meal and cover with a peel or piece of stiff cardboard. Invert and remove the banneton. Use an X-Acto knife or single-edge razor to cut a cross-hatch pattern in the top of the loaf.

8. Quickly open the oven and slide the loaf from the peel to the stone or baking tin. Quickly open the oven again and, averting your face, pour a couple of cups of water onto the tin or a cup or so of ice cubes into the frying pan. Wait 5 minutes, then decrease the oven temperature to 220°C/gas mark 7.

9. Bake the loaf until it is well risen and deep golden and its internal temperature is about 93°C, 25–30 minutes longer.

10. Let cool completely on a rack. Serve on the day the loaf is baked, or store in a paper bag at room temperature. An all-sourdough bread like this stays fresh for 3–4 days.

Sourdough bread made in San Francisco is characterised by its pronounced sour flavour, produced by a strong degree of lactic acid in the dough brought about by a particular species of *lactobacillus* called *L. sanfranciscensis*, a native to the Bay Area. It's possible to make a close imitation of it, though, even if you live several thousand miles away as I do. After a couple of near-misses, I spoke with my friend Ciril Hitz, formerly the department chair for the International Baking and Pastry Institute of Johnson and Wales University in Providence, Rhode Island. Ciril knows more about bread than anyone else in the universe. In about half a minute, he managed to explain to me the issues inherent in producing sourdough bread that has a really sour flavour. It all has to do with interrupting the proofing of your finished dough by letting it begin to puff and refrigerating it overnight so that the loaf proofs slowly and has a maximum amount of time to develop the strong sourdough flavour. If you start the process with the *levain* in the morning you can bake the proofed loaf some time the next morning.

1. Prepare the *levain* and the dough as for *Pain au Levain*, opposite, up to the end of step 5 but only let the loaf proof about 25% over its original size. Cover with oiled or sprayed clingfilm, leaving room for the loaf to expand, and refrigerate the banneton until the loaf has doubled in bulk, about 8–12 hours.

2. Proceed with the rest of the recipe, beginning with step 6.

Makes one large boule-shaped loaf

LEVAIN (SOURDOUGH SPONGE)

100g sourdough starter, page 128, fed twice in the previous 24 hours

100g room-temperature tap water, about 24°C

100g strong white bread flour

DOUGH

All the *levain*, above

225g room-temperature tap water, about 24°C

450g strong white bread flour

2 teaspoons fine sea salt

QUICK CHANGES

Instead of refrigerating the formed loaf, interrupt the fermentation at the end of step 4, cover and chill overnight. The next morning, start step 5. The loaf will take longer to proof because the dough is cold. A suggestion from my friend Tim Healea of little t american baker in Portland, Oregon.

'mozzarella in a carriage'

Makes about 8 antipasto servings, along with other dishes

8 slices from a large round loaf of *Pain au Levain*, page 130, or another 23cm round loaf

450g fresh mozzarella, thinly sliced

6 medium eggs

Salt and freshly ground black pepper

Light olive oil for frying

One wide slope-sided sauté pan and one swiss roll tin, lined with kitchen paper

This is a fun first course when served with a tomato salad, but it can also stand as a quick light meal on its own when there's nothing else available but a piece of bread, some mozzarella and a few eggs. There are countless variations on this recipe, some including a bit of anchovy along with the mozzarella, but this simple version is the best. In Naples it's common to use sandwich bread for this, but a good quality mild sourdough bread provides more flavour.

1. Arrange 4 of the slices of bread on the work surface and cover them with the sliced mozzarella, being careful not to let any of the cheese extend over the edges of the bread. Cover with the remaining slices of bread and press well to stick the bread and cheese together.

2. Whisk the eggs in a bowl with the salt and pepper and pour them into a rectangular tin that will just hold the 4 sandwiches. Place the sandwiches in the tin and let them stand for 10 minutes to absorb some of the eggs.

3. Turn the sandwiches over and let them stand for another 10 minutes.

4. Heat 2cm of olive oil in the sauté pan over a medium-high heat. Slip the sandwiches into the oil with a slotted spatula and cook them on the first side until they are deep golden, about 5 minutes. Turn them with tongs and repeat cooking on the other side.

5. Using a slotted spatula, transfer the sandwiches to the prepared tin. Let them drain for 1 minute on each side.

6. Cut each sandwich into 3 or 4 pieces and serve immediately.

ABOUT MOZZARELLA

Freshly made mozzarella makes a great filling for this Neapolitan classic, though you should try it anyway even if the only mozzarella available is the drier industrially made type. When purchasing fresh mozzarella, choose the salted as opposed to the unsalted variety. Mozzarella di bufala, or water buffalo milk mozzarella, is also a Neapolitan speciality, but is best used raw, perhaps in the classic insalata Caprese (Capri salad), where it's combined with sliced tomatoes, fresh basil, and a drizzle of olive oil. When melted it can exude an enormous amount of whey, making any dish you use it in a watery mess. Neapolitan pizza makers sometimes use it, but they bake their pizzas in ovens that heat to around 540°C – enough to evaporate any whey as the mozzarella melts.

french baked cheese sandwich

Makes 4 sandwiches

Eight 9mm slices Golden Sandwich Bread, page 60, or *Pain au Levain*, page 130, crusts trimmed

Soft butter for the bread

Eight 30g slices Swiss Gruyère, or a similar cheese, the same size as the bread

4 thin slices cooked ham or *prosciutto cotto*

One swiss roll tin lined with parchment paper

Making a really good *croque monsieur* is simple: rich sandwich bread like Golden Sandwich Bread is perfect, though some people like to substitute slices of a brioche loaf, or a gutsier bread like one of the sourdoughs in this chapter. All you need then are a few slices of Gruyère, Emmenthaler, or another similar cheese and a couple of slices of cooked ham. I like to bake the sandwich, as do most home cooks in France, but some people cook it slowly on both sides in butter. Here's the method I recently saw Adam Kaplan use when I was getting ready for a class at In Good Taste in Portland, Oregon.

1. Set a rack in the upper third of the oven and preheat to 200°C/gas mark 6.

2. Arrange the slices of bread on the prepared tin and butter the tops. Place the tin in the oven and reduce the temperature to 190°C/gas mark 5. Bake until the tops colour nicely but are not too dark, about 5 minutes.

3. Set the tin on the hob and use a metal spatula to flip the slices of bread over. Place 1 slice of cheese on each piece of bread. Add a slice of ham on top of the cheese on 4 of the slices.

4. Bake until the cheese is melted but not bubbling off the bread, 5–8 minutes.

5. Top the ham and cheese bread slices with the cheese-only bread slices (inverted cheese-side down) and gently press. Cut into halves or quarters diagonally and slide to a warm plate. Serve with a green salad or a tomato salad in season. Sip a glass of cool white wine and think of Paris.

QUICK CHANGES

Some like a little Dijon mustard spread between the cheese and ham before baking.

CROQUE MADAME: Prepare the *Croque Monsieur* and top the uncut sandwich with a fried egg.

The successful gastropub The Spotted Pig is one of my favourite places to meet friends for lunch. The menu features a grilled cheddar sandwich with onion marmalade, which I tried recently. The sandwich was predictably great, but the onion marmalade was flavoured with red wine and I didn't care for it. So I set to work on an onion marmalade of my own and I'm really pleased with it, especially because it has no added sugar in it and just a touch of sherry vinegar to add a slightly sharp contrast to the onions' sweetness. Of course, you can use any melting cheese you like, but good Gouda has a slightly salty flavour with overtones of caramel that's perfect with the bacon and onions. The instructions immediately below are for cooking the sandwiches in butter in a pan. See the Quick Changes for baking the sandwiches.

Makes 2 large sandwiches

4 slices cut from *Pain au Levain*, page 130

8 tablespoons home-made onion marmalade, see below

170g aged Dutch Gouda, thinly sliced

4 rashers streaky bacon, cooked and drained

2–4 tablespoons unsalted butter, softened

1. Arrange 2 slices of the bread next to each other on the work surface. Spread each with half the onion marmalade. Top each with a quarter of the Gouda, then half of the bacon, then the remaining Gouda. Place the second slice of bread on top and gently press to adhere.

2. Spread the tops of the two sandwiches with about half the butter.

3. Heat a non-stick sauté pan over a medium heat and invert the sandwiches into the pan, buttered sides down. Decrease the heat to very low and cook on the first side until nicely golden, 3–4 minutes.

4. Butter the tops of the sandwiches, then carefully turn them over without disturbing the filling. Cook on the reverse side until the cheese is uniformly melted and the bread is well coloured, 3–4 minutes longer.

5. Halve the sandwiches and serve them immediately.

ONION MARMALADE

Peel, halve, and thinly slice **900g large white onions or sweet onions, such as Vidalia,** from stem to root end. Put **3 tablespoons olive or vegetable oil** in a large Dutch oven and add the onions and **½ teaspoon fine sea salt**. Stir to coat the onions with the oil, turn the heat to medium and wait until the onions start to sizzle. Decrease the heat to very low and cook the onions until they're wilted, about 20 minutes, stirring occasionally. Continue cooking, stirring more often as the onions reduce in volume, until they're very soft and a light caramel colour, a total of about 1½ hours. Off heat, stir in **2 tablespoons sherry vinegar** and taste for seasoning. Adjust with more salt and vinegar if you like. Cool and pack into a clean plastic container. This makes about 225g and will keep refrigerated for a couple of weeks. Bring to room temperature before using.

QUICK CHANGES

To bake the sandwiches:
• Set a rack in the middle level of the oven and preheat to 200˚C/gas mark 6.
• Butter the sandwiches as in step 2, then invert them to a small swiss roll tin covered with parchment paper. Butter the tops.
• Place the tin in the oven and decrease the heat to 190˚C/gas mark 5. Bake them until well coloured (check that the bottoms are colouring too, and turn them if necessary) and the cheese has melted, about 15 minutes.
• Halve and serve immediately.

grilled gouda & bacon sandwich

baked open-faced swiss cheese sandwiches

Makes 4 substantial sandwiches

Four 2cm-thick slices cut from *Pain au Levain*, page 130, or a similar bread, lightly toasted

2–3 tablespoons dry white wine

340g Swiss Gruyère or *Vacherin Fribourgeois*, thinly sliced

30g butter

4 medium eggs

Salt and freshly ground black pepper

Four individual gratin dishes, bases lightly buttered, or one swiss roll tin lined with parchment paper

Kaeseschnitten, literally 'cheese slices', are a mainstay of *Beizli* and *pintes* – the respective names for casual bistros in the German- and French-speaking parts of Switzerland. Vacherin Fribourgeois is a sharp flavoured, strongly scented cheese similar to Gruyère. They can be used interchangeably in this open-faced sandwich. Feel free to add your own touches: a slice of cooked ham, a few rashers of cooked bacon (as pictured), or a couple of thin slices of ripe tomato under the cheese; a fried egg on top after it's baked (as in this version); or a spoonful of applesauce on the side. A *Kaeseschnitt* (the singular) is usually baked and served in an individual oval gratin dish. If you're baking multiple sandwiches, as we do here, and don't have individual baking dishes, bake them on a parchment paper-lined swiss roll tin and quickly slide them onto warm plates before serving.

1. Set a rack in the upper third of the oven and preheat to 200°C/gas mark 6.

2. Arrange a slice of the toasted bread in the bottom of each gratin dish and sprinkle the bread with a little of the white wine.

3. Top with the cheese, covering the bread completely, as any exposed bread surface might burn while baking.

4. Get everything ready to fry the eggs.

5. A few minutes before you're going to serve the *Kaeseschnitten*, place the gratin dishes in the oven and decrease the temperature to 190°C/gas mark 5.

6. To fry the eggs, melt the butter in a wide non-stick sauté pan over a medium heat. One at a time, crack an egg into a cup and slip it into the pan. Regulate the heat so that the eggs start to set but don't sizzle as they're cooking. Cook the eggs until the whites are completely set and the yolks have thickened and warmed, about 4–5 minutes.

7. Check the bread and cheese before the eggs are ready. The melted cheese is ready when it's bubbling just a little. If the cheese gets too hot, some of it will bubble off the bread onto the pan or it will become dry and crusty on top. Quickly remove the gratin dishes from the oven to the hob when they are ready.

8. Salt and pepper the eggs and use a wide spatula to slide an egg onto each of the *Kaeseschnitten*. Set each gratin dish on a plate and serve immediately. If you don't have the individual dishes, use a wide spatula to transfer each *Kaeseschnitt* to a warmed plate and top each with an egg.

A *bruschetta* (brew-SKET-ta) is one of many variations of toasted bread, olive oil and garlic from Italy and it is justly popular all over the world. Meant to be eaten as a dish in itself, today a *bruschetta* is often served with a topping, though then it's technically a *crostino* (literally 'little crust'). The traditional Roman way of preparing a *bruschetta* is to cook the bread in oil to toast it, while the Tuscan *fett'unta* ('anointed' slice) is toasted first, then drizzled with warmed olive oil, not only a little lighter but less work. And I've included a version of Italian-American garlic bread that won't make you expire from garlic poisoning.

BRUSCHETTA/FETT'UNTA

Cut some slices of **any type of sour-dough bread,** *Pane Sciocco*, page 113, or Sicilian Semolina Bread, page 110, about 1cm thick. Toast the bread on both sides on an outdoor grill, a hob grill pan, or a large non-stick sauté pan. Using the toaster or oven grill is fine too. Quickly rub the just-toasted bread with **a cut clove of garlic,** sprinkle with **fine or coarse sea salt** and drizzle with **best quality extra-virgin olive oil.** Serve and eat while still warm as an accompaniment to antipasti, soup, salad or nothing at all. Italian children eat this as an after-school snack.

<< CROSTINI

Cut some slices of **any baguette-shaped bread** about 1cm thick. If the loaf is fairly narrow in diameter, cut the slices on the diagonal to make them larger. Lightly brush both sides with **olive oil** and bake at 180°C/gas mark 4 until golden, about 10 minutes. Cool and serve with one of the following toppings, or with pâté or your favourite spread or dip.

CROSTINI CAPRESI

For about a dozen *crostini*, oil and toast them as above and rub one side with **a cut clove of garlic.** Rinse, cut away the stem end and cut **2 medium tomatoes** into 1cm dice. Place them in a bowl and mix with **170g fresh mozzarella** also diced, **6–8 torn leaves of fresh basil, 1 table-spoon of extra-virgin olive oil** and **salt and pepper.** Mix well, then spoon over the *crostini*; serve straight away or the *crostini* will become soggy. After summer is over, halved grape or cherry tomatoes are good in this; substitute a few pinches of dried oregano for the basil.

CROSTINI DI FEGATO

Mince **1 small onion** and combine it with **2 tablespoons olive oil** in a medium sauté pan. Place on a medium heat and cook until the onion starts to sizzle. Reduce the heat and cook, stirring occasionally, until the onion is soft and starting to colour a little, about 10–15 minutes. Increase the heat to high and add **340g chicken livers** that have been trimmed of fat and dark spots, rinsed and dried on kichen paper. **Salt and pepper** generously and cook, stirring or tossing, and regulating the heat if the onion is colouring too deeply, until almost cooked through (cut one of the livers open to see). Off heat, add **120ml medium dry sherry, Marsala or sweet Tuscan vinsanto.** Return to the heat and let the wine reduce almost dry as the livers finish cooking. Cool the mixture and pulse it in the food processor until finely chopped but not completely puréed. Spread on the *crostini* and sprinkle with **chopped chives, chopped parsley** or even some **crushed toasted sliced almonds.**

CROSTINI DI GORGONZOLA CON MARMELLATA DI CIPOLLE

Spread *crostini* with **Onion Marmalade,** page 137. Top the marmalade with a sprinkle of **crumbled Gorgonzola** or another blue-veined cheese. Sprinkle with **a pinch or two of chopped toasted walnuts.**

FORNINO GARLIC BREAD

From my friend Michael Ayoub, the pizza maven: grate **2–4 cloves of garlic** into a bowl and mix with **115g unsalted butter,** softened, **60ml extra-virgin olive oil, 3 tablespoons finely grated Parmigiano Reggiano, 1 tablespoon finely chopped flat-leaf parsley,** and **¼ teaspoon each fine sea salt and freshly ground black pepper.** Cut a baguette or other long loaf into 2cm diagonal slices and spread both sides with the seasoned butter. Arrange the bread on a foil-covered swiss roll tin. Set a rack in the upper third of the oven and preheat the grill. Right before serving, grill the bread slices until toasted, then turn and toast the other side. Quickly arrange on a serving plate, sprinkle with **a little more grated cheese and chopped parsley** and serve immediately. Garlic bread is a great snack with drinks, but is a little strong to accompany any other food.

CROSTINI DI TONNO E FAGIOLI

Drain and flake **one 140g tin of tuna in olive oil.** Fold together in a bowl with **70g cooked white beans such as cannellini.** Season with a little **salt, pepper, lemon juice and olive oil.** Sprinkle with **chopped parsley.**

catalan grilled bread rubbed with tomato

Makes 1 sandwich

6.5cm-thick slices firm textured bread, like
   Pain au Levain, page 130

1 ripe summer tomato

Fine sea salt

Best quality extra-virgin olive oil

Thinly sliced Serrano ham, optional

Food is central in Catalan life. Tapas bars and casual cafés serve *pa amb tomàquet* (bread with tomato) already assembled, but some restaurants merely deliver the components to the table: a piece of chewy bread grilled over a wood fire, a perfectly ripe tomato, fine salt, and local extra-virgin olive oil. Such a simple combination depends entirely on the quality of the ingredients – they have to be perfect. The instructions here are adapted from one of my favourite cookbooks, *Paula Wolfert's World of Food,* with her permission. This is the perfect starter for a casual late summer meal. Eat with a knife and fork!

1. Lightly toast the slices of bread or grill them over a wood fire.

2. Cut the tomato in half and rub the toast with it, on both sides if you'd like, while gently squeezing as you would an orange half.

3. Salt lightly and drizzle with extra-virgin olive oil. Serve with Serrano ham, if desired.

Makes 8 small toasts

115g coarsely grated Swiss
   Gruyère or a similar textured cheese

1 medium egg

Freshly ground black pepper

Pinch of freshly grated nutmeg

8 slices Baguette, page 107, or other bread, about
   9mm thick and about 7.5cm in diameter, lightly
   toasted

1 small baking sheet lined with parchment paper

These little treats take about 5 minutes to prepare and are perfect for a snack, with tea or as an accompaniment to a light soup or salad lunch. If you want to use another type of bread, just stamp out 7.5cm discs with a round biscuit cutter. Sometimes I add a teaspoon of Dijon mustard to the mixture.

1. Set a rack in the upper third of the oven and preheat to 190°C/gas mark 5.

2. In a small bowl, use a fork to mix the cheese, egg, pepper and nutmeg.

3. Spoon an equal amount of the cheese mixture on each slice of bread, spreading it to the edge.

4. Arrange the slices of bread on the prepared pan and bake until the cheese is melted and puffed, 5–7 minutes. Don't overbake or the topping will be lethally dry.

5. Serve immediately.

chapter nine

Wholegrain Breads

Although wholegrain breads are perceived as being healthier than their white flour counterparts, only breads made entirely from wholegrain flour qualify as true health foods. Most of us like wholegrain breads because of the variations in texture and flavour that they offer from white breads – whether the bread be made partially or wholly from wholegrain flour.

Wholemeal breads have an appealing nutlike flavour that pairs well with cheeses, hearty soups and other rustic-flavoured dishes. Rye is the bread of choice for deli meats such as corned beef, although most of the flavour that we associate with rye comes from the ground caraway added to the bread to flavour it. A close-to-100% rye experience may be enjoyed in the *Walliser Roggenbrot* pictured opposite, a rustic Swiss bread prepared without the addition of caraway flavouring. Untried by me before the writing of this book, spelt flour turned out to make one of my favourite breads here, the White Spelt and Caraway Bread on page 147. If you'd like to try using wholemeal spelt flour, substitute it for the dark rye flour in the *Walliser Roggenbrot* on page 149 or the Danish-style Rye Bread on page 153.

Makes one 30cm loaf

SPONGE

112g room-temperature water,
about 24°C

2 teaspoons fine granulated active dried yeast or
instant yeast

65g wholemeal flour

55g coarse rye meal or dark rye flour

DOUGH

225g room-temperature water, about 24°C

2 teaspoons fine granulated active dried yeast or
instant yeast

All of the sponge, above

2 tablespoons molasses or treacle

180g strong white bread flour

170g wholemeal flour

170g coarse rye meal or dark rye flour

2 tablespoons alkalised cocoa powder, sifted after
measuring (available online, or can be substituted for unsweetened cocoa powder)

4 teaspoons salt

One heavy baking sheet or swiss roll tin covered
with oiled parchment paper

This is a thoroughly Americanised version of the black bread that originated at Westphalia in Germany towards the end of the middle ages. That bread acquires its dark colour partly from the dark rye meal in the dough, but mostly from the long baking time of up to 24 hours in closed tins. The American version uses molasses, cocoa powder, and sometimes dark-brewed coffee to achieve the dark colour. Thinly sliced pumpernickel bread is a great replacement for a bagel when topped with smoked salmon, cream cheese, red onion and tomato. Slices of this bread are also great with cheese or just butter.

1. For the sponge, whisk the water and yeast together in a medium bowl. Stir in the flours. Cover with clingfilm and let ferment until more than doubled, about 2 hours.

2. For the dough, whisk the water and yeast together in the bowl of an electric mixer. Use a rubber spatula to stir in the sponge. Stir in the molasses or treacle, bread flour, rye meal, wholemeal flour and cocoa powder. Attach the dough hook and mix on lowest speed until the dough is smooth, firm and sticky, about 2 minutes. Increase the speed to low/medium and sprinkle in the salt. Beat until elastic but still sticky, about 2 minutes.

3. Scrape the dough into a lightly oiled bowl and turn it over so that the top is oiled. Cover with clingfilm and let it rise until fully doubled, 45 minutes to 1 hour, depending on the room temperature.

4. Set a rack in the middle level of the oven and preheat to 230°C/gas mark 8.

5. Scrape the dough to a floured work surface and gently flatten to a disc. Fold both sides about 2.5cm in towards the centre, then roll down from the top, swiss roll-style, leaving the seam on the bottom (see the photographs on page 151). Invert the loaf to the prepared tin and cover with oiled clingfilm. Proof until it begins to puff, 15–20 minutes.

6. Use an X-Acto knife or single-edge razor to slash the top of the loaf with three parallel lines across the width. Place the tin in the oven and decrease the temperature to 200°C/gas mark 6. Bake the loaf until it is well risen and has an internal temperature of 93°C, 30–40 minutes.

7. Cool the loaf on a rack and serve it the same day, though it will stay fresh for several days loosely covered at room temperature. Wrap and freeze for longer storage.

Spelt bread is nutty and delicious, and although it isn't permissible for people who are gluten intolerant, it can be enjoyed by some who suffer from sensitivities to wheat. White spelt flour (which can be purchased from wholefood shops and online) is the spelt equivalent of white flour – it has had the bran and germ removed and makes a delicately flavoured bread. In Scandinavia it's popular for open-faced sandwiches of smoked or marinated salmon for which rye bread is never used.

1. For the sponge, whisk the water and yeast together in a medium bowl and stir in the flour. Cover with clingfilm and let the sponge ferment at room temperature until it doubles in bulk, about 2–3 hours.

2. For the dough, whisk the water and yeast together in the bowl of an electric mixer and use a rubber spatula to stir in the sponge. Stir in the flour until it forms a dough, making sure there is no flour clinging to the side of the bowl.

3. Place the bowl on the mixer and attach the dough hook. Mix on the lowest speed until the dough is somewhat smooth, about 2 minutes, then let rest for 15 minutes.

4. Sprinkle in the salt and mix again on low/medium speed, sprinkling in the caraway seeds if using and mixing until the dough is smooth and elastic, 2–3 minutes.

5. Very lightly oil or spray a bowl and use a plastic scraper to transfer the dough to the bowl. Turn the dough over so that the top is oiled and cover the bowl with clingfilm. Let the dough ferment until it doubles in bulk, 1–2 hours.

6. Invert the dough to a floured work surface. Flatten the dough to a rough disc and fold both sides to meet in the centre.

Roll up from one of the unfolded sides. Invert the loaf to the prepared tin and cover it with oiled or sprayed clingfilm. Let the loaf proof just until it increases about 50% above its original bulk, 1–2 hours.

7. When the loaf is almost proofed completely, set a rack in the middle level of the oven and remove the racks above and below it. Place a cast iron frying pan or a medium roasting tin directly on the bottom of the oven. Preheat to 230°C/gas mark 8.

8. Use an X-Acto knife or single-edge razor to make three short parallel slashes in the top of the loaf. Spray the loaf with water and sprinkle with the caraway seeds if using. Place the tin in the oven and add 1 cup of ice cubes to the frying pan or 2 cups of water to the roasting tin. Quickly close the oven door and decrease the temperature to 200°C/gas mark 6. Bake the loaf until it is well risen and has an internal temperature of 93°C, about 30–40 minutes.

9. Cool the loaf on a rack and serve it the same day or wrap and freeze for longer storage.

Makes 1 large oval loaf

SPONGE

100g room-temperature tap water, about 24°C

¼ teaspoon fine granulated active dried yeast or instant yeast

100g white spelt flour

DOUGH

200g room-temperature water, about 24°C

1½ teaspoons fine granulated active dried yeast or instant yeast

All the sponge, above

360g white spelt flour

1½ teaspoons fine sea salt

1 tablespoon caraway seeds, optional, if you wish to add them to the dough or sprinkle them on the outside of the loaf

A baking sheet or swiss roll tin covered with parchment or maize meal

white spelt and caraway bread

The mountainous areas of the Valais canton in the middle west of Switzerland are home to commercial vineyards located at the highest altitude in Europe outside the village of Vispertsterminen. The mountains aren't suitable for growing wheat, so rye is the grain of choice for bread baking in the Valais. *Walliser roggenbrot* is protected by an AOC designation, which means that it may only be sold as such if it meets the standards set out by the Swiss Federal Office of Agriculture. The recipe isn't a secret, but it's only leavened with sourdough, so it's not easy to prepare unless you have some starter. My recipe uses a little bit of bread flour in the sponge to help keep the gases formed during fermentation from leaking out. Aside from its chewy texture and strong rye flavour, the bread is unique in appearance – the lack of strong gluten in the dough makes the surface of the loaf crack attractively under its coating of rye flour while it's proofing.

1. For the sponge, stir the water and sourdough starter together in a medium bowl. Stir in the bread and rye flours. Cover the bowl with clingfilm and let the sponge ferment for 6–8 hours. If it's warm in the kitchen, it will be ready after 6 hours.

2. For the dough, stir the water and sponge together in the bowl of an electric mixer. Stir in the rye flour and salt.

3. Place the bowl on the mixer and attach the dough hook. Mix on the lowest speed until the dough is smooth, about 2 minutes – it will be heavy and quite sticky.

4. Very lightly oil or spray a bowl and use a plastic scraper to transfer the dough to the bowl. Turn the dough over so that the top is oiled and cover the bowl with clingfilm. Let the dough rest for 30 minutes – it will begin to puff slightly.

5. Set a rack in the middle level of the oven and preheat to 230°C/gas mark 8.

6. Invert the dough to a floured work surface. Pull a section of dough around its perimeter into the centre and press it in place. Continue all around the dough until it's round and fairly even. Invert the loaf to the prepared tin and dust it with a heavy even coating of rye flour. Let the loaf proof just until the surface is covered with a series of small cracks, about 30 minutes.

7. Place the tin in the oven and immediately reduce the temperature to 200°C/gas mark 6. Bake the loaf until it is firm and has an internal temperature of 93°C, 35–45 minutes.

8. Cool the loaf on a rack and serve it the same day, though it will stay fresh for several days loosely covered at room temperature. Wrap and freeze for longer storage.

swiss sourdough rye bread from the valais

Makes one 15–18cm round loaf

SPONGE

100g room-temperature tap water, about 24°C

40g sourdough starter, page 128, fed twice during the previous 24 hours

50g strong white bread flour

50g dark rye flour

DOUGH

200g room-temperature tap water, about 24°C

All of the sponge, above

350g dark rye flour, plus more for dusting

1½ teaspoons fine sea salt

One swiss roll tin or round pizza pan dusted with maize meal

walliser roggenbrot

deli rye bread

aka jewish rye bread

Makes one 25cm oval loaf

RYE SOUR

75g room-temperature water, about 24°C

20g sourdough starter, page 128, fed twice during the previous 24 hours

90g dark rye flour

DOUGH

300g room temperature tap water, about 24°C

1¼ teaspoons fine granulated active dry yeast or instant yeast

All the rye sour, above

500g strong white bread flour

1 tablespoon ground caraway seeds

1 ½ teaspoons whole caraway seeds

2 teaspoons fine sea salt

A baking sheet or swiss roll tin covered with parchment or maize meal

This is the rye bread that you'll get when you order a sandwich at a kosher deli – it's flavourful, slightly chewy and a perfect complement to corned beef, pastrami and other deli specialities, such as chopped liver. Rye flour accounts for only about 20% of the total flour in the dough, but in a higher concentration the bread would lose its characteristic texture. The dough is flavoured with ground caraway and may also have whole caraway seeds added either to the dough or to the outside of the loaf; I wouldn't do both. Thanks to my friend Tim Healea of little t american baker in Portland, Oregon, and Maggie Glezer, author of A *Blessing of Bread*, for sharing their recipes.

1. For the rye sour, late the night before you intend to bake the bread, stir the water and sourdough starter together in a medium bowl. Stir in the rye flour. Cover the bowl with clingfilm and let the sponge ferment until bubbly, 6–8 hours. If it's warm in the kitchen, it will be ready after only 6 hours.

2. For the dough, the following morning, whisk the water and yeast together in the bowl of an electric mixer. Stir in the rye sour, followed by the bread flour and ground caraway seeds. You can add the whole caraway seeds in the dough or add them on the outside of the loaf before baking.

3. Place the bowl on the mixer and attach the dough hook. Mix on the lowest speed until the dough is smooth, about 4 minutes. Scrape the bowl and dough hook and let the dough rest for 15 minutes. Mix again on low speed, sprinkling in the salt. After the last of the salt is added, let the dough mix for 2–3 minutes longer.

4. Using a plastic scraper, transfer the dough to a lightly oiled bowl. Turn the dough over so that the top is oiled and cover the bowl with clingfilm. Let the dough ferment until it is about 50% larger than its original volume, about 1 hour. If the room is warm it will ferment more quickly.

5. Scrape the dough to a floured surface and flatten it to a disc. Fold the two sides in to overlap at the centre, then roll the top towards you, swiss roll-style. Return the dough to the bowl smooth (bottom) side upward, and let it rest again as in step 4.

6. Set a rack in the middle level of the oven and remove the racks above and below it. Place a roasting tin directly on the bottom of the oven. Preheat to 230°C/gas mark 8.

7. Invert the dough to a floured work surface. Pull a section of the dough around its perimeter to the centre and press it in place. Continue all around the dough until it's round and fairly even. Cover the dough with a tea towel or oiled or sprayed clingfilm and let it rest for 20 minutes.

8. Invert the dough, smooth (top) side down, flatten it to a rough disc, and fold both sides to meet in the centre. Roll the dough up from one of the unfolded sides. Invert the loaf to the prepared tin and cover it with oiled or sprayed clingfilm. Let the loaf proof just until it begins to puff visibly, about 30 minutes.

9. Use an X-Acto knife or single-edge razor to make three short parallel slashes in the top of the loaf. If using the caraway seeds on the outside of the loaf, spray or brush with water and sprinkle with the seeds. Place the tin in the oven and add 2 cups of water to the roasting tin. Quickly close the oven door and decrease the temperature to 200°C/gas mark 6. Bake the loaf until it is well risen and has an internal temperature of 93°C, about 30–40 minutes.

10. Cool the loaf on a rack and serve it the same day, though it will stay fresh for several days loosely covered at room temperature. Wrap and freeze for longer storage.

chapter ten

Flatbreads & Crispbreads

Probably the most ancient of all breads, flatbreads are found in almost every nation and culture in the world. The fact that flatbreads, such as pitta, are still common in the Middle East, often called the cradle of civilisation, emphasises their early origin. These are the breads to make when you don't have the patience to fuss over forming a perfect baguette or the time to wait for the multiple risings and turnings of a bread that needs to hold a specific shape while baking. Flatbreads are easy, fun (you can involve guests in making their own pittas if you have space in the kitchen), and, above all, rewarding in taste.

I had considered some more complicated focaccia recipes that use pre-ferments or sourdough, but after testing a few I reverted to my old faithful – the simplest, easiest and best focaccia I know. Try it and you'll see that great bread doesn't have to be either complicated or difficult to prepare.

Makes one 28 x 43cm focaccia

BASIC FOCACCIA DOUGH

450g room-temperature tap water, about 24°C

7g sachet fine granulated active dried yeast or instant yeast

110g olive oil

675g strong white bread flour

2 teaspoons salt

TOPPING

3 tablespoons olive oil

2 teaspoons kosher salt or Maldon sea salt

One 28 x 43cm swiss roll tin or 30 x 46cm sheet pan

QUICK CHANGES

Add one of the following to the dough right before completing the mixing at the end of step 3:
• 4 tablespoons finely chopped fresh rosemary leaves or coarsely chopped fresh sage leaves
• 85g pitted black or green olives, coarsely chopped
• 85g sun-dried tomatoes, coarsely chopped, plus 1 teaspoon dried oregano.

OVERNIGHT FOCACCIA
• Prepare the focaccia recipe using only 1½ teaspoons yeast up to the end of step 3. The dough should take 2–4 hours to ferment at room temperature.
• Once it is doubled in bulk, scrape it to a floured work surface and flatten the dough to a disc. Fold the two sides in to overlap at the centre, then roll the top toward you, swiss roll-style. Invert, flatten and repeat.
• Place the dough in a clean oiled bowl seam side up, then turn over so that the top is coated with oil. Cover with clingfilm and refrigerate until the next day.
• Resume the recipe at step 4, but the chilled dough will take much longer to proof, up to 2 hours depending on the temperature of the room.

Focaccia is one of the best and easiest of all yeast-risen baked goods to prepare. Technically more related to pizza than it is to bread, focaccia also has a strong link to yeast-risen pastries because of the oil used in, under and on the dough. In Italy, *focacce* (the plural) come in all shapes, sizes and thicknesses. Some are baked on pans, while others are baked directly on the oven's hearth or on a baking stone in a home oven. While you can make an excellent focaccia that's out of the oven only a couple of hours after you mix the dough, you can also mix the dough and refrigerate it until the next day. The ones below are all baked on pans, but the next recipe for a Roman *pizza bianca* is baked on a stone or a heated pizza pan.

1. Whisk the water and yeast together in the bowl of an electric mixer. Wait 30 seconds, whisk again, and whisk in half the oil.

2. Use a large rubber spatula to stir in the flour about one quarter at a time. Place the bowl on the mixer with the dough hook and mix on the lowest speed for 2 minutes – the dough will be soft. Stop the mixer and let the dough rest for 10 minutes.

3. Start the mixer again on medium speed and sprinkle in the salt. Mix until the dough is smoother, about 2 more minutes. Leave the dough in the mixer bowl and cover it with oiled or sprayed clingfilm. Let the dough ferment until it doubles in bulk, 45 minutes to 1 hour.

4. Coat the baking pan with the remaining 4 tablespoons olive oil, remembering to coat the sides, too. Use a plastic scraper to remove the dough from the bowl, letting it fall onto the pan without folding it over on itself. Oil your hands and, pressing and stretching with your fingertips spread apart from each other, dimple and ease the dough to fill the pan. Try not to pierce the dough all the way through, but at this stage any holes should close while the dough is proofing.

Cover the dough with oiled or sprayed clingfilm and let it proof until it doubles in bulk, about 30–45 minutes.

5. When the dough is almost proofed, set a rack in the lowest level of the oven and preheat to 220°C/gas mark 7.

6. Uncover the dough. If most of the impressions you made earlier have closed up, use oiled fingertips to dimple it again, without pressing through to the bottom, at unevenly spaced 2.5cm intervals. For the topping, drizzle on the oil and sprinkle with the salt. See box opposite for more toppings.

7. Bake the focaccia until well risen and well coloured, 30–40 minutes. After about 20 minutes, use a metal spatula to lift a corner of the focaccia and check to see whether the bottom is getting too dark. If so, slide another pan of the same size under the baking pan to insulate the bottom and turn the oven down to 190°C/gas mark 5. Once baked, slide the focaccia to a rack to cool. Use a sharp serrated knife or pizza wheel to cut the focaccia into 7.5cm squares and serve warm or at room temperature.

ABOUT FOCACCIA TOPPINGS

Here are a few suggestions for simple toppings that can enhance rather than obscure the fine flavour and texture of a focaccia. For all of these, apply them in step 6 before the oil and salt; exceptions are noted in the individual entries.

One batch Onion Marmalade, page 137; omit the vinegar if you wish. Use your fingertips to drop the marmalade all over the top of the risen focaccia, then to spread it fairly evenly.

45g finely grated Parmigiano Reggiano or Pecorino Romano; omit the salt with the Romano. 15g finely shredded fresh sage leaves or 4 tablespoons finely chopped rosemary leaves; sprinkle them on the risen focaccia before dimpling the dough so they'll stick inside the impressions made by your fingertips.

300g well drained, chopped tinned plum tomatoes or ripe fresh tomatoes that have been skinned, deseeded, and chopped. Sprinkle with 4 tablespoons Pecorino Romano and 1 teaspoon dried oregano.

Drain a 340g jar of roasted red peppers (not the kind packed with vinegar and sugar) and cut them into 5mm strips. Mix them with 3 peeled and thinly sliced cloves garlic and 4 tablespoons olive oil. Let them marinate while the focaccia is rising in the pan. Distribute the whole mixture over the risen focaccia before dimpling it. Sprinkle with salt but no added oil. Sprinkle with dried oregano too if you wish.

Though this pizza is anything but pure white, it's relatively unadorned, since it has no tomato or other topping. It's basically a thin focaccia sprinkled with oil and salt. In Rome, many pizzerias that also serve other food make freshly baked *pizza bianca* to serve at the table in place of bread.

1. In the bowl of an electric mixer, whisk the yeast into the water and then whisk in the oil. Add the flour to the bowl and use a rubber spatula to mix, scraping up from the bottom of the bowl, until all the flour is moistened.

2. Place the bowl on the mixer with the dough hook and mix on the lowest speed for 2 minutes, then let rest for 10 minutes.

3. Sprinkle in the salt and mix the dough on medium speed until smooth and elastic, about 2 minutes longer.

4. Scrape the dough into an oiled bowl and turn it so that the top is oiled. Cover with oiled or sprayed clingfilm and let the dough rise until doubled in bulk, about 1 hour.

5. When almost risen, set a rack in the middle level of the oven (remove any racks above it) and preheat to 260°C/gas mark 10. Place the pan or baking stone into the oven to heat.

6. Once the oven is heated, scrape the dough in one piece, without folding it over, to a floured work surface. Gently pull and stretch to a 30cm diameter, keeping it as round as possible. Cover the dough and let it rest for 10 minutes, then use your fingertips to dimple the surface all over.

7. Fold the dough into quarters and transfer it to a peel or piece of stiff cardboard covered with maize meal. Unfold the dough.

8. Generously drizzle the top of the dough with olive oil and sprinkle on about ¾ teaspoon coarse salt. Immediately slide the *pizza bianca* onto the preheated pan or stone. Bake until the pizza is well coloured, about 15 minutes.

9. Remove the pan from the oven, or use the same peel to remove it from the baking stone and set it on a rack to cool for 5 minutes. Serve immediately or allow to cool to room temperature.

roman white pizza

Makes one focaccia, about 30cm in diameter

1½ teaspoons fine granulated active dried yeast or instant yeast

225g room-temperature tap water, about 24°C

2 tablespoons olive oil, plus more for drizzling

350g strong white bread flour

¾ teaspoon fine sea salt

kosher salt or Maldon sea salt for sprinkling

Maize meal for the peel

One 30m diameter or larger round pizza pan, or a baking stone

pizza bianca

hazar turkish flatbread

Makes six 15cm round flatbreads

DOUGH

250g room-temperature tap water, about 24°C

7g sachet fine granulated active dried yeast or instant yeast

1 teaspoon sugar

450g strong white bread flour

1½ teaspoons fine sea salt

EGG WASH

1 teaspoon water

1 teaspoon yogurt

1 teaspoon beaten egg

One large or two smaller swiss roll tins lined with parchment paper

A friend and I happened upon Hazar, in the Bay Ridge section of Brooklyn, by accident one day. After ordering an aubergine salad and some *acili ezme*, a spicy red pepper salad, we tore into the basket of flatbreads and were impressed with all. We also ordered *lahmacoun*, a thin individual flatbread with a minced lamb topping, and I asked for lemon and parsley, the traditional accompaniments. The man at the oven brought them and when I told him how good the bread was, he told me that he makes it fresh three times a day. Two weeks later I was in the basement prep room with Ramazan, the owner, making his bread. Since he makes it so often it's fairly simple and quick to prepare. Once the dough is risen, it's divided, rounded, shaped into dimpled discs and baked straight away.

1. Whisk the water and yeast together in the bowl of an electric mixer. Wait 30 seconds and whisk in the sugar.

2. Use a rubber spatula to stir the flour into the liquid.

3. Attach the dough hook and beat for 2 minutes on the lowest speed. Stop the mixer and let the dough rest for 10 minutes.

4. Start the mixer again on medium speed and sprinkle in the salt. Mix until the dough is smoother and elastic, about 2 minutes longer. Cover the bowl with oiled or sprayed clingfilm and let the dough ferment until it doubles in bulk, about 1 hour.

5. Set racks in the upper and lower thirds of the oven and preheat to 230°C/gas mark 8. Scrape the dough onto a floured work surface and divide it into 6 pieces, each about 50g. To round each piece of dough, move one to a flour-free place in front of you.

Cup your right hand over the piece of dough so that the top of your palm just beyond your fingers is touching the dough. Press the piece of dough and move your hand in a circular motion at the same time. If you're pressing hard enough you'll be able to feel the dough turning into a sphere. Repeat with the remaining pieces of dough.

6. When you're ready to bake, make the egg wash by combining the ingredients and lightly brush the top of each piece of dough.

7. One at a time, form the breads by pressing down on the rounds of dough with the joined fingertips of each hand meeting in the middle making a line across the dough. Mark 4 lines equidistant from each other on the dough, then turn the flatbread 90 degrees and repeat, making a grid pattern on the dough. Place on one of the prepared pans and repeat with the remaining pieces of dough.

8. After all the flatbreads have been formed, pick one up by the edge and let it stretch a little downward, moving along the outside edge of each. Return to the pan after the stretching and repeat with the remaining flatbreads. Spray with water and place in the oven. Wait 2 minutes, then spray again.

9. Reduce the temperature to 220°C/gas mark 7 and bake the flatbreads until golden, a total of about 15 minutes. Halfway through, move the bottom pan to the top rack and vice versa, turning the pans back to front.

10. Cool the flatbreads on a rack and serve them soon after baking. At Hazar they always reheat the breads in a hot oven for a couple of minutes before serving.

swedish rye crispbread

Makes 12 crispbreads

200g strong white bread flour

200g dark rye flour

1½ teaspoons caraway seeds, finely ground in a spice grinder

1½ teaspoons fine sea salt

112g milk, scalded and cooled

112g room-temperature tap water, about 24°C

7g sachet fine granulated active dried yeast or instant yeast

Two baking sheets or swiss roll tins lined with foil

*K*nägebröd (KNAY-guh-brawd) is about as Swedish as you can get. It's the nucleus of the popular light lunch called SOS for the Swedish words for crisp bread, herring, and butter, all washed down with beer and/or *akvavit*, the Scandinavian caraway-flavoured spirit distilled from grain. Easy to prepare, *knägebröd* is crisp and chewy and in Sweden it's always buttered. Though most Swedes now buy their crispbread from a bakery or supermarket, it used to be a popular item to bake at home. The disc-shaped breads were baked with a hole cut in the centre so they could be strung onto a pole suspended from the ceiling, presumably to keep them out of reach of mice. Thanks to Annike Benjes of Visit Sweden for her help with this recipe.

1. Mix the bread flour, rye flour, ground caraway and salt and set aside.

2. Mix the cooled milk and water in the bowl of an electric mixer and whisk in the yeast. Wait 30 seconds and whisk again.

3. Use a large rubber spatula to stir in the flour mixture a little at a time until it is completely absorbed.

4. Place the bowl on the mixer fitted with the dough hook and mix on the lowest speed for 2 minutes. Stop the mixer and let the dough rest for 10 minutes.

5. Start the mixer on medium speed and mix the dough until smooth and elastic, about 2 more minutes – the dough will be dry and firm. Cover the bowl with oiled or sprayed clingfilm and let the dough ferment until it doubles in bulk, about 1 hour.

6. Scrape the dough onto a floured work surface and divide into 12 pieces, each about 50g. To round each piece of dough, move one to a flour-free place in front of you. Cup your right hand over the piece of dough so that the top of your palm just beyond your fingers is touching the dough. Press the piece of dough and move your hand in a circular motion at the same time. If you're pressing hard enough you'll be able to feel the dough turning into a sphere. Repeat with the remaining pieces

of dough. (See the video on my website for a demonstration of rounding.) Cover with a tea towel, and let them rest for 30 minutes. Or wrap them individually in clingfilm and refrigerate them for 12–18 hours.

7. When you're ready to roll and bake, set racks in the upper and lower thirds of the oven and preheat to 220°C/gas mark 7.

8. To form the crispbreads, place one of the rounded pieces of dough on a floured surface and flour it. Use the palm of one hand to press it into a disc. Roll the dough as thinly as possible, keeping a circular shape, until it is about 20cm in diameter. Pierce the dough all over at 1cm intervals with a fork and place on one of the prepared tins, putting 2 of the breads on each tin. Bake the crispbreads until deeply coloured and dry, about 5 minutes. Cool them on a rack.

9. While baking the first crispbreads, continue rolling 4 more while watching the oven and continue baking and rolling in shifts this way until all the breads are baked and cooled.

10. Serve the crispbreads with butter and herring, creamed or otherwise, or just with butter or any favourite spread. Store leftovers indefinitely in a tin or tightly sealed plastic container.

Back when I was in high school, my friend Sandy and I would often grab a commuter train in New Jersey and head to Greenwich Village. We spent $3 on lunch at Amy's on University Place, a vegetarian sandwich and salad shop where we always ordered a salad pitta and helped ourselves to the added bonus: coolers of free spring water or mint tea. One of the pittas that follows is filled with a Greek salad mixture (like the one at Amy's), while the other has a Turkish-style aubergine salad that I make all summer long. Both salads are also perfect as starters or side dishes with pitta or other bread.

SALAD PITTAS

4 pittas, page 164, warmed right before filling

Greek Salad or Aubergine Salad, see below

Cut the top 2.5–5cm from the pittas and divide the salad equally among them. Serve immediately.

GREEK SALAD

65g 1cm ribbons of sliced cos lettuce

1 large or 2 medium ripe tomatoes, 170–225g, halved, deseeded, and cut into 1cm dice

1 medium cucumber, 115–140cm, peeled, halved, and thinly sliced

½ small red or green pepper, about 55g, cut into thin slices

¼ medium red onion, about 55g, thinly sliced from stem to root end

2 tablespoons coarsely chopped pitted Kalamata or other flavourful black olives

About 85g crumbled feta cheese

3 tablespoons extra-virgin olive oil

1 tablespoon lemon juice, strained before measuring, or more or less to taste

1 teaspoon dried oregano, crumbled

Freshly ground black pepper

Combine all the vegetables in a mixing bowl. Sprinkle on the crumbled cheese, olive oil, lemon juice, oregano and pepper. Use a rubber spatula to fold everything together thoroughly. Taste for seasoning – it might need a pinch of salt, but be careful since both the olives and cheese are quite salty.

AUBERGINE SALAD

You can prepare this with aubergine that has been baked whole until it collapses, scraping out the flesh to a colander, rinsing it under running cold water, squeezing it dry, and chopping it by hand, but I prefer the diced aubergine below, which is a little chewier.

BAKED AUBERGINE

2 tablespoons olive oil

2 medium aubergines, about 675g, peeled and cut into 1cm dice

½ teaspoon coarse sea salt

SALAD

1 medium clove garlic, peeled and finely grated

1½ tablespoons lemon juice, strained before measuring

3 tablespoons olive oil

4 tablespoons chopped flat-leaf parsley

Freshly ground black pepper

½ small cucumber, about 55g, peeled, deseeded, and cut into 5mm dice

1 small tomato, about 85g, halved, deseeded, and cut into 5mm dice

½ small red or green pepper, about 55g, cut into 5mm dice

3 spring onions, white part only, rinsed, trimmed, and thinly sliced

1. To cook the aubergines, set a rack in the middle level of the oven and preheat to 190°C/gas mark 5. Grease a swiss roll tin or half sheet pan with the olive oil, spread out the diced aubergine on it, and sprinkle with the salt. Bake until cooked through and softened, opening the oven and stirring occasionally, 20–25 minutes.

2. Cool the aubergine on the pan, then scrape it into a medium mixing bowl.

3. Stir the garlic and lemon juice together and sprinkle over the aubergine, followed by the oil, parsley and pepper. Use a medium rubber spatula to fold everything together.

4. Sprinkle on the cucumber, tomato, pepper and spring onions and fold again. Taste for seasoning and adjust salt, pepper, and lemon juice if necessary.

5. For advance preparation, cover and chill the salad and bring it back to room temperature before serving. After being refrigerated, it may need to be perked up again with a little salt or lemon juice.

chapter eleven

Filled Breads

Filled breads are portable and delicious and in the case of all but the Neapolitan *calzone*, easy to prepare in advance. Like flatbreads, they're universal – I can't think of a place where they don't have at least one savoury dish wrapped in bread dough – while many cultures, especially in Asia, excel at producing all types of elaborately filled steamed, fried and baked dumplings.

The ones here are simple and practical, and aside from the plait on page 182, all are either turnovers or are baked in tins for easy unmoulding.

Most of the recipes have suggestions for elaborating on the filling, but you can also take off in any direction you like, as long as you keep one important rule in mind: when making a filled bread never use raw vegetables, meat or fish, which generate juices while steaming inside the dough. The juices prevent the interior dough from baking and your delicious filling will be surrounded with pasty unbaked dough.

If you like to picnic, filled breads are perfect – just bring some drinks, a knife, paper napkins and some fruit for dessert and you're ready to go.

Makes enough dough for 4 *calzoni* or 8 smaller ones

2 teaspoons fine granulated active dried yeast or instant yeast

450g room-temperature tap water, about 24°C

2 tablespoons olive oil

675g strong white bread flour

2 teaspoons fine sea salt

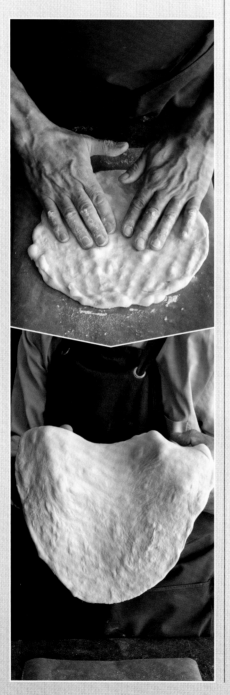

This is essentially the same dough I used for thin-crusted pizza in *BAKE!*, and I'm really happy with the way it easily stretches to the round shape you need for making a *calzone*. The dough is soft, so I recommend pressing it out directly on a piece of parchment paper that you can easily transfer to the baking tin to avoid having to pick up the *calzone* once it's formed, which might stretch it out of shape. See the *calzone* recipe opposite for filling, assembling, and baking.

1. In the bowl of an electric mixer, whisk the yeast into the water, then whisk in the oil.

2. Use a rubber spatula to stir the flour into the liquid, scraping the side of the bowl and folding up any unmixed flour from the bottom of the bowl.

3. Mix on the lowest speed with the dough hook until the dough starts to pull away from the bowl. Stop, scrape and let rest for 10 minutes.

4. Sprinkle in the salt and start the mixer on medium speed and mix the dough until it is smooth and more elastic, about 2 minutes. Cover the bowl with clingfilm and let the dough ferment until halfway doubled in bulk, 20–30 minutes.

5. Scrape the dough onto a floured work surface and flatten to a disc. Fold the two sides in to overlap at the centre, then roll the top towards you all the way to the end, swiss roll-style. Invert, flatten and repeat. Oil a bowl, place the dough in the bowl seam side up, turn it over so that the top is oiled and let ferment until almost doubled. If you don't intend to bake the *calzoni* straight away, give the dough another turn, return it to the bowl seam side down, cover with oiled or sprayed clingfilm and refrigerate for up to 24 hours before using.

6. When you're ready to make the *calzoni*, scrape the risen dough onto a floured work surface. Use a bench scraper to divide the dough into 4 equal pieces. Fold the sides of each piece of dough into the top centre to round them; invert, then move them to a floured place on the work surface. Cover with a tea towel or oiled or sprayed clingfilm and let the pieces of dough rest for 5 minutes.

7. To form the *calzone* crusts, cut four 30cm squares from parchment paper. To form a crust, generously flour one of the squares of paper and place a piece of the dough on it. Flour the top of the dough and press it with the palms of your hands to flatten it, always trying to maintain an even round shape. Reach under the dough with both hands and gently pull from the centre outward to make it thinner, then pull from the edges outward from the top with a hand on either side of the dough and moving around the entire circumference. Check often during this whole process to be sure the dough isn't sticking and add more flour to the paper under the dough if necessary.

8. For advance preparation, pull the square of paper onto a large plate or pizza pan, generously flour the top, cover loosely with clingfilm, and refrigerate for up to 6 hours. Stack 4 crusts on the same pan and cover well with clingfilm.

Here are the ingredients for one *calzone*, which you can increase if you're making multiples. There is a base filling that's common to all, plus extras to add for each type. If you have room in the kitchen, you can let guests make their own.

1. Set a rack in the lower third of the oven and preheat to 230°C/gas mark 8.

2. For the base filling, use a rubber spatula to stir the ingredients together. Stir in the garnish of your choice, or wait and sprinkle it on the base filling when assembling the *calzone* — the same goes for the mozzarella.

3. Remove a *calzone* crust from the refrigerator and make sure it isn't stuck to the paper. Mound the filling in a semicircle shape 2.5cm away from both the diameter and the edge of the crust. Brush a little water on the crust around the filling and fold the unfilled half of the dough over to meet it. Press the two edges together to seal.

4. Starting at one of the corners of the crust, pinch and pull the beginning of the folded edge out by about 5mm, then fold it back onto the edge at a 45-degree angle, firmly pressing it into place. Repeat all around the folded edge of the crust.

5. Transfer the *calzone* to the pan and cut away any excess paper around it. If you're using a round pan and are baking another *calzone* on it, face the folded edge to the diameter of the pan. Use an X-Acto knife or the point of a pair of sharp scissors to cut 3 or 4 vents in the top of the crust, then brush with olive oil.

6. Bake until deep golden and firm, about 20 minutes. If you're baking more than one pan at a time, set racks in the lowest level and a couple of notches above, then switch racks about halfway through the baking.

7. Serve the *calzone* immediately and eat with a knife and fork.

Makes 1 calzone, 1 large or 2 smaller servings

BASE FILLING

225g whole milk ricotta, preferably freshly made

Freshly ground black pepper

1 tablespoon finely grated pecorino Romano

3–4 medium leaves fresh basil, rinsed, dried and stacked and cut into 5mm ribbons

GARNISHES

Any one of the following:

85g thinly sliced prosciutto, stacked and cut into 5mm ribbons

85–115g sweet or hot dried sausage or *soppressata*, peeled and cut into 5mm dice

85–115g cooked ham, stacked and cut into 5mm ribbons

170g sausage and pepper mixture on page 97

225g mushrooms, rinsed, sliced, and sautéed in 1 tablespoon olive oil with a little salt

225g grilled or roasted vegetables such as asparagus, courgettes, aubergines or onions, or a combination

55g sun-dried tomatoes, soaked in warm water for 1 hour, drained and seasoned with 1 tablespoon olive oil

115g fresh mozzarella, finely sliced or diced (may be used in combination with any of the above or on its own)

Note: If you want to mix fillings, reduce the amount of each proportionately to avoid overfilling

One *calzone* crust, page 174, chilled

Olive oil for brushing

One 30–36cm round pizza pan or swiss roll tin at least 28cm across the short side (if you are baking 2 at a time, one tin will do; if you are baking 3 or 4 at a time, you'll need two tins)

vegetable & tuna pie from galicia in spain

Makes one 23 or 25cm empanada, 8 servings

EMPANADA DOUGH

400g plain flour

1½ teaspoons sugar

1½ teaspoons fine sea salt

170g room-temperature tap water, about 24°C

7g sachet fine granulated active dried yeast or instant yeast

100g olive oil, plus more for brushing

1 medium egg

FILLING

2 tablespoons olive oil

2 medium white onions, about 450g total, peeled, halved, and cut into 1cm dice

2 medium red peppers or pimentos, about 240–450g halved, stemmed and deseeded and cut into 1cm dice

60g green Spanish olives, pitted and coarsely chopped

2 x 140g tins tuna packed in olive oil, well drained and flaked

2 hard-boiled eggs, page 74, coarsely chopped

Freshly ground black pepper

Salt, if necessary

One 23cm square or 25cm round tart tin with removable base, ungreased

QUICK CHANGES

Replace the tuna with 200g peeled and diced Spanish cooked *chorizo*, or thinly sliced and shredded *jamon Iberico*, Spanish ham similar to prosciutto.

Though we tend to think of an *empanada* as a kind of turnover, in Galicia, Spain, it's a kind of pie made with a yeast dough enriched with olive oil. Fillings may vary, but this one of onions, peppers, olives and tuna is a popular one. In Spain, this is usually made in a square or rectangular tin, but you can use a square or round tart tin. You'll have some scraps of dough left after lining the tin and covering the filling with the top crust – make some breadsticks and bake them on a maize meal-dusted tin on an upper rack while you're baking the *empanada*.

1. For the dough, mix the flour with the sugar and salt and set aside.

2. Whisk the water and yeast together in the bowl of an electric mixer, then whisk in the oil and egg. Use a large rubber spatula to stir in the flour mixture.

3. Attach the dough hook and beat on the lowest speed until fairly smooth, about 2 minutes. Remove the dough from the mixer and knead it for a minute.

4. Place the dough in a lightly oiled bowl and turn it so that the top is oiled. Cover with clingfilm and let the dough ferment until it doubles in bulk, 30–45 minutes.

5. For the filling, pour the oil into a wide sauté pan and add the onions and peppers. Place on a medium heat and wait until the vegetables start to sizzle. Toss, decrease the heat to medium-low, and cook, tossing occasionally, until soft, about 20 minutes. Off heat, stir in the olives, tuna and eggs. Taste and adjust the seasoning, if needed.

6. Scrape the filling to a thin layer on a large plate or a metal pan covered with clingfilm and chill while you roll the dough.

7. Set a rack in the lower third of the oven and preheat to 220°C/gas mark 7.

8. Scrape the dough from the bowl to a floured surface and gently press to deflate. Divide the dough into two pieces, one of which is slightly larger than the other. Flour the surface, form the large piece of dough into a rough disc without folding it over on itself, and roll it to a 30–33cm square (or disc if using a round pan). Fold the dough in half and transfer the dough to the tin, lining up the fold with the diameter of the tin. Unfold the dough into the tin and press it well against the bottom and sides of the tin, letting the excess dough extend over the edge of the tin.

9. Scrape the cooled filling into the lined tin and spread it evenly.

10. Roll the remaining piece of dough to a 28–30cm square or disc and centre it on the filling. Use your fingertips to press the two layers of dough together, then use scissors to cut away all but 5mm of the excess dough. Pull a piece of the overhanging dough upward and fit it into the space between the edges of the tin and the side of the crust all around to make a flat top on the *empanada*.

11. Cut 3 or 4 vent holes in the top crust then brush with olive oil.

12. Bake the *empanada* until it is deep golden and firm, 20–30 minutes. Remove to a rack and cool for 5 minutes before serving, or cool completely and serve at room temperature.

13. To unmould, stand the tart tin on a wide base, such as a large tin of tomatoes and let the side of the tin fall away. Slide the *empanada* to a round cutting board or serving plate to serve.

POOLISH

7g sachet fine granulated active dried yeast or instant yeast

56g room-temperature tap water, about 24°C

56g whole milk, scalded and cooled

100g strong white bread flour

DOUGH

2 medium eggs at room temperature

2 medium egg yolks at room temperature

1½ tablespoons sugar

All the poolish, above

265g strong white bread flour

1½ teaspoons fine sea salt

115g unsalted butter, softened

This is similar to the brioche dough in *BAKE!* but is both saltier and less sweet, making it perfect for filled breads like the recipes that follow in this chapter.

1. For the poolish, whisk the yeast into the water and wait a couple of minutes. Whisk in the milk, then use a rubber spatula to stir in the flour. Cover with clingfilm and let the sponge ferment until more than doubled, about 30 minutes.

2. Once the sponge has risen, use a rubber spatula to break up the eggs and yolks in the bowl of an electric mixer. Stir in the sugar. Scrape the risen poolish into the bowl and mix it into the eggs. Add the flour to the bowl and stir.

3. Place the bowl on the mixer fitted with the dough hook and mix on medium speed until the dough comes away from the sides of the bowl, 3–4 minutes. Let the dough rest for 10 minutes.

4. Sprinkle in the salt and beat the dough on medium speed for 1 minute. Add a third of the butter and beat until the butter is completely absorbed. Repeat with the remaining two-thirds of the butter. After all the butter has been incorporated, continue to mix until the dough is very smooth, elastic and shiny, 2–3 minutes longer.

5. Scrape the dough into a buttered bowl and turn it over so that the top is buttered. Cover with clingfilm and let rise until doubled in bulk, about 30 minutes.

6. To make forming the dough easier, deflate the dough and press it into a thick rectangle on a baking sheet covered with floured clingfilm. Cover with clingfilm and refrigerate until firm, about 2 hours.

QUICK CHANGES

BRIOCHE LOAF FOR SLICING OR SWEET BREAD PUDDINGS:
- Increase the sugar above to 3 tablespoons and decrease the salt to 1 teaspoon.
- At the end of step 5, scrape the dough to a lightly floured work surface. Flour your hands and gently round the dough without deflating it too much by pushing inward at the bottom with your flat upturned palms all around the piece of dough – you'll see the outside skin of the dough tighten and it will become more spherical.
- Stretch the rounded piece of dough into a rough rectangle and slide both hands under it, palms upward, and transfer to a buttered 23 x 12 x 7.5cm loaf tin. Cover the tin with a piece of buttered clingfilm and let the dough rise 4cm above the rim of the tin, about 30 minutes.
- About 20 minutes before the loaf is completely risen, set a rack in the lower third of the oven and preheat to 190°C/gas mark 5.
- Bake the loaf until well risen and deep golden, with an internal temperature over 93°C. Unmould the loaf to a rack and cool on its side to prevent deflating.

My departed friend Anna Tasca Lanza, Marchesa di Mazzarino, learned to cook as an adult directly from Mario Lo Menzo, a monzu chef, tying into a tradition of elegant hybrid French/Italian cooking begun when French chefs first came to work in noble households in Sicily and Naples during the 19th century. This is a loose adaptation of Chef Mario's recipe, first prepared in honour of a visit by Prince Charles, the Prince of Wales, to Regaleali.

1. Scrape the chilled dough from the bowl to a floured surface and gently press to deflate. Divide the dough into two pieces, one of which is slightly larger than the other. Flour the surface, form the large piece of dough into a rough disc without folding it over on itself, and roll it to a 36–38cm disc. Fold the dough in half and transfer the dough to the tin, lining up the fold with the diameter of the tin. Unfold the dough into the tin and press it well against the base and sides of the tin, letting the excess dough extend over the edge of the tin.

2. Scatter the filling ingredients onto the crust, ending with the peas.

3. Roll the remaining piece of dough to a 36cm disc and centre it on the filling. Use your fingertips to press the two layers of dough together, then use scissors to cut away all but 5mm of the excess dough. Pull a piece of the overhanging dough upward and fit it into the space between the edges of the tin and the side of the crust all around to make a flat top.

4. Let proof for 20–30 minutes while you set a rack in the lower third of the oven and preheat to 190°C/gas mark 5.

5. Right before placing in the oven, cut several vent holes in the top crust and brush with the egg wash.

6. Bake until the top crust is deep golden and baked through, about 30 minutes. Unmould and slide to a rack to cool. Transfer to a serving plate and serve slightly warm or at room temperature.

sicilian filled brioche from regaleali

Makes one 30cm filled bread, about 12 servings

One batch Brioche Dough for Filled Breads, opposite, chilled in the covered mixer bowl for about 2 hours

450g mixed cheeses such as Gruyère, Gouda, Edam, and Fontina (use at least 2 types), cut into 1cm dice

225g best-quality cooked ham, cut into 1cm dice

280g frozen tiny peas, defrosted, brought to the boil in water to cover, cooked for 3 minutes, drained and cooled

Egg wash: 1 egg well whisked with a pinch of salt

One 25cm tart tin with removable base, ungreased

When Easter comes to southern Italy, it's time to use up all the dried sausages and other home-made cured meats before the weather starts to heat up. Due to that practice, and to the fact that milk and consequently cheeses are more plentiful in the Spring, Easter pastries like *pizza rustica* and other savoury pies are brimming over with both. *Casatiello* is a Neapolitan filled bread made by rolling salami, prosciutto and cheese into a yeast dough enriched with lard, shaping it into a ring, usually in a mould and decorating the top with eggs that cook through while the bread is baking. I've decided to make a totally non-traditional *casatiello* from brioche dough, and to incorporate the eggs, already cooked, right into the filling. A Neapolitan traditionalist might scoff at this version, but it's delicate, flavourful, and very much in keeping with the spirit of the original.

1. Invert the chilled brioche dough to a floured surface and flour the dough. Use the palms of your hands to press the dough to a rough rectangle. Roll the dough, moving it often and adding more flour under it to prevent sticking, until it is about 60 x 30cm.

2. Position the dough so that the 60cm side is parallel with the edge of the work surface; spray or brush it lightly with water.

3. One at a time, evenly scatter all the filling ingredients except the eggs on the dough, leaving a 2.5cm margin uncovered closest to the edge of the countertop.

4. Fold over about 4cm of the dough at the far end, then fold again, and roll the folded dough halfway towards you. Stop and add a line of the eggs on the still unrolled part of the dough closest to the rolled part, then continue rolling, ending with the seam side down.

5. Slide your hands, palms upward, in from each of the ends of the roll, and supporting the dough on your forearms, drop it into the prepared tin, seam side down.

6. Cover the tin with a tea towel or oiled or sprayed clingfilm and let the bread proof until it has increased 50% in bulk over its original size, about 45 minutes.

7. Meanwhile, set a rack in the lower third of the oven and preheat to 190°C/gas mark 5.

8. Bake until well risen and deep golden and a thermometer inserted 5cm deep midway between the side of the tin and the central tube reads 93°C, about 60 minutes. Don't neglect to check the temperature – the outside might look done while there is still raw dough in the centre.

9. Cool in the tin for 5 minutes, then invert to a flat tin or cutting board and lift off the baking tin. Cover with a rack and invert again. Cool completely on the rack.

10. Cut the *casatiello* into 1cm slices and serve as a first course with other antipasti or as an hors d'oeuvre with drinks.

neapolitan easter bread with salami, cheese & eggs

One batch Brioche Dough for Filled Breads, page 178, chilled for about 2 hours

115g sweet dried sausage or Italian salami, skinned if necessary and cut into 5mm dice

65g finely grated Parmigiano Reggiano

65g finely grated pecorino Romano

115g thinly sliced prosciutto, stacked and cut into 5mm dice

115g provolone, rind removed and cut into 5mm dice

5 hard-boiled eggs, page 74, sliced or coarsely chopped

One 3–4 litre ring mould or tube tin (don't use a Bundt tin), well buttered and sprayed with vegetable cooking spray

casatiello napoletano

Makes one 38cm plait, 6–8 servings depending on the rest of the menu

340g mild fresh goat's cheese, such as Montrachet, at room temperature

115g cream cheese, at room temperature

2 tablespoons small capers in brine, rinsed and finely chopped

1 tablespoon finely chopped flat-leaf parsley

2 tablespoons finely snipped fresh chives

1 teaspoon finely grated lemon zest

Freshly ground black pepper

340g smoked salmon, sliced paper thin

One batch Brioche Dough for Filled Breads, page 178, chilled for about 2 hours

One baking sheet or swiss roll tin at least 30cm long

This is a transformation of a Danish pastry shape paired with a savoury filling, though like a sweet Danish, it would make a perfect brunch dish. It's impressive looking, easy to get ready in advance and adaptable to other fillings. The plaited top of the bread looks complicated, but it's really simple to do – you cut both sides of a rectangle of dough into thin strips and, after arranging the filling on the central and intact part of the dough, alternate folding the strips over the filling to give the bread an appealing woven top.

1. For the filling, use a rubber spatula to beat the cheeses together until smooth, then beat in the capers, parsley, chives and lemon zest. Grind some pepper over the filling, mix it in, and taste for seasoning; add more pepper if necessary. Separate the slices of smoked salmon and have them ready nearby.

2. Invert the chilled brioche dough to a floured surface and flour the dough. Use the palms of your hands to press the dough to a rough rectangle. Roll the dough, moving it often and adding more flour under it to prevent sticking, until it is about 30 x 38cm.

3. Slide the dough to a piece of parchment paper the same size as your baking tin, lining up the 30cm side of the dough with the shorter side of the paper. Turn the paper so that the 30cm side of the dough is facing you. Use a fingertip to mark the dough into 3 sections, each 4 x 15 inches. With a sharp pizza wheel, cut the two outer sections of dough into 1cm strips that are still attached to the centre section.

4. Spread half the cheese filling on the centre section of dough, then evenly arrange the salmon on it. Spread the remaining filling on the salmon (drop a dab of it here and there all over the salmon, then spread; easier than trying to spread a single blob of it the length of the plait).

5. Cut away the first and last two 1cm strips of dough on both sides of the filling. This will leave you with a 2.5cm flap of dough on each end of the filling. Fold the flap to cover the end of the filling and close off the end of the plait. Then one strip at a time, and alternating one from each side, fold the strips over the filling starting at a slight angle to the centre rectangle and continuing the whole length of the plait. At the end, tuck the end of the last strip under.

6. Carefully slide the paper to your baking tin (if your tin has sides, slide the paper to a flexible cutting board or a piece of cardboard first, then slide it onto the tin). Cover with clingfilm and let the plait proof until it puffs slightly to about a 50% increase over its original bulk, about 30–45 minutes.

7. To prep in advance, cover and refrigerate, remembering that you'll need at least a couple of hours for the plait to come to room temperature and proof before baking.

8. About 30 minutes before the plait has finished proofing, set a rack in the lower third of the oven and preheat to 190°C/gas mark 5.

9. Bake the plait until it is well risen and deep golden, 35–40 minutes.

10. Slide the plait to a rack to cool to room temperature before serving – both dough and filling taste much better after cooling than hot from the oven.

chapter twelve

Enriched & Sweetened Breads

While industrially made bread products are labelled as 'enriched', this simply means that the factory that produces them adds certain nutrients to them. When I use the term 'enriched', I mean that these breads have a small amount of fat and/or sugar added to them, which gives them a tender texture and a delicate crumb. These two types of 'enriched' breads could not be more different. The enriched breads in this chapter probably came about when a creative baker experimented with adding butter or oil and/or sugar to already existing bread dough. So many are concentrated in the German-speaking part of Europe and the area immediately east of it that it's easy to assume that they originated in one of those areas.

Preparing a *challah* or Sally Lunn isn't any more complicated than mixing up a simple bread dough, except for one important point: many of the ingredients, such as butter, eggs or cream, are stored refrigerated and need to be brought to room temperature before mixing the dough or fermentation will be vastly slowed down. A room temperature of under 22°C can also delay doughs of this type; my home-made solution is to fill your pasta-cooking pot with water, bring it to the boil, and let the water simmer while the dough is fermenting or proofing. The steam escaping into the air efficiently warms it enough to help the dough to ferment at a normal rate. If your kitchen is large, it's probably better to move the bowl of dough to a warmer spot in the house.

This branch of bread baking is the one that I first learned, as it's so closely linked to the world of pastry and desserts. *Challah* and company led me to explore other breads, and for that reason I've always felt a particular fondness for these yeast-risen specialities.

jewish plaited sabbath bread

Makes two 41–46cm challahs

SPONGE

112g warm tap water, about 38°C

2 x 7g sachets fine granulated active dried yeast or instant yeast

100g strong white bread flour

DOUGH

225g room-temperature tap water, about 24°C

100g mild-flavoured vegetable oil, such as safflower or rapeseed

65g light brown sugar

3 medium eggs, at room temperature

1 medium egg yolk (save the white for the egg wash)

All the sponge, above

800g strong white bread flour

1 tablespoon fine sea salt

EGG WASH

1 medium egg white (from egg above)

1 teaspoon sugar

2 teaspoons water

Poppy seeds for the outside of the loaf, optional

Two 28 x 43cm swiss roll tins or 30 x 45cm half sheet pans, lined with parchment paper

In most observant Jewish homes, the mother begins the Friday evening Sabbath meal by lighting candles and the father recites a blessing over the *challah*, a plaited bread enriched with oil and eggs. The plaited shape of the loaf symbolises the bond between man and the deity and is always used – except for Rosh Hashanah, the celebration of the New Year, when a spiralled round *challah* is baked to recall the continuous circuit of time and Passover, when *matzo*, the unleavened flatbread is eaten. My dear friend, award-winning cookbook author and baking teacher Carole Walter, shared her own recipe, which I've adapted here.

1. For the sponge, whisk the water and yeast together in the bowl of an electric mixer. Wait 30 seconds and whisk again. Use a rubber spatula to smoothly stir in the flour. Cover the bowl with clingfilm and let the sponge ferment until doubled in bulk, about 30 minutes.

2. For the dough, use a rubber spatula to stir the water, oil, brown sugar, eggs and yolk into the sponge. Stir in half the flour, then gradually stir in the remaining flour until it is absorbed and there is no flour clinging to the side of the bowl.

3. Place the bowl on the mixer fitted with the dough hook and mix on the lowest speed until smooth, about 2 minutes. Let the dough rest for 15 minutes.

4. Start the mixer again on medium-low speed and sprinkle in the salt. Mix the dough until smooth and elastic, 4–5 minutes. Scrape into an oiled bowl and turn it so that the top is oiled. Cover the bowl with clingfilm and let the dough ferment until doubled in bulk, about 1 hour.

5. Once the dough has risen, scrape it onto a floured work surface and divide it in half. Set half aside covered while you form the first *challah*, which is composed of a large plait and a smaller one on top of it.

6. Use a bench scraper to cut off a third of the dough, which will be used to form the smaller plait, and set it aside, covered. Divide the large piece of dough into 3 equal pieces. To round each piece of dough, move one to a flour-free place in front of you. Cup your right hand over the piece of dough so

that the top of your palm just beyond your fingers is touching the dough. Press the piece of dough and move your hand in a circular motion at the same time. If you're pressing hard enough you'll be able to feel the dough turning into a sphere. Repeat with the remaining pieces of dough. (See the video on my website for a demonstration of rounding.). Set aside, covered, to rest for 5 minutes, then divide the smaller piece of dough into 3 pieces, round, and cover.

7. To form the strands for the plaits, invert the 3 larger pieces of dough to the work surface and use the palm of your hand to flatten them to discs. Roll each disc of dough from the far end toward you and seal the edge. Form the smaller pieces of dough the same way and set aside covered.

8. Roll the larger pieces of dough under the palms of both hands to lengthen them to about 35cm, tapering them at the ends. Arrange them on one of the prepared tins side by side and, starting from the middle, plait them together to one end, pinching the ends of the strands together at the end; turn the tin and plait from the middle to the other end the same way.

9. Repeat step 7 with the smaller pieces of dough, making them 2.5–5cm longer than the plait on the tin. Repeat step 8 to plait the smaller pieces of dough. Brush the centre line of the larger plait on the tin with water and carefully pick up the smaller plait and arrange it down the length of the larger one, pinching the ends to the ends of the bottom plait and turning them under on each end. Cover with a tea towel. *Continued*

10. Repeat steps 6 through 9 with the other half of the *challah* dough.

11. Cover the two *challah* loaves with tea towels or pieces of oiled or sprayed clingfilm and let them proof until almost doubled, 45-60 minutes.

12. About 20 minutes before the *challah* is fully proofed, set racks in the upper and lower thirds of the oven and preheat to 180°C/gas mark 4. Whisk the egg wash ingredients together in a small bowl.

13. Gently brush the risen *challah* with the egg wash and sprinkle with poppy seeds, if using. Bake until well risen and deep golden, with an internal temperature of about 88°C, 40–45 minutes. After about 25 minutes, switch the tins from top to bottom, turning them back to front at the same time for even baking.

14. Cool on the tins for a few minutes, then slide on the paper to a rack to cool. Loosely cover to serve on the day they're baked, or wrap and freeze for longer storage. Defrost and reheat at 180°C for about 5 minutes, then cool before serving.

Oddly, saffron breads are not baked in the traditional places where saffron is used in cooking such dishes as Marseillaise *bouillabaisse*, Valencian *paella*, and Milanese *risotto*. Instead, saffron breads and buns appear in southern England, as well as in Scandinavia, where they're baked for the December 13th celebration of St. Lucy's feast day. The Cornish saffron bread here is adapted from a recipe of Wilfred J. Fance, who wrote brilliantly about British baking in the middle years of the twentieth century. Serve it for breakfast, brunch or tea.

1. For the sponge, whisk the yeast into the water; wait 30 seconds and whisk again. Stir in the flour smoothly and cover the bowl. Let ferment until more than doubled in bulk, about an hour.

2. Meanwhile, bring the milk to a simmer in a small pan. Off the heat, stir in the saffron. Let cool until the sponge is ready.

3. Pass the milk through a fine-meshed sieve over the sponge and stir; set aside.

4. Put the flour and sugar in the bowl of an electric mixer and use a rubber spatula to combine. Place the bowl on the mixer fitted with the dough hook and add the butter. Mix on the lowest speed until the butter is absorbed by the flour, about 1 minute.

5. Add the sponge and saffron mixture to the bowl and mix on the lowest speed until there are no longer any dry bits of flour, about 2 minutes. Stop the mixer and let the dough rest for 15 minutes.

6. Sprinkle in the salt and mix the dough on low/medium speed for a minute, then add the dried currants, sultanas and candied peel. Continue to mix until the dough is smooth and elastic and the fruit is evenly distributed, about 2 minutes longer.

7. Scrape the dough into an oiled bowl and turn it over so that the top is oiled. Cover with clingfilm and let the dough ferment until doubled in bulk, about 1–1½ hours.

8. Scrape the dough onto a lightly floured surface and divide it in half. Form each half into a rough square, then roll each up, swiss roll-style, and drop into the prepared tins, seam side down. Cover the loaves with sprayed or oiled clingfilm and let them proof until they are risen about 2.5cm over the rim of the tins.

9. About 20 minutes before the loaves are fully proofed, set a rack in the lower third of the oven and preheat to 200°C/gas mark 6.

10. Place the fully proofed loaves in the oven and reduce the temperature to 190°C/gas mark 5. Bake until well risen and deep golden, with an internal temperature of 93°C, about 45 minutes. Check after 20 minutes and if the tops of the loaves are colouring too quickly, reduce the temperature to 180°C/gas mark 4.

11. Unmould the loaves and cool them on racks on their sides to prevent deflating.

Makes two 21cm loaves

SPONGE

1 tablespoon fine granulated active dried yeast or instant yeast

150g warm tap water, about 38°C

150g strong white bread flour

DOUGH

225g whole milk

⅛ teaspoon crumbled saffron threads

370g strong white bread flour

70g sugar

70g unsalted butter, cut into 10 pieces and softened

1 teaspoon fine sea salt

150g dried currants

100g sultanas

50g candied orange peel, cut into 5mm dice, or more sultanas if you prefer

Two 22 x 11.5 x 7cm loaf tins, buttered or sprayed with vegetable cooking spray

cornish saffron loaf

swiss plaited bread

Makes one 30-35cm plait

SPONGE

62g warm water, about 38°C

7g sachet fine granulated active dried yeast or instant yeast

66g strong white bread flour

DOUGH

All the sponge, above

112g whole milk, warmed to about 38°C

2 medium eggs, at room temperature

2 tablespoons sugar

450g strong white bread flour

30g unsalted butter, softened

1 teaspoon fine sea salt

Egg wash: 1 egg well whisked with a pinch of salt

One baking sheet or swiss roll tin lined with parchment paper

Like fried potatoes in Belgium, this Sunday morning plaited bread might be the only food that truly unites Switzerland's diverse ethnic and linguistic groups. I've given the recipe name in the country's four languages: German, French, Italian, and Rumantsch Grischun, this last a compiled language of ancient dialects spoken in Canton Graubünden. The version here comes from Zurich baker Reto Hausammann, acknowledged by critics and the public alike for preparing one of the very best versions of *Zopf* in the country. The precise and creative Swiss have figured out dozens of ways to plait a *Zopf*. This version is what I consider the most popular and widely seen: a four-stranded plait that has an attractive woven shape.

1. For the sponge, whisk the water and yeast together in the bowl of an electric mixer. Wait 30 seconds and whisk again. Use a rubber spatula to stir in the flour until smooth. Cover the bowl with clingfilm and let the sponge ferment until it more than doubles, 30-45 minutes.

2. Use a rubber spatula to stir the sponge down, then stir in the milk, eggs and sugar. Stir in the flour and the butter, cut into 10 or 12 pieces, on the surface of the dough.

3. Place the bowl on the mixer fitted with the dough hook and mix on low speed until smooth. Stop and let rest for 10 minutes.

4. Sprinkle in the salt and beat on low/medium speed until the dough is smooth and elastic, 2-3 minutes. Cover the bowl again and let ferment until almost doubled in bulk, 30-45 minutes.

5. Once the dough has risen, scrape it onto a floured work surface and divide it into 4 equal pieces and round each according to the instructions in step 6 on page 186. Set aside, covered, to rest for 5 minutes.

6. To form the strands for the plait, invert the pieces of dough to the work surface and use the palm of your hand to flatten them to discs. Roll each disc of dough from the far end towards you and seal the edge and set aside, covered, for 5 minutes.

7. Roll each piece of dough under the palms of both hands to lengthen them to about 35cm, slightly tapering them at the ends. Arrange on the prepared tin side by side.

8. To plait the loaf, weave the left strand over the one to its right, under the next one, then over the far one. Repeat with the strand that is now on the far left. Continue repeating until you come to the end. Once you see the photos, opposite, it's easy. Tuck the ends under at both ends and cover the *Zopf* with a tea towel or oiled or sprayed clingfilm and let proof until almost doubled in bulk, about 30 minutes.

9. Immediately set a rack in the middle level of the oven and preheat to 190°C/gas mark 5.

10. Gently brush the risen *Zopf* with the egg wash, making sure to clean the brush against the side of the bowl or cup to eliminate excess egg wash every time you dip the brush. Bake until well risen and deep golden, with an internal temperature of about 88°C, 40-45 minutes.

11. Cool on the tin for a few minutes, then slide on the paper to a rack to cool. Loosely cover to serve on the day it's baked or wrap and freeze for longer storage. Defrost and reheat at 180°C/gas mark 4 for about 5 minutes, then cool before serving.

umbrian cheese bread

Makes one 20 or 23cm round bread

1 tablespoon fine granulated active dried yeast or instant yeast

55g room-temperature tap water, about 24°C

400g strong white bread flour

115g unsalted butter or leaf lard, at room temperature

5 medium eggs, at room temperature

80g finely grated *Grana Padano*, see Note

40g pecorino Romano, finely grated

50g Swiss Gruyère, cut into 5mm dice

½ teaspoon salt

¼ teaspoon freshly ground black pepper

One 5cm deep, 20 or 23cm round tin, buttered and the base lined with a disc of parchment paper

I n 1988, when I was in Italy researching my book about Italian baking, I was fortunate enough to be introduced to Maria Carla Schucani-Sandri, chef/owner of the town's top pastry shop, Sandri, maker of the best *crescia* in Perugia. Traditionally baked in a glazed earthenware mould similar in shape to a flowerpot, *crescia* is also a family speciality of my friend Rosalinda Mariotti, a native of Perugia who now lives in Eugene, Oregon. Rosa's aunt used to work for the Schucani family and this is her recipe. It makes a *crescia* very similar to the one sold at Sandri – and is perfect as a breakfast bread or as a simple hors d'oeuvre with drinks.

1. In a small bowl, whisk the yeast and water together and set aside.

2. Combine the flour and butter in the bowl of an electric mixer fitted with the paddle and beat on medium-low speed until the butter is finely mixed into the flour and no pieces of butter remain visible, stopping and scraping the bowl and beater several times while mixing.

3. Switch to the dough hook and add the eggs to the bowl; whisk the yeast and water again and add. Mix on low for 1 minute to combine. Add the 3 cheeses, salt and pepper and mix on low speed to combine. Increase the speed to low-medium and beat the dough until smooth and elastic, about 3 minutes longer.

4. Remove the bowl from the mixer and cover it with clingfilm. Let the dough ferment until it starts to puff, 15–20 minutes.

Set a rack in the lower third of the oven and preheat to 180°C/gas mark 4.

5. Scrape the dough into the prepared tin and cover it with a piece of oiled or sprayed clingfilm. Let proof until it reaches the top of the tin, about 45 minutes.

6. Bake the *crescia* until well risen and deep golden, with an internal temperature of about 88°C.

7. Cool in the tin for 5 minutes, then invert to a rack, remove the paper, and cover with another rack. Invert again and remove the top rack. Cool completely before serving on the day it's baked.

Note: Grana Padano is used instead of Parmigiano Reggiano because the former is much less expensive in Italy. Outside Italy it might be more difficult to find, so feel free to substitute Parmigiano Reggiano.

I love recipes whose very names are the subject of controversy. Some suggest the name of this recipe is a corruption of *soleil-lune* (sun-moon) in French. Another explanation is that in the 18th century there was a bakery in Bath, England, run by a Sally Lunn. Whatever the origin of the name, Sally Lunn is a breakfast and tea bread, usually made as a large individual roll; in bakeries and tea rooms, it is sold split and buttered or filled with clotted or whipped cream. I'm departing from tradition here and making a single large loaf that can be baked in a round cake tin. Please make sure that all the ingredients are at room temperature or the dough will take forever to ferment.

Makes one 20 or 23cm round loaf

45g warm water, about 38°C

7g sachet fine granulated active dried yeast or instant yeast

85g whipping cream, at room temperature

3 medium eggs, at room temperature

2 teaspoons finely grated lemon zest

340g strong white bread flour

2 tablespoons sugar

1 teaspoon fine sea salt

85g unsalted butter, softened

One 5cm deep, 20 or 23cm round tin, buttered and the base lined with a disc of parchment paper

1. Whisk the water and yeast together in the bowl of an electric mixer; wait 30 seconds and whisk again. Whisk in the cream, eggs and lemon zest.

2. Use a rubber spatula to stir in the flour and sugar. Sprinkle the salt and distribute the butter, cut into 10 or 12 pieces, on the dough. Place on the mixer fitted with the dough hook and mix on low speed until the butter is absorbed and the dough is smoother, about 3 minutes.

3. Stop and scrape the bowl and dough hook and continue mixing on low-medium speed until the dough is smooth and elastic, 2–3 minutes longer. Scrape the dough into an oiled bowl and turn it so that the top is oiled. Cover the bowl with clingfilm and let the dough ferment until it is almost doubled in bulk, about 45–60 minutes.

4. Invert the dough to a floured work surface and pull the edges of dough all around the perimeter into the centre and press them in place to form a rough sphere. Turn the dough over and form it into a boule shape, page 28. Transfer the dough to the prepared cake tin. Cover the loaf with oiled or sprayed clingfilm and let it proof until doubled in bulk, 30–45 minutes.

5. About 15 minutes after setting the loaf to proof, set a rack in the middle level of the oven and preheat to 180°C/gas mark 4.

6. Bake the Sally Lunn until well risen and deep golden, with an internal temperature of 88–93°C, about 45 minutes.

7. Cool on a rack for 5 minutes, then use oven mitts to unmould and quickly turn it over onto the rack. Cool completely and serve the loaf on the day it is baked. It's traditional to cut a Sally Lunn into 1cm thick horizontal slices but it's more practical to cut the loaf in half, then stand it on the cut side and cut 1cm slices. Serve as is or toasted with butter and/or your favourite marmalade or jam.

barmbrack

Makes one tall 23cm loaf

225g room-temperature tap water, about 24°C

1 tablespoon fine granulated active dried yeast or instant yeast

225g milk, scalded and cooled

650g strong white bread flour

70g sugar

1½ teaspoons salt

¼ teaspoon each ground cinnamon, freshly grated nutmeg and ground cloves

60g unsalted butter, softened

150g sultanas

75g dried currants

50g diced candied orange peel

One 6cm deep, 23cm round springform tin, buttered and the base lined with a disc of parchment paper

I first tasted barmbrack when my friend Sandy Leonard brought some back from a trip to Ireland. Barmbrack is an enriched and sweetened bread. It has some butter and sugar added along with sultanas, dried currants and candied peel. It's perfect as a breakfast or brunch bread, since it's neither too rich nor too sweet, and it certainly deserves the nickname I gave it long ago: the *panettone* of Ireland.

1. Whisk the water and yeast together in a small mixing bowl; whisk in the cooled milk and set aside.

2. Stir together the flour, sugar, salt and spices in the bowl of an electric mixer. Place on the mixer fitted with the paddle and mix on the lowest speed for 1 minute, adding the butter in 5 or 6 additions. Mix until the butter is no longer visible.

3. Switch to the dough hook and add the yeast mixture to the bowl. Beat on the lowest speed until the dough comes together around the hook, 2–3 minutes.

4. Increase the speed to medium and beat the dough until smooth and elastic, about 2 minutes longer.

5. Decrease the speed to the lowest and add the sultanas, currants and orange peel a little at a time. Mix until the fruit is evenly distributed, about 2 minutes.

6. Scrape the dough into an oiled bowl and turn it so that the top is oiled. Cover the bowl with clingfilm and let the dough ferment until doubled in bulk, about 1 hour.

7. Invert the dough to a lightly floured work surface and round it by pulling the sides and folding them over toward the centre. Invert the dough to the tin, smooth side upward, and cover it with a piece of oiled or sprayed clingfilm. Let the barmbrack proof until it fills the tin, about 1 hour, depending on the temperature of the room.

8. About 30 minutes before the barmbrack is fully proofed, set a rack in the middle level of the oven and preheat to 190°C/gas mark 5. Bake the barmbrack until it is well risen and dark golden, about 1 hour.

9. Invert to a rack, turn right side up, and cool completely. Serve the barmbrack on the day it's baked with butter and marmalade. For advance preparation, wrap and freeze; defrost and bring back to room temperature before serving.

italian christmas cake

Makes one tall 23cm cake, 12–16 servings

SPONGE

7g sachet fine granulated active dried yeast or instant yeast

112g whole milk, warmed to 38–43°C

90g strong white bread flour

DOUGH

All the sponge, above

3 medium eggs, at room temperature

3 medium egg yolks, at room temperature

70g sugar

4 ½ teaspoons home-made *millefiori*, below (if you buy a prepared version use amount recommended on the package)

400g strong white bread flour

½ teaspoon fine sea salt

140g unsalted butter, softened

50g raisins

50g sultanas

50g diced candied orange peel

One 7.5cm deep, 23cm round cake or springform tin, buttered and the base lined with a disc of parchment paper

A home-made *panettone* doesn't stay fresh as long as a bought one, but it's your own and easy to prepare. If you want to prepare it days or even weeks in advance, freeze it and your *panettone* will be fresh and moist when you serve it.

The traditional flavouring for *panettone* is called *millefiori* (thousand flowers) or *fiori di Sicilia* (Sicilian flowers) and can sometimes be found in Italian groceries. It usually comes packaged in little glass vials – one is usually enough for a batch of *panettone*, but you may want to ask for a translation where you buy it, since the recommended dosage is usually written only in Italian. I developed my own version, which is provided at the end of the recipe.

1. For the sponge, whisk the yeast into the milk and stir into the flour in a small bowl. Cover with clingfilm and ferment until bubbly, about 30 minutes.

2. Once the sponge has fermented sufficiently, scrape it into the bowl of an electric mixer and use a rubber spatula to stir in the eggs and yolks. Stir in the sugar, *millefiori* and flour, one at a time.

3. Beat the mixture on low speed with the paddle for 4 minutes, then stop the mixer and let the dough rest for 10 minutes.

4. Beat the dough on medium speed and add the salt. Add the butter in 4 or 5 additions, continuing to beat until the butter is absorbed and the dough is relatively smooth. Beat in the raisins, sultanas and candied orange peel.

5. Cover the bowl and let the dough ferment until doubled, about 1 hour.

6. Scrape the dough onto a floured work surface and using a bench scraper, flatten the dough to a disc. Fold the two sides in to overlap at the centre, then roll the top towards you all the way to the end, swiss roll-style. Turn the dough seam side down and round it, palms upward, by pushing in toward the centre all around the piece of dough. Drop the dough in the tin rounded (smooth) side upward. Cover with buttered clingfilm and let the dough rise to the top of the tin, about 30–60 minutes.

7. When the dough is almost completely risen, set a rack in the lower third of the oven and preheat to 180°C/gas mark 4. Bake until well risen and deep golden, with an internal temperature of 93°C, about 40 minutes.

8. Unmould, turn right side up and cool on a rack. Double wrap in clingfilm to store.

MILLEFIORI FOR *PANETTONE*

This makes enough for 2 batches of the dough above.

1 tablespoon vanilla essence

1 ½ tablespoons white rum

¼ teaspoon lemon essence

¾ teaspoon orange flower water

¼ teaspoon anisette

¼ teaspoon rose water

Stir together and store in a tightly capped dark-coloured bottle in a cool place or in the refrigerator for up to 6 months.

ABOUT CANDIED FRUIT

Candied fruit ranks shoulder to shoulder with lard and anchovies as an ingredient that sends ordinarily calm people running out screaming at the thought of using it. Unlike pork fat and smelly little fish, candied fruit ought to be easy to swallow – it's sweet, citrusy when made from fruit peel and tender. But pick some up at your local supermarket and you'll open the packet only to discover dry bitter bits of what tastes like fruit-coloured plastic. Worst of all are mixtures of candied fruit to be used for making fruitcake, because they're loaded with grapefruit peel, slightly bitter when correctly candied and worse than a mouthful of unsweetened cocoa powder in the supermarket version.

Money, as usual, is the root of this evil, because really good candied fruit is expensive to prepare – not because the peel is expensive (it can probably be bought for next to nothing by the truckload from juice factories), but because it requires time. Citrus peel is naturally bitter and the only way to remove the bitterness is by repeated blanching: covering the peel with water, bringing the pot to the boil, draining and repeating as many as 6–12 times with long soaking in cold water between every blanching. Then comes the candying itself, a lengthy process that replaces the water molecules within the peel with sugar molecules. The best candied fruit is made in batches of only several kilograms at a time.

If you buy candied fruit imported from France or Italy, it's never cheap, but you can be assured that it's prepared correctly.

• Candied orange or lemon peel is as its name implies, made from peels of those fruits with most of the bitter white pith under the skin trimmed away.

• Candied citron is made from a thick-skinned relative of lemons, but unlike candied lemon peel, the pith is the part that's candied. Around Easter you can usually find good-quality candied citron in Italian grocery shops – it keeps indefinitely tightly wrapped and refrigerated.

• Candied cherries are probably the most innocuous of candied fruit, mostly because small amounts are used as decorations.

• Candied pineapple lacks bitterness and even industrially made kinds can be good.

• Candied or crystallized ginger also lack bitterness, so inexpensive versions can be good. Be careful that it hasn't dried out and hardened – it should be soft and moist.

Though *Gugelhupf* is made in various forms all over the German-speaking and nearby Slavic world, it has reached its highest form in Vienna, where there are many variations on the basic slightly sweet and butter-enriched cake. The recipe here is strictly a *Germgugelhupf*. *Germ* in German means yeast. Other versions may be marbled with chocolate, chocolate glazed, or leavened with baking powder, and there is even an imperial version called *Kaiser's Gugelhupf*. For a 2.9–3.8 litre mould, double the recipe (but not the yeast).

1. Place the raisins or sultanas in a small pan. Add water to cover and bring to the boil. Drain and transfer the raisins to a small bowl. Stir in the rum and set aside.

2. For the sponge, whisk the milk and yeast together in a small bowl and stir in the flour. Cover with oiled clingfilm and let ferment until doubled in bulk, about 1 hour.

3. For the dough, beat the butter and sugar in the bowl of an electric mixer fitted with the paddle attachment on medium speed until well mixed, about 1 minute. Beat in the egg and yolk, one at a time, until smooth, then beat in the lemon zest and vanilla essence.

4. Decrease the mixer speed to the lowest and beat in the sponge, then the flour, a little at a time. Once all the flour has been added, let the dough rest for 10 minutes.

5. Sprinkle in the salt and start the mixer on low-medium speed and beat the dough until it is smooth and elastic, about 2 minutes longer. Halfway through, beat in the raisins and rum.

6. Scrape the dough by large spoonfuls into the prepared mould, distributing evenly, then smooth the top. Cover with oiled or sprayed clingfilm and let the dough ferment until it fills the mould, about 1 hour.

7. Once the dough has started puffing, set a rack in the lower third of the oven and preheat to 190°C/gas mark 5.

8. Bake the *Gugelhupf* until well risen and deep golden, with an internal temperature of 93°C. Cool in the tin for a minute, then invert the mould to a rack, lift off the mould, and let the *Gugelhupf* cool completely. Dust with icing sugar and slide to a serving plate before serving.

viennese yeast-risen coffeecake

Makes one 16.5cm tube cake, 6–8 servings

RUM SOAKED RAISINS

50g raisins or sultanas

1½ tablespoons dark rum

SPONGE

100g whole milk, scalded and cooled to room temperature

7g sachet fine granulated active dried yeast or instant yeast

100g strong white bread flour

DOUGH

90g unsalted butter, softened

3 tablespoons sugar

1 medium egg

1 medium egg yolk

Grated zest of 1 large lemon

2 teaspoons vanilla essence

All the sponge, above

150g strong white bread flour

½ teaspoon fine sea salt

Icing sugar for serving

One 1.2–1.4 litre (9.5cm deep x 16.5cm diameter) *Gugelhupf* (sometimes called *Kugelhopf*) mould, buttered

Makes one 25cm tube cake, about 16 servings

POPPY SEED FILLING

300g ground poppy seeds

225g whole milk

170g honey

110g sugar

¼ teaspoon fine sea salt

Grated zest of 1 large lemon

100g raisins

DOUGH

150g whole milk, scalded and cooled to lukewarm, about 38°C

1 tablespoon fine granulated active dried yeast or instant yeast

80g sugar

60g unsalted butter, melted

400g strong white bread flour

2 medium eggs

½ teaspoon fine sea salt

Icing sugar for serving

One 1 or 2-piece 2.9–3.8 litre tube or bundt tin, buttered

QUICK CHANGES

WALNUT BABKA: Substitute finely chopped but not ground walnuts for the poppy seeds in the filling. Add 1 teaspoon ground cinnamon along with the sugar and salt. A tablespoon of dark rum will add a gentle sweet aroma to the walnut filling. Pecans or hazelnuts would work well, too.

Babka is a wonderful bakery-café in Melbourne, Australia, run by Sasha Lewis and her son Nico, who is the head baker. When I decided to include a babka recipe in this book, I asked Sasha if she had one. I had never tasted the babka at Babka, but I loved it as soon as I tried the recipe. You can purchase ground poppy seeds online. One small word of warning: if you're not sure whether you like poppy seeds, try the walnut filling. An entire filling made from poppy seeds is more intensely flavoured than a few seeds sprinkled on a roll. Babka is great with coffee or tea any time of the day, but it isn't necessarily a dessert.

1. For the filling, combine the ground poppy seeds, milk, honey, sugar and salt in a medium saucepan and set over a low heat. Cook, stirring often, until the filling comes to a simmer and has a moderately thick jam-like consistency, about 5 minutes. Off heat, stir in the lemon zest and raisins. Transfer to a shallow bowl and let cool to room temperature.

2. For the dough, whisk the cooled milk and yeast together in the bowl of an electric mixer. Whisk in the sugar and melted butter. Use a rubber spatula to stir in half the flour. Attach the dough hook and beat on the lowest speed until the flour is incorporated, then add the eggs, one at a time, beating until incorporated after each addition. Add the remaining flour and beat until the dough is fairly smooth, then let rest for 15 minutes.

3. Sprinkle in the salt and beat on medium speed until the dough is smooth and elastic, 2–3 minutes. Scrape into an oiled bowl and turn it so that the top is oiled. Cover with clingfilm and let ferment until doubled in volume.

4. To form the babka, invert the dough to a floured surface and pull it to a rough rectangle. Gently roll the dough in both directions, moving it often to make sure it doesn't stick, until the rectangle measures about 30 x 60cm. Leaving a 1cm margin all around the dough, drop tablespoons of the filling all over the dough, then use a small spatula to spread the filling fairly evenly. Fold over 2.5cm or so of the top 60cm edge and roll the dough, swiss roll-style towards you, pinching the end to the rest of the roll. Slide both hands in from opposite edges of the roll; quickly lift and arrange it in the tin seam side up. Tightly press the two ends to each other to form a ring so that they securely join while the babka is proofing.

5. Cover the tin with oiled or sprayed clingfilm and let the babka proof until almost doubled in size, about 45 minutes.

6. About halfway through the proofing, set a rack in the lower third of the oven and preheat to 200°C/gas mark 6. Once the babka is fully proofed, place it in the oven and reduce the temperature to 190°FC/gas mark 5. Bake until well risen and deep golden, with an internal temperature of about 93°C.

7. Place the tin on a rack, cover with aluminium foil and a damp tea towel, and let the babka cool to room temperature. Covering it as it cools minimises the dough shrinking away from the filling.

8. Once cooled, invert a serving plate over the tin and then invert the whole thing. Lift off the tin. Lightly dust the babka with icing sugar before serving in thick slices.

Gubana, a traditional cake from Friuli in Northern Italy, is related to strudel, babka and a host of other Slavic, Czech and other Eastern European pastries. What distinguishes all of them is the construction. Each is made by rolling up a filling in a dough that is then coiled in a tin so that when the finished cake is cut, you see an attractive spiral pattern of filling in each slice. A visit to Gubana Vogrig, a bakery in Cividade del Friuli, and a talk with Lucio Vogrig, the bakery's owner, gave me all the information I needed to attempt my first version of *gubana* over 20 years ago. Since then I have made a few adjustments, but it didn't seem to improve noticeably until I decided to use a variation of brioche dough – the result was excellent.

fruit & nut filled cake from friuli

Makes one 25m cake, about 12 generous servings

SPONGE

112g whole milk, scalded and cooled to lukewarm, about 38°C

7g sachet fine granulated active dried yeast or instant yeast

100g strong white bread flour

DOUGH

2 medium eggs at room temperature

2 medium egg yolks at room temperature

110g sugar

2 teaspoons vanilla essence

Grated zest of 1 large lemon

All the sponge, above

300g strong white bread flour

½ teaspoon fine sea salt

115g unsalted butter, softened

FILLING

150g sultanas

75g candied orange peel, cut into 5mm dice

4 tablespoons dark rum

100g dark brown sugar

60g unsalted butter

40g dry breadcrumbs, page 36

170g walnut pieces, lightly toasted and finely chopped, but not ground

1 medium egg, lightly beaten

One 23cm round, 7.5cm deep cake or springform tin, buttered and lined with a disc of parchment paper

1. For the sponge, whisk the milk and yeast together in a small bowl. Wait 30 seconds and whisk again. Use a small rubber spatula to stir in the flour. Cover with oiled or sprayed clingfilm and let ferment until more than doubled in size, about 1 hour.

2. For the dough, whisk the eggs, yolks, sugar, vanilla essence and lemon zest by hand in the bowl of an electric mixer. Use a rubber spatula to stir in the sponge.

3. Attach the dough hook and add the flour. Mix until smooth on lowest speed. Let rest for 15 minutes.

4. Sprinkle in the salt and mix on low/medium speed until the dough comes away from the side of the bowl, then beat in the butter a little at a time. Cover and let rise until doubled in bulk, about 1 hour.

5. Flour a baking sheet and place the dough on it. Flour the dough and press it out flat to about 20 x 30cm. Cover with clingfilm and refrigerate for 1 hour.

6. For the filling, place the sultanas in a small pan, add water to cover, then bring to the boil. Drain and transfer to a large bowl with the orange peel and add the rum. Scatter the brown sugar on top.

7. In a medium sauté pan, melt the butter and cook the breadcrumbs in it over a low heat until they are golden, then add to the filling. Add the nuts and egg and fold the filling together until evenly sticky. Let cool.

8. Invert the dough to a floured work surface and roll it to a rectangle about 30 x 45cm. Spread the filling evenly over the dough, leaving a 2.5cm margin. Beginning from a wide end, roll up the dough and filling. Form the dough into a loose spiral and drop into the tin, leaving room between the curves for the dough to grow while it's rising. Loosely cover the tin with clingfilm and let the *gubana* proof until there are no longer any gaps in the dough, about 1 hour, but possibly longer.

9. About 30 minutes into the proofing, set a rack in the lower third of the oven and preheat to 160°C/gas mark 3.

10. Bake the *gubana* until well risen and deep golden, with an internal temperature of 93°C, 65–75 minutes.

11. Place the tin on a rack and cover with foil and a slightly damp tea towel so that it cools slowly. Unmould when cooled. Wrap and serve the day after it's baked.

cranberry pecan coffeecake

SPONGE

200g whole milk, scalded and cooled to 38°C

4 teaspoons fine granulated active dried yeast or instant yeast

200g strong white bread flour

DOUGH

150g dried cranberries

45g orange juice

180g unsalted butter, softened

100g light brown sugar or turbinado sugar

2 medium eggs, at room temperature

2 medium egg yolks, at room temperature

1 tablespoon finely grated orange zest

2 teaspoons vanilla essence

300g strong white bread flour

1 teaspoon fine sea salt

FILLING

100g turbinado sugar or moist light brown sugar

1½ teaspoons ground cinnamon

150g pecan pieces, lightly toasted and coarsely chopped

ICING

215g icing sugar

3 tablespoons fresh orange juice, strained before measuring

One 3.8 litre tube or Bundt tin, thickly buttered

Perfect for a fall or winter brunch, this versatile cake can be made with almost any combination of dried fruits and nuts you like. I love the tangy flavour of dried cranberries, and they're a perfect contrast to the sweet dough and icing and the richness of the nuts in this cake.

1. For the sponge, whisk the milk and yeast together in a small bowl and stir in the flour. Cover with oiled or sprayed clingfilm and let the sponge ferment until it is doubled in bulk, about 1 hour.

2. Immediately after preparing the sponge combine the dried cranberries and orange juice in a small bowl and set aside.

3. Once the sponge is risen, beat the butter and brown sugar in the bowl of an electric mixer fitted with the paddle attachment on medium speed until well mixed, about 1 minute. Beat in the eggs and yolks, one at a time. Beat until smooth, then beat in the orange zest and vanilla essence.

4. Decrease the mixer speed to lowest and beat in the sponge, then the flour a little at a time. Once all the flour has been added, let the dough rest for 10 minutes.

5. Sprinkle in the salt and beat on low/medium speed until the dough is smooth and elastic, about 2 minutes longer. Halfway through, beat in the dried cranberries and orange juice.

6. For the filling, stir the brown sugar, cinnamon, and pecans together.

7. To assemble, spoon a little less than a third of the dough into the bottom of the mould and spread it evenly. Sprinkle with half the sugar and pecan mixture. Spoon in half the remaining dough and level; top with all the remaining sugar and pecan mixture. Spoon in the last of the dough and level the top. Cover with oiled or sprayed clingfilm and let the dough ferment until it fills the mould, about 1 hour.

8 Once the dough has started puffing, set a rack in the lower third of the oven and preheat to 190°C/gas mark 5.

9. Once the cake is fully proofed, bake until well risen and deep golden, with an internal temperature of about 93°C, about 1 hour.

10. Invert a rack on the top of the tin and using oven mitts, invert them together. Lift off the tin and let the cake cool completely. Once cooled, invert the cake to a rack over a piece of parchment paper or a tin.

11. To make the icing, stir the icing sugar and orange juice together in a small saucepan and place over a low heat. Cook the icing, stirring constantly, until it is just warm, about 43°C. Use a spoon to drizzle the icing onto the cooled cake. Let the icing dry, then slide the cake to a serving plate. Serve it on the day you baked it for brunch or tea.

one-step sweet brioche dough

Makes about 900g dough

112g whole milk, scalded and cooled
    to lukewarm, about 38°C

4 teaspoons fine granulated active dried yeast or
    instant yeast

400g strong white bread flour

110g sugar

¼ teaspoon ground mace

2 medium eggs, at room temperature

2 medium egg yolks

Grated zest of 1 large lemon

1 teaspoon fine sea salt

145g unsalted butter, softened

Classic brioche dough is often made using a poolish that incorporates part of the liquid and flour and all of the yeast in the formula. In this quicker and somewhat richer version, the ingredients are mixed as they are for a one-step bread dough. I've added a little lemon zest and a pinch of mace to emphasise the sweet flavour. This is the right amount of dough for all the recipes in this chapter that call for it.

1. Whisk the milk and yeast together in the bowl of an electric mixer. Wait 30 seconds and whisk again. Use a rubber spatula to stir in one-third of the flour. Let the mixture rest for a few minutes while you gather the remaining ingredients.

2. Stir in the sugar, mace, eggs, yolks and lemon zest, followed by the remaining flour. Make sure all the flour is thoroughly integrated.

3. Place the bowl on the mixer and attach the dough hook. Mix on the lowest speed until the dough comes together on the hook, about 2 minutes. Scrape the dough off the hook and let rest for 15 minutes.

4. Sprinkle in the salt and start the mixer on low-medium speed and beat the dough until it is smoother and more elastic, about 2 minutes. Increase the speed to medium and beat in the butter about 30g at a time, beating until smooth after each addition. By the time all the butter has been incorporated, the dough should be very smooth and elastic.

5. Scrape the dough into a buttered bowl and turn it so that the top is buttered. Cover the bowl with clingfilm and let the dough ferment until it doubles in bulk.

6. Use the dough straight away in any of the following recipes, or flour a swiss roll tin and press the dough into a 2.5cm thick square; cover with clingfilm and refrigerate until needed, but use it within a few hours.

Though Lent isn't observed with the fervour it was when I was a child, hot cross buns still appear during the pre-Easter season. Departing from tradition as I like to do, I'm using the one-step brioche dough in this chapter for the buns – it makes them rich and tender and not overly sweet. I'm also making the crosses with icing sugar icing, which appeals more to me than using the traditional thin flour and water dough for them.

By the way, if you can't find really sweet good-quality candied citron or orange peel, use some sultanas instead.

Makes 15 buns

1 batch One-Step Sweet Brioche Dough, page 208, including the lemon zest and omitting the mace, prepared up to step 4

½ teaspoon ground cinnamon

½ teaspoon ground ginger

¼ teaspoon freshly grated nutmeg

¼ teaspoon ground cloves

100g dried currants

50g candied citron or orange peel, cut into 5mm dice

30g unsalted butter, melted

GLAZE

2 tablespoons caster sugar

1 tablespoon water

ICING

115g icing sugar

1 tablespoon water

One 23 x 33 x 5cm tin, lined with buttered foil

1. To finish the dough, start the mixer on low speed and beat in the spices and then the currants and candied citron or orange peel until evenly distributed throughout.

2. Scrape the dough into a buttered bowl and turn it so that the top is buttered. Cover the bowl with clingfilm and let the dough ferment until doubled, about an hour.

3. Invert the dough to a floured work surface and divide it into 15 x 70g pieces. Round each according to the directions on page 162, step 5. Brush the sides of the formed buns with the melted butter to keep them from sticking together and arrange them in the prepared tin in 3 rows of 5 buns.

4. Cover the tin with oiled or sprayed clingfilm and let proof until they almost grow together, 45 minutes to 1 hour.

5. About 20 minutes before the buns are fully proofed, set a rack in the middle level of the oven and preheat to 190°C/gas mark 5.

6. Bake the buns until well risen and fully extended together, with an internal temperature of 93°C.

7. While the buns are baking, make the glaze: stir the sugar and water together in a small saucepan and bring to the boil over a low heat, stirring to dissolve the sugar.

8. Brush the glaze on the buns as soon as you remove them from the oven. Cool the buns in the tin for 5 minutes, then, grasping one side of the tin with an oven mitt, pull the foil on the opposite side lifting it upward over a rack. Pull the tin away and lower the buns on the foil to a rack. Let the buns cool on the rack until you can handle them, then separate them while still warm.

9. To make the icing for the crosses on the buns, combine the icing sugar and water in a small saucepan and stir with a small wooden spoon. Heat the icing until it is just lukewarm. Use a spoon to drizzle two perpendicular lines on each bun, or pour the icing into a non-pleated plastic bag, force it into a corner, snip the end and pipe the crosses onto the buns. Let the icing dry before serving.

10. Serve the buns on the day they are baked. For advance preparation, omit the glaze when the buns come out of the oven and wrap and freeze the buns either separated or together. Defrost and reheat before brushing with the glaze. Then cool and add the crosses with the icing, as in step 9.

cinnamon knots

Makes sixteen 10cm rectangular buns

DOUGH

75g warm tap water, about 38˚C

1 tablespoon fine granulated active dried yeast or
 instant yeast

400g strong white bread flour

2 tablespoons sugar

1 teaspoon fine sea salt

140g unsalted butter, cold and cut into 10 pieces

1 medium egg, at room temperature

1 medium egg yolk, at room temperature

80g soured cream, at room temperature

2 teaspoons vanilla essence

CINNAMON SUGAR

200g granulated sugar

1 teaspoon ground cinnamon

Two baking sheets or swiss roll tins, lined
 with parchment paper or foil

When my friend Nancy Nicholas shared this recipe, I had to try it immediately. Though it doesn't bear much resemblance to the original, these sweetly rich knotted buns are perfect for a special breakfast, brunch, or tea. Don't neglect to chill the dough when indicated or it might become too soft to handle easily.

1. For the dough, whisk the water and yeast together in a medium bowl and set aside.

2. Combine the flour, sugar and salt in the bowl of a food processor fitted with the metal blade and pulse a couple of times to mix. Add the butter and pulse at 1-second intervals until the butter is reduced to pieces no larger than 5mm, 6–8 pulses.

3. Whisk the egg, egg yolk, soured cream and vanilla essence into the yeast mixture and add to the work bowl. Pulse several times until the dough just begins to form a ball.

4. Invert the dough to a floured work surface and carefully remove the blade. Fold the dough over on itself several times to incorporate any dry bits — don't overdo it or the butter will start to melt. Form the dough into a rough square and drop it into an oiled bowl. Cover it with clingfilm and let it ferment until it just starts to puff, 1–2 hours.

5. Invert the dough to a floured work surface and press it into a square. Slide the dough to a floured baking sheet and cover it with clingfilm. Chill the dough until it is firm, about 1 hour – you can leave the dough refrigerated overnight if you wish.

6. To roll the dough, mix the cinnamon sugar. Cover the work surface with one-third of the cinnamon sugar and place the dough on it. Sprinkle another one-third of the cinnamon sugar on the dough. Roll the dough to a 30 x 40cm rectangle and sprinkle it with half the remaining

cinnamon sugar. Fold one of the 30cm sides over to meet the opposite edge to make a 15 x 40cm rectangle. Sprinkle the remaining cinnamon sugar under and on the dough and roll the dough to a 20 x 40cm rectangle. If the dough is starting to soften too much to handle, slide it onto a baking sheet and chill it for 1 hour.

7. To form the buns, use a pizza wheel to cut the dough into two 10 x 40cm rectangles. Cut the 40cm edge of each into 5cm lengths, making eight 10 x 5cm buns from each strip of dough. Use the pizza wheel to make a slash about 4cm long in the centre of each running lengthways. To knot the buns, pass the top or bottom of the rectangle of dough through the slashed centre and pull it to form a rectangle again. Place the knots on one of the prepared tins as they are formed, keeping them 5cm apart on all sides.

8. Cover the tins with clingfilm and let the buns proof until they just start to puff, 30–45 minutes. About 20 minutes in, set racks in the upper and lower thirds of the oven and preheat to 200˚C/gas mark 6.

9. Place the tins in the oven and immediately reduce the temperature to 190˚C/gas mark 5. After 10 minutes, switch the bottom tin to the upper rack and vice versa, turning the tins from back to front at the same time. Bake the buns until risen, firm and light golden, 10–15 minutes longer. Cool the buns on a rack and serve them the day they are baked.

chapter fourteen

Desserts

Bread and dessert seem an unlikely combination, but both sliced and cubed bread and fresh breadcrumbs add substance and body to many desserts. Some of the recipes here use the Brioche Loaf on page 178, while others may be made using *Pain de Mie* or Golden Sandwich Bread in Chapter 5, and one recipe uses a baguette for crisp round slices of toasted bread atop a pudding. For the most part though, bread with a large open crumb, like *ciabatta* and some of the slow-rise breads, isn't the best choice for either fresh breadcrumbs or slices of bread – their texture isn't dense enough to keep fillings from leaking through them.

While leftover bread has long been used in homely desserts such as custardy bread puddings, bread also figures in many delicate desserts. Used as both the lining of the mould and as a binder for the filling, bread is what defines a French apple charlotte. Untoasted bread lines the mould for a light and elegant summer pudding while dry breadcrumbs bind the batter for a Viennese apricot pudding. Fresh breadcrumbs find their way into a rich chocolate cake that also happens to be based on a Viennese recipe.

If you're baking bread on a regular basis and wind up eating most of what you bake, save scraps and ends of your bread in a plastic bag in the freezer for desserts that require either diced bread or fresh or dry crumbs.

french apple charlotte

Makes one 23cm charlotte, 6–8 servings

LINING THE MOULD

170g unsalted butter, melted and slightly cooled

One 23cm loaf *Pain de Mie,* page 66, or Golden Sandwich Bread, page 60, cut into 5mm slices, crusts trimmed away

APPLE FILLING

40g unsalted butter (possibly left from lining the mould)

1.35kg Golden Delicious apples, peeled, halved, cored, and each half cut into 4 or 5 wedges

100g granulated sugar

1– 2 tablespoons dark rum or Calvados

1 tablespoon lemon juice, strained after measuring

½ teaspoon ground cinnamon

130g dried currants

80g fresh white breadcrumbs made from the trimmings of the bread used to line the mould

APRICOT SAUCE

280g apricot jam

1 tablespoon water

1 tablespoon dark rum or Calvados

One 1.5 litre metal charlotte mould or porcelain soufflé dish, plus one large pan or sheet of aluminium foil for the floor of the oven

A classic apple charlotte is made in a bucket-shaped metal mould lined with buttered white bread and filled with cooked sweetened apples. Served unmoulded and still warm, it's a perfect old-fashioned autumn dessert. I learned this version from André René, the opening chef at Windows on the World. Chef René's secret touch was a few handfuls of fresh crumbs made from the trimmings of bread. The breadcrumbs disappear into the filling and bind it just enough so that the charlotte doesn't sag after it's unmoulded. Although you can get everything ready in advance, the charlotte can't be made so far ahead that the filling needs to be refrigerated, as chilled filling won't warm up sufficiently while the charlotte is baking. But you can easily line the mould with the bread and wrap and refrigerate it a day in advance. Charlotte moulds are available online.

1. Skim any foam from the surface of the butter and pour it into a shallow bowl, leaving most of the water behind.

2. Use a round biscuit cutter to stamp out a 4cm disc from one slice of the bread. Dip one side in the butter and set the disc, buttered side down, in the bottom centre of the mould.

3. Stack 5 slices of bread and cut them diagonally into triangles; then take one stack of the bread triangles and cut the shortest side so that it forms a straight base for the now-isosceles triangle. Repeat with the second stack. One at a time, dip the bread triangles into the butter and arrange them in the bottom of the mould with the short bases snugly against the side of the mould, overlapping each other by 5mm, pinwheel style, and the points converging over the central disc. When you come to the last triangle, lift the side of the first one and insert the edge of the last one under it.

4. To line the sides of the mould, trim the bread 9mm shorter than the inside of the mould to control leaks of butter while the charlotte is baking. Cut each slice vertically to make two pieces, each approximately 5cm wide. Dip into the butter and press against the side of the mould, overlapping the rectangles of bread by 5mm. When you come to the last rectangle, lift the side of the first one and insert the edge of the last one under it. Cover the lined mould loosely with clingfilm, making sure you have enough

scraps of bread and butter left to make the charlotte's base on top of the filling.

5. Pulse any remaining scraps or diced pieces of leftover bread in the food processor to make crumbs. You can add a few pieces of the trimmed away crust of the bread, but not too much or they'll darken the filling.

6. For the filling, melt the butter in a wide pan or large Dutch oven and add the apples. Cook over a medium-high heat until the apples start to sizzle. Quickly stir in the sugar, rum, lemon juice, cinnamon and dried currants. Decrease the heat to medium-low and cover the pan. Let the apples steam until they release their juices and soften slightly, floating in the water, 7–8 minutes.

7. Increase the heat so that the water evaporates quickly and the apples cook through (about half the apple slices will have disintegrated and the other half should remain intact). Increase the heat to high, scatter in the breadcrumbs and use a silicone spatula to fold them in without breaking up the apples. When you slide the pan back and forth on the hob, the filling should move as a single unit.

8. Cool the filling slightly, pack it into the prepared mould and cover the filling with any leftover pieces of bread (use any odd leftover pieces from cutting the other shapes), buttered side up. Cover loosely with clingfilm. The assembled charlotte can sit several hours before baking.

9. To make the sauce, combine the apricot jam with the water and rum in a small saucepan and bring to a simmer over a medium-low heat, stirring occasionally. Sieve into a bowl, rinse the pan, and pour the sauce back in so you can reheat it and serve it warm. If the jam is very chunky, pulse it in a food processor to reduce the size of the solid pieces before heating.

10. If you need to get the filling ready further in advance, cook the filling but don't add the breadcrumbs. Just before you're ready to bake the charlotte, reheat the filling and add the breadcrumbs as in the middle of step 7, then follow with step 8.

11. About 1½ hours before you intend to serve the charlotte, set a rack in the lower third of the oven and preheat to 180°C/gas mark 4.

12. Bake the charlotte when you know you'll be ready to serve it as soon as it's ready. Bake until the bread is well toasted and dark golden and the temperature of the filling is about 88°C, about 45 minutes.

13. Let the charlotte cool for a couple of minutes (if you leave the baked charlotte in the mould too long the bread will become soggy), then, using oven mitts, place a serving plate over the mould and invert the charlotte onto the plate. Lift off the mould and serve immediately, cutting wedges and serving both filling and bread in each portion. Serve the sauce on the side.

A real summer pudding has only three ingredients besides the bread: sugar, raspberries and redcurrants, the last almost impossible to find in the United States. I decided to substitute redcurrant jelly for the currants and some of the sugar. The key to making a summer pudding that doesn't collapse when you unmould it is to make a small one. If you're making it for more than 4 or 5 people, make multiples – it certainly isn't difficult or time-consuming to prepare.

summer pudding

Makes 4 servings

One 340g jar redcurrant jelly

675g fresh raspberries, picked over but not washed

½ Brioche Loaf, page 178 Quick Changes, *Pain de Mie*, page 66 or Golden Sandwich Bread, page 60, cut into 9mm slices, crusts trimmed away

One 1-litre round-bottomed bowl, lightly oiled and lined with clingfilm (the oil helps to keep the clingfilm in place)

Crème fraîche, whipped cream, or clotted cream for serving

1. Scrape the jelly into a wide saucepan and place it over a low heat. Let the jelly melt, stirring occasionally, until it comes to a simmer. Cook at a gentle simmer for 5 minutes to reduce it slightly.

2. Add the raspberries to the pan and gently slide the pan back and forth several times to moisten them with the reduced jelly. Increase the heat to medium and cook, sliding the pan again occasionally (stirring would crush the berries), until the mixture approaches a simmer, about 3 minutes, no longer. Pour into a medium bowl and cool to room temperature.

3. Use a biscuit cutter or a small plate as a pattern to cut as wide a disc as possible from one of the slices of bread and place it in the bottom of the prepared bowl. Add more slices of bread (easier if you trim them to a trapezoid shape) around the disc already in place to line the side of the bowl, fitting them tightly together without overlapping.

4. Use a slotted spoon to fill the lined bowl with the berries, adding only as much of the juices as necessary to fill the bowl to within about 2.5cm of the top. Cover the fruit with a layer of bread, piecing it together. Reserve any leftover juices.

5. Cover with clingfilm, then set a small plate or saucer that fits inside the bowl on top; put the bowl inside a larger bowl to catch any leaks. Place a weight such as a large tin of tomatoes on the plate and refrigerate overnight.

6. When you want to serve the pudding, remove it from the refrigerator and remove the weight and plate from the top of the dessert. Bring it to room temperature for 1 hour. Invert a deep serving plate over the dessert, then invert again holding the bowl against the plate; lift away the bowl (you might have to tug gently on the clingfilm a little to ease it out). Pour the reserved juices over the pudding, especially on any areas that haven't been completely coloured by the absorbed juices. Use a couple of large spoons to serve the pudding on plates and pass the cream on the side.

strawberry brioche pudding

Makes about 6 servings

1 Brioche Loaf, page 178, crusts trimmed and cut to make 300g of 1cm cubes

280g whole milk

70g granulated sugar

360g double cream

3 medium eggs

1½ teaspoons vanilla essence

280g strawberries, rinsed, drained, hulled and sliced

4 tablespoons flaked almonds

2 tablespoons granulated sugar for topping

One 2-litre gratin dish or other baking dish, buttered

QUICK CHANGES

Substitute raspberries, blackberries, blueberries or a combination for the strawberries.

So many horrors exist under the name of bread pudding that I hesitated even to try making one for years. There are a few 'secrets' to a perfect bread pudding: let the bread cubes dry slightly in the oven so that they absorb the liquid easily; mix any solid elements with the dry bread cubes before moistening; and add the liquid in several stages so that the bread absorbs it completely. Here, the bread mixture is dotted with quartered strawberries and finished with a sugary almond topping, a perfect complement to the rich and moist pudding under it.

1. Set a rack in the middle level of the oven and preheat to 180°C/gas mark 4.

2. Scatter the brioche cubes on a swiss roll tin and bake until slightly dry, but not toasted, about 10–15 minutes. Transfer the bread cubes to a large bowl.

3. Whisk the milk and sugar together in a saucepan and heat, stirring occasionally, until the sugar is dissolved. Off the heat, whisk in the cream, eggs and vanilla essence.

4. Fold the berries into the brioche cubes; pour over half the custard mixture. Let stand for 15 minutes. Pour in the rest of the custard and let stand for another 15 minutes.

5. Scrape the mixture into the prepared baking dish and level the top.

6. Bake the pudding for 45 minutes, then sprinkle with the almonds and sugar. Continue baking until set, another 15 minutes or so.

7. Cool to lukewarm before serving.

I never tire of paging through Eduard Mayer's brilliant 1968 *Wiener Suss-speisen* (Viennese sweet dishes), a never-ending source of inspiration for one of my favourite branches of dessert making. In Vienna, a *koch* is a baked breadcrumb-based dessert that lies halfway between a baked pudding and a soufflé. Though Mayer doesn't give a recipe for an apricot version, this is loosely based on his method for preparing a *koch*.

1. Combine the apricots and water in a non-reactive saucepan and bring to the boil. Remove from the heat, cover and allow to soak for an hour. Return to a low heat and slowly simmer until the apricots are soft and the liquid is all but boiled away, about 15–20 minutes. Let cool.

2. Stir the rum, lemon juice and lemon zest into the apricots and purée them in the food processor. Set aside.

3. Set a rack in the middle level of the oven and preheat to 200°C/gas mark 6.

4. Use a rubber spatula to beat the butter and half the sugar in a large mixing bowl, then beat in the egg yolks, one at a time, beating until smooth after each addition. Beat in the apricot purée. Scatter the breadcrumbs over the top but do not mix them in.

5. Whisk the 5 egg whites with the salt on medium speed until white and opaque, then increase the speed to medium-high and whisk in the remaining 50g of sugar about a tablespoon at a time, continuing to whisk the egg whites until they hold a soft peak.

6. Scrape the egg whites over the breadcrumbs in the bowl. Fold everything together, making sure to scrape the bottom of the bowl as you fold to avoid any unmixed batter at the bottom.

7. Scrape the batter into the prepared baking dish and smooth the top. Place the baking dish in the oven and decrease the heat to 190°C/gas mark 5. Bake the pudding until it is slightly puffed and set, about 25 minutes.

8. Cool the pudding on a rack for 15–20 minutes before serving with some sweetened lightly whipped cream.

viennese baked apricot pudding

Makes about 6 servings

340g dried apricots, snipped into 6 or 8 pieces each

450g water

1 tablespoon white or golden rum

1 tablespoon strained lemon juice

2 teaspoons grated lemon zest

115g unsalted butter, very soft

100g granulated sugar

4 medium eggs, separated, plus an extra egg white

80g dry breadcrumbs, page 36

Pinch of salt

One 2-litre gratin dish, buttered and sugared

Sweetened lightly whipped cream, to serve

marillenkoch

Makes about 6 servings

675g whole milk

450g double cream

200g granulated sugar

Pinch of salt

1 vanilla pod, split

5 medium eggs

4 medium egg yolks

1 Baguette, page 107, sliced 5mm thick

55g unsalted butter, melted and slightly cooled

One 2-litre oval gratin dish, buttered
and set in a larger roasting tin

Back when I was working at Windows on the World, our general manager Alan Lewis, never known for his diplomatic ways, walked into the pastry shop and said, 'Why don't we have a [expletive] bread pudding on the lunch menu?' After a failed attempt by the assistant pastry chef, I bought a copy of James Beard's *American Cookery*. Next morning we tried his recipe for bread and butter pudding from the Coach House, which happened to be right across the street from my first apartment in New York City. We cut into one as soon as they came out of the oven and there was a thick layer of custard topped with a thin layer of buttery toasted bread. This excellent bread and butter pudding is loosely adapted from James Beard's recipe. At the Coach House, this was always served with a raspberry sauce, but I think it's best plain.

1. Set a rack in the upper third of the oven and preheat to 160°C/gas mark 3.

2. Whisk the milk, cream, sugar and salt in a medium saucepan; add the vanilla pod and bring to the boil over a medium heat.

3. Whisk the eggs and yolks just to break them up in a large bowl.

4. Whisk the boiled mixture into the eggs a little at a time. Put it back into the pan, quickly rinse and dry the bowl and pass the mixture through a fine mesh sieve back into the bowl.

5. Dip a slice of bread into the butter and arrange it, buttered side up, at one end of the baking dish. Continue with the remaining slices of bread, overlapping them slightly, to fill the dish.

6. Skim any foam from the surface of the custard and pour it over the bread in the baking dish – the bread will float to the surface of the custard.

7. Carefully place the tin containing the baking dish into the oven and quickly add about 750ml hot water to the larger tin. Bake until the bread is deep golden and the custard has set, about 45 minutes. Test the custard in the centre of the pudding with the point of a small paring knife – the knife should emerge moist but clean.

8. Carefully remove the roasting tin from the oven without splashing water into the pudding and lift the baking dish out to a rack. Cool the pudding to room temperature and serve the day it is baked. Wrap and refrigerate leftovers and bring to room temperature before serving again.

This was a speciality of Marie Smith Leonard, my friend Sandy's mother. She had adapted it from an early *Joy of Cooking* (Bobbs Merrill, 1943), though it disappeared from later editions. I liked Mrs. Leonard a lot – she had a great sense of humour and always chatted with Sandy's schoolmates as though they were her own friends. This sweet and tangy pudding always makes me remember her and smile.

1. Set a rack in the middle level of the oven and preheat to 160°C/gas mark 3.

2. Warm the milk to about 49°C, no more, and pour over the breadcrumbs into a small bowl. Don't stir or the mixture might turn gluey. Let the moistened crumbs cool while you prepare the rest of the ingredients.

3. In a medium mixing bowl, use a rubber spatula to beat the butter and sugar together. Beat in the egg yolks, one at a time, beating until smooth after each addition.

4. Switch to a whisk and mix in the lemon zest and juice.

5. Make sure the crumb mixture is completely cooled or the milk will curdle when it meets the lemon juice. Use the rubber spatula to gently fold in the crumb mixture.

6. Scrape the pudding mixture into the prepared dish and bake until set, 30–35 minutes. Cool to room temperature on a rack before making the meringue – if you put the meringue on a warm pudding, a watery layer of condensation will develop and leak out when you cut into the pudding.

7. When you're ready to prepare the meringue, set a rack in the upper third of the oven and preheat to 150°C/gas mark 2.

8. Half fill a medium saucepan with water and bring it to the boil. Whisk the egg whites with the salt, vanilla essence and sugar in the bowl of an electric mixer. Adjust the heat so that the water just simmers actively, place the bowl on the saucepan, and whisk gently until the egg whites are hot (55–60°C) and the sugar is dissolved, about 3 minutes. Place the bowl on the mixer fitted with the whisk and whip the meringue until it is well risen in volume and firm, but still creamy textured and not dry.

9. Scrape the meringue onto the cooled pudding and use the back of a spoon to spread it, swirling it into short peaks. Make sure the meringue touches the edge of the baking dish all around or it might slide off after it's baked.

10. Bake the pudding again until the meringue is set and light golden, about 15 minutes. Cool and serve at room temperature or chilled with or without some slightly sweetened whipped cream.

Makes about 6 servings

PUDDING

450g whole milk

100g fresh white breadcrumbs, page 36

55g unsalted butter, softened

100g caster sugar

3 medium egg yolks (save the whites for the meringue)

2 teaspoons finely grated lemon zest

3 tablespoons strained lemon juice

MERINGUE

3 medium egg whites (from above)

Pinch of fine sea salt

½ teaspoon vanilla essence

100g caster sugar

One 2-litre gratin dish, buttered

Slightly sweetened whipped cream to serve (optional)

lemon meringue bread pudding

Makes one 23cm round cake, 8-10 servings

CAKE BATTER

75g finely ground almonds or
  prepared almond flour

50g fresh breadcrumbs (no need
  to remove the crust), page 36

170g unsalted butter, softened

135g granulated sugar

¼ teaspoon ground cinnamon

¼ teaspoon pure almond essence

115g plain chocolate, melted and cooled

8 medium eggs, separated

CHOCOLATE GLAZE

115g double cream

4 tablespoons light corn syrup or golden syrup

200g plain chocolate,
  melted and cooled

40g lightly toasted flaked almonds to finish

Whipped cream for serving, optional

One 6.25–7.5cm deep, 23cm springform tin,
  buttered and the base lined with a disc of
  buttered parchment paper

Back when I was a partner in the Total Heaven Baking Company, a wholesale baking company founded by Bill Liederman and me, having a pastry chef was still a rare phenomenon, and so this chocolate almond cake was an immediate top seller to New York City restaurants. The original recipe had called for dry breadcrumbs; I switched to fresh breadcrumbs and got a much moister cake. Like a lot of rich chocolate cakes, this one falls a little in the centre while cooling and we had to trim it before pouring on the glaze. After the initial batch, we saved the trimmings and used them in later cakes in place of the breadcrumbs for an even more moist and dense result. Try it and see.

1. Set a rack in the middle level of the oven and preheat to 180°/gas mark 4.

2. Stir the almonds and breadcrumbs together and set aside.

3. Beat the butter and half the sugar in the bowl of an electric mixer fitted with the paddle attachment on medium speed until light, 3-4 minutes. Stop the mixer and add the cinnamon, almond essence and chocolate. Beat on low speed to combine, then stop and scrape the bowl and beater.

4. Start the mixer again on low-medium speed and separate the eggs, adding the yolks to the chocolate batter as it's mixing and transferring the whites to another mixer bowl. (If you only have one mixer bowl, put the whites in a small bowl and transfer the chocolate batter to a medium mixing bowl after all the yolks have been added. Wash the bowl in hot soapy water, rinse well, and dry before using for the egg whites.)

5. Take the bowl off the mixer and use a large rubber spatula to stir in the almond and breadcrumb mixture.

6. Whisk the egg whites on medium speed, using the whisk attachment, until they are white, opaque and beginning to hold their shape. Increase the speed to medium-high and add the remaining sugar in a slow stream, continuing to whisk the egg whites until they hold a soft peak.

7. Stir about one third of the egg whites into the chocolate batter to lighten it, then fold in the rest until no streaks of white remain. Scrape the batter into the prepared tin and smooth the top.

8. Bake the cake until well risen but still moist in the centre when tested with the point of a paring knife, 35-40 minutes. Cool in the tin for 5 minutes, then invert to a card board. Leave the paper on the cake and invert to a rack to cool completely.

9. Wait until the cake has cooled completely before preparing the glaze. Whisk the cream and corn syrup together in a small saucepan and heat just until there are a few bubbles around the edge of the liquid. Remove from the heat and cool to about 38°C - it should feel just slightly warm when tested with a fingertip. Pour the cooled cream mixture over the melted chocolate and use a rubber spatula to stir them together to avoid creating bubbles in the glaze.

10. Use a long, sharp serrated knife to trim the top of the cake evenly, then place a card board on the cake; invert so that the smooth bottom side of the cake is upward and remove the paper. Set the cake on a rack over a tin to catch drips and pour the glaze over the cake, using a metal spatula to sweep excess from the top and to touch up the sides where necessary. Let stand until the glaze sets, then press the flaked almonds against the sides. Transfer to a serving plate and cut the cake into wedges, remembering to wipe the knife with a damp cloth between cuts. Serve a spoonful of whipped cream on the side if you wish.

brown bread ice cream

Makes about 2 litres ice cream

ICE CREAM MIXTURE

900g whole milk

265g caster sugar

1 vanilla pod, split

Three 7.5cm strips lemon zest, yellow part only, removed with a vegetable peeler

5cm piece of cinnamon stick

10 medium egg yolks

225g double cream, chilled

CARAMELISED BROWN BREAD CUBES

100g crustless wholemeal bread, sliced 5mm thick and cut into 5mm dice

115g water

100g granulated sugar, plus 2 tablespoons for sprinkling

Pinches of fine sea salt

15g unsalted butter, melted

One swiss roll tin or small roasting tin, base lined with parchment paper

When I first started outlining this book, I had a long talk with my favourite baking guru, Kyra Effren, whose teaching and baking experience spans a lifetime. She made some great suggestions and then added, 'And don't forget brown bread ice cream – it's one of my favourites.' Baking crumbled bread with caramel, a pinch of salt, and just a small bit of butter produces sweet cubes that stay crisp once added to the ice cream. The ice cream recipe is based on the one I learned from Monsieur Alex Frolla, the pastry chef when I did my three summer seasons working at the Sporting Club and the Hotel de Paris in Monte Carlo. It was the best ice cream I've ever tasted.

1. For the ice cream, set a medium saucepan in a bowl of ice water; place a fine mesh sieve over the pan.

2. Whisk the milk and sugar in another saucepan and add the vanilla pod. Bring to the boil over a medium heat. Remove from the heat, add the lemon zest and cinnamon stick and let cool for 10 minutes. Meanwhile, whisk the egg yolks in a bowl just enough to break them up.

3. Use a slotted spoon to remove the vanilla pod, lemon zest and cinnamon stick and return the milk mixture to the boil. Whisk about one-third of it into the yolks, then return the pan to a low heat. Starting to whisk before pouring, pour the yolk mixture into the pan and whisk constantly until the mixture thickens slightly – it won't be very thick. Immediately strain it into the prepared pan and whisk the strained mixture several times in the next few minutes while it's cooling. Once cooled, pour it into a non-reactive bowl and cover loosely with clingfilm. Refrigerate until the next day. Just

before you intend to churn the ice cream, whisk in the cream.

4. For the brown breadcrumbs, set a rack in the middle level of the oven and preheat to 180°C/gas mark 4. Scatter the bread on the tin and bake until dry, but not toasted, 5–7 minutes. Remove the pan from the oven but leave the oven on.

5. Combine 4 tablespoons water and the sugar in a small saucepan and place over a medium heat. Bring to the boil and continue to cook until the sugar starts to colour. Pull the pan off the heat so that the caramel doesn't get too dark – it will continue to darken from the heat retained by the pan. Quickly heat the remaining water in a small pan. Check the colour of the caramel; if it is not yet a deep amber colour, return the pan to the heat for 2 additional minutes, then repeat. When the caramel is ready, cover your hand and forearm with a towel and add the hot water to the caramel, averting your face. The caramel will bubble up, then settle. If the caramel has cooled and hardens on contact with the water, place the pan back

on a low heat and cook for a minute or two, stirring, until the caramel is liquid. Use a tablespoon to drizzle the diluted caramel over the bread cubes on the tin, sprinkle with the 2 tablespoons sugar, a few pinches of salt and the butter, then use 2 spoons to toss the bread cubes to distribute the caramel, sugar, and salt evenly.

6. Bake the bread cubes again, stirring them every 2 minutes, until they are well toasted and crisp, 6–7 minutes.

7. Slide the paper off the pan to a rack to cool the bread cubes. They'll become quite crunchy when the caramel hardens; if necessary, break apart any that have stuck together while cooling.

8. Before you churn the ice cream, place a stainless steel bowl in the freezer. Churn in an ice cream maker according to the manufacturer's directions. Scrape into the prepared bowl and quickly fold in the cooled bread cubes. Cover with clingfilm and freeze until serving time.

Afterword

Baking bread, like eating it, is a totally natural activity. Neither is difficult or complicated and both involve sharing. Start baking bread at home and you'll be amazed at the reaction you get from your family and friends – home-baked bread is always better than anything you can buy, even if you don't have any previous experience.

Because I see writing as an extension of teaching people to bake, which I've been doing for almost 35 years, I've given you a lot of background information about the nature of the main ingredients for bread baking and what they accomplish when you use them. I've also used (and defined) foreign terms sometimes, but only to be more accurate rather than to make the process more complex.

Once you master a few essential steps needed for bread baking you'll be able to tackle any bread formula you encounter, even the ones that yield very soft doughs.

While developing the formulas for the different breads throughout the book was challenging and an immense learning experience for me, I loved reaching back into my memory (and the memories of many of my friends and colleagues) for ideas to use bread in creative savory and sweet dishes. And as in the bread recipes, I've tried to suggest many and varied applications for the dishes made from bread, though you can certainly feel free to take off on your own with them. The only important thing is, as I've said before, bake something!

Calvel, Raymond. *La Boulangerie Moderne,* 9th edition. Paris: Éditions Eyrolles, 1980.

_____. *Le Goût du Pain.* Paris: Éditions Jérôme Villette, 1990.

Coria, Giuseppe. *Profumi di Sicilia.* Palermo: Vito Cavallotto, 1981.

Couet, Alain and Éric Kayser. *Pains Spéciaux et Décorés.* Paris: Éditions St.-Honoré, 1989.

David, Elizabeth. *English Bread and Yeast Cookery,* American edition. New York: Viking Press, 1980.

École Professionnelle Richemont. *La Boulangerie Suisse.* Lucerne: École Professionnelle Richemont, 1983.

Fance, Wilfred James. *The New International Confectioner.* London and Coulsdon, England: Virtue & Company, 1981.

_____. *The Students' Technology of Breadmaking and Flour Confectionery.* London: Routledge & Keegan Paul, 1976.

Glezer, Maggie. *A Blessing of Bread.* New York: Artisan Books, 2004.

Hahnemann, Trina. *The Scandinavian Cookbook.* Kansas City: Andrews McMeel, 2008.

Hitz, Ciril. *Baking Artisan Bread.* Beverly, MA: Quarry Books, 2008.

Jacob, H.E. *Six Thousand Years of Bread.* New York: Doubleday, 1944.

Kaltenbach, Marianne. *Aus Schweizer Küchen.* Bern, Switzerland: Hallwag, 1977.

Laverty, Maura. *Full& Plenty: Breads & Cakes,* vol. 1. Dublin: Anvil Books, 1985.

Mayer, Eduard. *Wiener Süßspeisen.* Linz, Austria: Trauner Verlag, 1968.

Olney, Richard. *Simple French Food.* New York, Atheneum, 1974.

Pagrach-Chandra, Gaitri. *Warm Bread and Honey Cake.* Northampton: Interlink Books, 2010.

Polshenke, Paul. *Gebäck aus Deutschen Landen.* Alfeld, Germany: Gildeverlag, 1949.

Standard, Stella. *Our Daily Bread.* New York: Bonanza Books, 1970.

Vogt, Ernst, et al. *Der Schweizer Bäcker-Konditor,* vol. 2. Thun, Switzerland: Ott Verlag, 1944.

Vogt, Ernst and Josef Mattle. *Die Schweizer Bäckerei,* vol. 1. Thun, Switzerland: Ott Verlag, 1953.

A fter such an enormous undertaking as this book there are many people to thank. There's only room to list everyone, but my heartfelt thanks goes out to each:

My agent, Phyllis Wender; my publisher at Kyle Books, Anja Schmidt; and Natalie Danford who helped me with every aspect of writing and editing this book.

Cara Tannenbaum and Patricia LaMorte who helped with bread production for photography and assisted in the studio.

Dirk Kaufman for design, Romulo Yanes and his staff for the fabulous photography, and my old friend Paul Grimes for brilliant food styling.

I don't know what I would have done without the help and advice I received from bread experts Ciril Hitz of Johnson and Wales University, Tim Healea of little t american baker, Sim Cass of the Institiute of Culinary Education, Bill Weekley of General Mills, and Kelly Olson of Red Star Yeast.

The following friends, colleagues, chefs, authors, and associates contributed or tested recipes or double-checked recipes I wrote. They are Jean Anderson, Ramazan Ay of Hazar, Annike Benjes of Visit Sweden, Gerard Bertolino, Tim Brennan of Cravings, Dara Bunjon, Aurelia Carlen of Zurich Tourism, Mark di Giulio and Peter Meltzer of Quatorze Bis, Phyl Divine, Kyra Effren, Vincent Florizoone of Grand Cabaret, Alessandro Frassica of 'ino, Maggie Glezer, Reto Hausammann, Maida Heatter, Christina Heinze Johansson of Visit Denmark, Adam Kaplan of In Good Taste, Siegfried Kroepfl, Albert Kumin, Ris Lacoste of Ris, Jim Lahey of Sullivan Street Bakery; Eleanor, Sharon, Jack, Joshua, and Jeremy Lebewohl and Steve Cohen of the Second Avenue Deli; Sandy Leonard, Sasha and Nico Lewis of Babka, Erika Lieben, Rosalinda Mariotti, Fred Morin of Joe Beef, Jennifer Morris and Hosni Emam of Habibi, Nancy Nicholas aka Sourdough Jack, Ann Nurse, Jack Parker of O'Connell's, Barbara Pugliese, Kerrin Rousset, Marie-Isabelle Rousset, Roberto Santibañez and Marco Diaz of Fonda, Thierry Saxe of Café au Bon Vin, Cenk Sonmezsoy, Carole Walter, and Ari Weinzweig and Roger Bowser of Zingerman's Delicatessen.

At the Institute of Culinary Education: Rick Smilow, president; Andrea Tutunjian, director of the career baking program; Shawana Jones, director of purchasing and all her staff; Mary Bartolini, schedule and operations manager; and students Elissa Beerman, Kristina Marie Brunswick, Rita Choulee, Alexandra Curran, Jennifer Fallon, Zoe Galanopoulos, Erynn Henderson, Adeline Lau, Jasmine Lopez, Hector Ortiz, and Shari Tanaka who assisted in the studio or with prep for photography.

Special and infinite thanks to Ciril Hitz who read the manuscript, provided suggestions and corrections, and was always available to answer questions and offer guidance.

acknowledgements

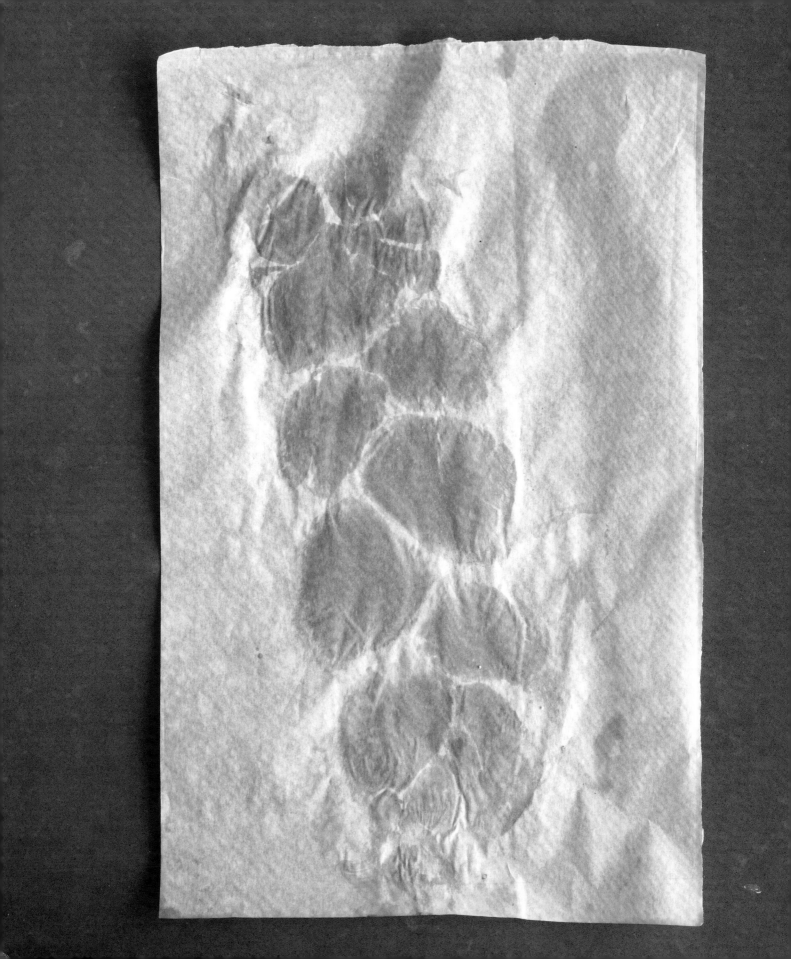